DATE DUE			

Writing North Carolina History

Writing North Carolina History

Edited by Jeffrey J. Crow
and
Larry E. Tise

The University of North Carolina Press
Chapel Hill

© 1979 The University of North Carolina Press
All rights reserved
Manufactured in the United States of America
Library of Congress Catalog Card Number 79-439
ISBN 0-8078-1369-9

975.6007
W93
116566
Jan. 1981

Library of Congress Cataloging in Publication Data

Main entry under title:

Writing North Carolina history.

Includes index.
1. North Carolina—Historiography—Addresses,
essays, lectures.   I. Crow, Jeffrey J.   II. Tise,
Larry E.
F253.2.W74   975.6'007'2   79-439
ISBN 0-8078-1369-9

To Larry, Nicholas, Jason, Kevin,
and other students
of North Carolina's past

Contents

Introduction

"The history of the State is unknown," declared Joseph Seawell "Shocco" Jones in 1834. "The great events of her annals are buried amidst the musty papers of her ancient families, and are not celebrated by the 'historians of the adjacent States,' because they were ignorant or careless of their existence." Jones, of course, had a highly partisan and romantic view of North Carolina history, and his purpose in writing the history of the Old North State in the American Revolution bore a political intent (an attack on Thomas Jefferson and the Democratic party) as much as a pedagogical one. Even so his words still resonate with surprising relevance for this volume and may be taken as a point of departure. "It is the duty, and the most sacred duty, of the historian to preserve the integrity of history," Jones intoned. "Ignorance and wickedness may misrepresent with impunity the character of her [North Carolina's] history, if efforts are not made to break away the darkness which surrounds it; and such are the inducements to this publication."[1]

   In the nearly 150 years since Jones took up the gauntlet and unsheathed a rapierlike pen, scores of works on North Carolina history have appeared.[2] With varying success, all have

1. Joseph Seawell Jones, *A Defence of the Revolutionary History of the State of North Carolina from the Aspersions of Mr. Jefferson* (Boston and Raleigh, 1834), pp. 11, 16.
2. Other Tar Heel historians, to be sure, preceded Jones. For their identities and works, see the essays by William S. Powell, Alan D. Watson, and Robert M. Calhoon in this volume. Two helpful bibliographies on North Carolina history are becoming outdated: Mary Lindsay Thornton, comp., *A Bibliography of North Carolina, 1589–1956* (Chapel Hill: University of North Carolina Press, 1958);

attempted to record, interpret, and explain the people and events, tragedies and triumphs, that have shaped the Old North State. Yet no single historian nor any single volume has ever undertaken a full assessment of North Carolina's historical literature. The reasons for this strange lacuna may be traced in part to the comparative dearth of writings on Tar Heel history. All too often North Carolina's history has been seen as an antilogism to South Carolina's erratic course and Virginia's phlegmatic conservatism. This prevailing view seems somehow peculiar, because North Carolina boasts the oldest pedigree, having been the site of the first English colony in 1585, a full two decades before the settlement of Jamestown, Virginia, in 1607. Nonetheless, North Carolina has usually been over-shadowed by the flamboyance of its southern neighbor and the smug self-image of its northern neighbor. Wedged between these two "mountains of conceit," in the words of a favorite Tar Heel saw of unknown origin, North Carolina has been the perennial "vale of humility."

The notion of North Carolina as a "vale of humility," conceived early and still persisting, has frequently animated the writing of the state's history. Virginian William Byrd set the tone and the trend with his roguish *History of the Dividing Line betwixt Virginia and North Carolina* in 1728. Byrd considered North Carolina a "Lubberland" because of the "great felicity of the Climate, the easiness of raising Provisions, and the Slothfulness of the People." Nor did he find North Carolinians to be particularly pleasant folks. "The Truth of it is," the aristocratic Byrd archly sniffed, "these People live so much upon Swine's flesh, that it don't only encline them to the Yaws, & consequently to the downfall of their Noses, but makes them likewise extremely hoggish in their Temper, & many of them seem to Grunt rather than Speak in their ordinary conversation."[3] North

---

and Hugh T. Lefler, *A Guide to the Study and Reading of North Carolina History*, 3d ed. (Chapel Hill: University of North Carolina Press, 1969).

3. William K. Boyd, ed., *William Byrd's Histories of the Dividing Line betwixt*

Carolina historians clearly have had to face formidable prejudices from two overpowering and highly critical neighbors.

As a result, much of the impetus for an examination of the state's history has found its origin in a comparison of North Carolina's place next to South Carolina's or Virginia's. When a group of historically minded North Carolinians formed an organization in 1900 to write and discuss publicly the history of the Old North State, a dispute with Virginia over the relative contributions of the two states in the Civil War galvanized their movement. A stirring notice in the *Raleigh News and Observer* at the time of the founding of the seminal North Carolina Literary and Historical Association asserted, "No State has been more misrepresented than our own; therefore, we must tell our own story; from our midst must come the man or woman in each generation whose voice will be heard above the jargon of those who belittle us at home and traduce us abroad." J. Bryan Grimes, longtime secretary of state for North Carolina and chairman of the North Carolina Historical Commission, provided the most gallant defense, however. Responding to yet another Virginia critic, he declared, "I do not intend to reflect upon Virginia, . . . but North Carolina has suffered enough in the past by being denied credit for her achievements. Our State has always acted the part of a loving sister to Virginia. . . . Whenever Virginia has suffered North Carolina has bled. We would disdain to pluck one laurel from Virginia's brow—we love her still—but we say calmly to our beloved sister that she must pause and give us justice."[4]

Virginia and North Carolina (Raleigh: North Carolina Historical Commission, 1929), pp. 55, 92. For an equally harsh view of North Carolina by a South Carolina Anglican itinerant who deplored the religious and cultural backwardness of colonial Tar Heels, see Richard J. Hooker, ed., *The Carolina Backcountry on the Eve of the Revolution: The Journal and Other Writings of Charles Woodmason, Anglican Itinerant* (Chapel Hill: University of North Carolina Press, 1953), esp. pp. 76–81.

4. William J. Peele, ed., *Literary and Historical Activities in North Carolina, 1900–1905* (Raleigh: North Carolina Historical Commission, 1907), pp. 2, 22–23, 416–99.

Rival claims among Virginia, South Carolina, and North Carolina have plagued the Tar Heel state's historiography. The insidious effects of this three-state squabble have tended to obfuscate the unique aspects of North Carolina's past. Moreover, when not using North Carolina history as a convenient foil to the red-hot extremism of South Carolina or the blue-blooded elitism of Virginia, scholars have traditionally studied North Carolina's past to shed new light on broad national and regional problems. This pilferage of North Carolina history is perhaps best illustrated in Carl Degler's splendid book *The Other South: Southern Dissenters in the Nineteenth Century*.[5] In this astute study Degler details the views and activities of an uncommon number of Tar Heel freethinkers and dissenters including Eli W. Caruthers, Benjamin Hedrick, Hinton R. Helper, Daniel R. Goodloe, Jonathan and Daniel Worth, Zebulon Baird Vance, William Woods Holden, and Daniel Lindsay Russell, Jr. Yet while these figures admirably serve Degler's purposes in illuminating a forgotten side of southern history, the social, economic, and cultural forces in North Carolina that produced them remain something of a mystery.

This is not to say that capable historians have ignored North Carolina's past or have not tried to define its unique features as well as its typically southern characteristics. But even the standard textbook on Tar Heel history, *North Carolina: The History of a Southern State*, by Hugh T. Lefler and Albert Ray Newsome, is now a quarter of a century old, despite modest revisions in the 1963 and 1973 editions, and it becomes increasingly unsatisfactory as modern scholars dissect southern history with new methodological tools and different sets of questions.[6] Moreover, vast areas of North Carolina history

5. Carl N. Degler, *The Other South: Southern Dissenters in the Nineteenth Century* (New York: Harper & Row, 1974).

6. Hugh T. Lefler and Albert Ray Newsome, *North Carolina: The History of a Southern State* (Chapel Hill: University of North Carolina Press, 1954). Even as valuable a work as Arthur S. Link and Rembert W. Patrick, eds., *Writing Southern*

remain understudied if not unknown. Such American favorites
as the Revolution, Civil War and Reconstruction, the Progressive
era, and the New Deal have attracted only a handful of North
Carolina historians. Able works exist in each of these areas of
Tar Heel history, but larger interpretive views, trenchant
comparisons with other states, and overall syntheses are for the
most part lacking.

What makes this general historiographical situation
doubly ironic is the fact that North Carolina claims many of
the nation's leading scholars in its own institutions and some
of the best research facilities found anywhere. Within a thirty-
mile radius are two excellent research libraries at Duke
University and The University of North Carolina at Chapel Hill;
three outstanding manuscript collections at Duke, the Southern
Historical Collection in Chapel Hill, and the North Carolina
State Archives in Raleigh that holds the largest centralized
collection of county and local records in the nation; and the
unparalleled North Carolina Collection in Chapel Hill, the
repository for all printed matter on the state. The parade
of scholars who visit Raleigh, Durham, and Chapel Hill each
year is impressive. And this listing does not include the
manuscript collections at other universities in the state, notably
East Carolina University and Wake Forest University, and the
archives of many religious denominations: Lutherans, Baptists,

---

History: Essays in Historiography in Honor of Fletcher M. Green (Baton Rouge:
Louisana State University Press, 1965), which cites numerous studies on North
Carolina, reflects the status of southern writings only to the early 1960s. A major
new assessment of southern historiography is clearly in order. To take but one
example, the New South, Charles B. Dew wrote a massive 112-page bibliographical essay in a new edition of C. Vann Woodward's *Origins of the New South,
1877–1913* (Baton Rouge: Louisiana State University Press, 1971) that updated
merely two decades of scholarship on the period. Other recent syntheses of the
thrust of scholarship on the New South in the past two decades are Harold D.
Woodman, "Sequel to Slavery: The New History Views the Postbellum South,"
Journal of Southern History 43 (November 1977): 523–54; and James Tice Moore,
"Redeemers Reconsidered: Change and Continuity in the Democratic South,
1870–1900," ibid. 44 (August 1978): 357–78.

Methodists, Quakers, German Reformed, Presbyterians, and
Roman Catholics.

With the wealth of resources available in the state, North
Carolina would seem a likely and popular subject for study.
Sadly it is not. At a time when state and local history is enjoying
a renaissance of interest among the public and among historians,
North Carolina remains neglected. Virginia and South Carolina
continue to attract more attention than other South Atlantic
states. And even Maryland claims its own "Maryland Mafia"
—a group of energetic young scholars studying colonial
Chesapeake society virtually on a county-by-county basis.

Much of the foregoing relates to professional concerns,
but there are public ones as well. Two paradoxical trends have
manifested themselves in recent years. The first, a serendipitous
one, has already been noted. Interest in state and local history
is booming. The nation's bicentennial anniversary and the
phenomenal popularity of Alex Haley's *Roots* are only meteoric
traces of Americans' rising historical consciousness. Neophyte
genealogists are uncertainly climbing family trees. Historic
preservationists, capturing the ecological mood of the nation, are
recycling historic and not-so-historic buildings and structures.
Local lay historians, with sometimes bewildering results, are
writing county histories and narratives of obscure, if not
forgotten, episodes.[7]

This renewed interest in the past has coincided with a
disturbing and perplexing trend in public education. History
as an independent entity has been dropped from the curricula of
many primary and secondary schools and has been eliminated
as a requirement in many colleges and universities.[8] The decline

7. For cogent discussions of the uses and abuses of local history, see Alan
D. Watson, "What's Wrong with the Writing of North Carolina Local History?"
Carolina Comments 25 (May 1977): 66–71; Brent D. Glass, "Industrialization in
North Carolina: Sources for Historians," ibid. 26 (May 1978): 69–75; and Edward
W. Phifer, Jr., "The Place of the County in the Study of American History: An
Appraisal," ibid. 26 (September 1978): 117–22.

8. On this point, see H. G. Jones, "The Rape of History," *North Carolina*

in the formal study and teaching of history is a complex issue
that yields no simple solution. But if professional historians
abdicate their responsibility to demonstrate the pertinence of
historical inquiry and perspective, if they withdraw into the
insular walls of academia, if they permit the ahistorical and
untutored to interpret the past's meaning for the present,
then state and local history in North Carolina and elsewhere will
become by default the province of hagiographers, antiquarians,
and local chambers of commerce.

In the absence of discourse between historians and the
general public, dangerous misconceptions and misinformation
can be propagated. A case in point is a 1976 editorial in the
Charleston News and Courier. Pondering Herbert G. Gutman's
study of the black family, the editorial writer decided that if the
black family survived the "wrenching power of slavery" and was
still intact on the eve of the Great Depression, then the apparent
breakdown of the black family's stability in the 1960s and 1970s
might be attributed to the effects of welfare.[9] Such an
interpretation of Gutman's work stretches his evidence beyond
its bounds, and certainly historians enter a minefield when they
address explosive contemporary social issues or see their
arguments politicized. But if historians do not mediate between
the past and the present, who will?

Professional and public concerns, then, prompted the
North Carolina Division of Archives and History to convene a
symposium on the study and writing of North Carolina history
in June 1977. Over the course of two days the first systematic
analysis of writing on the state's history took place. The
eight scholars selected to participate in the symposium were

Historical Review 54 (Spring 1977): 158–68; Richard S. Kirkendall, "The Status of
History in the Schools," *Journal of American History* 62 (September 1975): 557–70;
and "History in the Public Schools" (A Position Paper by the Joint Committee on
the Status of History in the Public Schools), *Carolina Comments* 26 (March 1978):
43–47.

9. Herbert G. Gutman, *The Black Family in Slavery and Freedom, 1750–1925*
(New York: Pantheon Books, 1976); *Charleston News and Courier*, October 18, 1976.

eminently qualified for the task, having demonstrated skill and originality in their own work in the period assigned them. The papers they delivered have been revised and edited for publication in this volume.

Each historian was asked to identify the major literature for a selected period, to evaluate the content and perspective of the general studies on North Carolina history, and to review the germane monographs and articles in various professional periodicals. Each was also asked to explore the development of standard interpretations and the principal themes on which historians have concentrated. In the end, of course, each historian was free to determine the best manner in which to treat the history and historiography of the respective periods.

But besides interpreting the paths and byways of North Carolina's historical literature, each scholar was asked to concentrate on topics, themes, and source materials that remain untapped, underutilized, or even unaddressed in the history of the Tar Heel state. This book, then, constitutes the first comprehensive statement on the status of North Carolina's historical writings and an agenda for what needs to be done.

Collectively the essays reveal an unexpected consensus on a wide range of subjects. All recognize the monumental contributions of such well-known Tar Heel historians as William L. Saunders, Walter Clark, J. G. de Roulhac Hamilton, Robert D. W. Connor, Samuel A'Court Ashe, Guion Griffis Johnson, Christopher Crittenden, and others. But all agree that too often the seminal work of these historians has inhibited later historians from probing deeper or asking different questions. William S. Powell, Alan D. Watson, and Allen W. Trelease all note the need for larger interpretive works on their periods. Trelease in particular points out that with only a few exceptions neo-Whig and Negrophobic attitudes have dominated the interpretation of North Carolina in the Civil War and Reconstruction. Robert M. Calhoon ambitiously approaches the history

of the early national period as one filled with social tensions
and cultural turmoil. Harry L. Watson delves the contradictions
evident in standard interpretations of antebellum North Carolina
and like Calhoon suggests new points of departure. Robert F.
Durden cites the nearly total neglect of North Carolina's
agricultural and industrial history despite the primacy of both
in the state's distant and not-so-distant past. Upon reaching the
twentieth century, however, Sarah M. Lemmon and H. G. Jones
confront a different problem. After the other contributors have
reviewed hundreds of works on North Carolina history before
1900, Lemmon and Jones must contend with the paucity of
studies dealing with the Tar Heel state in the twentieth century.
Jones in particular turns, however reluctantly, to the social
sciences for relevant material. His comments on why historians
continue to shun recent history provide a philosophical capstone
for the book and a challenge to the profession.

No single symposium or book can hope to alter the flow
of historiography or influence the predilections of the historical
community. But each may serve as a starting point. Shocco
Jones's ghost can rest easy. The outlines of North Carolina
history are now known and the unfamiliar territories, if not
charted, are identified. New generations of historians and
graduate students can approach the history of North Carolina
with a fresh perspective, thanks to the efforts of the essayists
in this volume. For the study and writing of North Carolina
history truly belong to the future. As Christopher Hill has so
aptly expressed it, "History has to be rewritten in every
generation, because although the past does not change the
present does; each generation asks new questions of the past,
and finds new areas of sympathy as it re-lives different aspects
of the experiences of its predecessors."[10] This volume offers
enough new questions to engage the talents of the next

10. Christopher Hill, *The World Turned Upside Down: Radical Ideas during the
English Revolution* (New York: Viking Press, 1972), p. 13.

generation of North Carolina historians and to enliven those
classrooms where the teaching and study of North Carolina
history are not dead disciplines.

Raleigh, North Carolina   Jeffrey J. Crow
February 1978   Larry E. Tise

Writing North Carolina History

1

Colonial North Carolina, 1585–1764

by William S. Powell

To review what has been written about North Carolina during the 179-year period between 1585 and 1764 is a monumental undertaking for several reasons. Not only is that a very long period of time during which great and impressive events occurred, but it also anticipates that one must have at least passing acquaintance with what has been written about the period from 1585 until the present, which is a staggering 394 years. Touching even lightly on the publications of nearly four hundred years about events in North Carolina during that long-removed century and three-quarters anticipates a bibliographical and a historical knowledge of great proportions. To such I make no claim. By contrast, the next greatest period of time being reviewed by any of my colleagues at this symposium is a mere forty-four years, and he has nearly two hundred fewer years of writing time to survey. The briefest time span to be considered is one of only fifteen years (1861 to 1876) that ended just a century ago.

The enormity of the assignment became apparent when I took stock of the entries in the card catalog of the North Carolina Collection at The University of North Carolina in Chapel Hill. Under the appropriate subject headings I discovered approximately seven hundred cards representing books, monographs, pamphlets, scholarly and popular articles, theses and dissertations, biographies, bibliographies, and source books on this period. I can claim familiarity with only a small portion of this mass of material and perhaps an even more limited understanding of the events that occurred between 1585 and 1764. It must be clear at the outset, therefore, that I am by no means master of this period or of the literature dealing with it. The trite saying about the tip of the iceberg was perhaps never better applied than in this instance. Instead of a single paper, a whole symposium might easily be devoted to this one period alone. Perhaps the pending four-hundredth anniversary of the Roanoke Expeditions will provide the incentive for such a symposium.

North Carolina was the site of England's first attempt to discover and settle North America, and North Carolina is the only one of the United States that can claim an Elizabethan background. Our historical literature dates from that same beginning since Thomas Hariot and Richard Hakluyt rushed to press with contemporary reports.[1] Neither ancient Virginia nor Massachusetts can claim so early an English heritage, either historical or literary.

It would be of considerable interest if something of the sense of history or more precisely the extent of the historical knowledge of early North Carolinians were known. As H. G. Jones has reminded us, history as an academic discipline is only a century old in the United States and even younger in North Carolina.[2] Although the human desire to know and understand the past is ancient indeed, the utilitarian value of history came to be recognized among English-speaking people only a short while

1. Thomas Hariot, *A briefe and true report of the new found land of Virginia* (London, 1588). This little book has been reprinted a number of times. Richard Hakluyt, *The Principal Navigations, Voiages, and Discoveries of the English Nation* (London: George Bishop and Ralph Newberie, 1589). This work has also been reprinted in facsimile, the most recent being that of the Cambridge University Press in two volumes for the Hakluyt Society in 1965, with an introduction by David B. Quinn and a magnificent index by Alison M. Quinn. Also essential for a study of Raleigh's efforts at colonization is David B. Quinn, ed., *The Roanoke Voyages, 1584–1590*, 2 vols. (London: The Hakluyt Society, 1955).

2. H. G. Jones, "The Rape of History," *North Carolina Historical Review* (hereafter cited as *NCHR*) 54 (April 1977): 158.

before the beginning of the period that we are considering here. England's colonial expansion sparked a desire for knowledge of important events. Such knowledge was thought to produce the wise man. Elizabethan culture placed emphasis on history and kindled a demand for historical literature. The glories of England and the growth of her power were related in many histories published in the days of the Tudors and the Stuarts.[3] Under the Tudors, North Carolina was discovered and explored by Englishmen. Under the Stuarts, North Carolina was named, settled, and established. Yet I find little evidence that North Carolinians of the colonial period had any interest in history, especially their own.

John Lovick in 1727 willed his copy of "Lord Clarenden's History" to his friend William Little. Dr. John Eustace owned books described simply as "Sharp's Information to Universal History," "Rudiments of Ancient History," and a "Compendious History of England." Jeremiah Vail about the same time owned Bundy's *Roman History* and books identified as "Present State of England" and a "History of Georgia," while James Milner owned William Stith's "History [of the First Discovery and Settlement of Virginia?]" and a history of England. The Reverend James Reed owned a six-volume history of England and a "Roman History" in Latin.[4] Yet none of these dealt with North Carolina. The truth is, except for some brief sixteenth-century accounts, some promotional tracts, and a few summary reports in broader works, nothing dealing with the colony was available.

With the permanent settlement of the English at Jamestown in 1607, the history of Sir Walter Raleigh's colonies at Roanoke Island came to be viewed as the first step that led to the establishment of the colony of Virginia. It was because of

3. Michael Kraus, *A History of American History* (New York: Farrar & Rinehard, Inc., 1937), p. 16.

4. J. Bryan Grimes, *North Carolina Wills and Inventories* (Raleigh: Edwards & Broughton Printing Co., 1912), pp. 292, 490–92, 563, 516–17, 539.

Raleigh's reconnaissance reports from Roanoke Island that the country had been named Virginia. Captain John Smith's book, *The Generall Historie of Virginia, New-England, and the Summer Isles*, published in London in 1624, related the complete history of Raleigh's efforts as they were then known. From the reports of Amadas and Barlowe in 1584 through an account of John White's Lost Colony of 1587, and the efforts in 1590 to locate the missing colonists, the whole story was told. Smith established the precedent, and Robert Beverley's *The History and Present State of Virginia* (London, 1705) repeated the same information and added over a dozen engravings based on John White's drawings. Richard L. Morton's recent two-volume history of colonial Virginia opens with a chapter entitled "Beginnings," which summarizes the Roanoke voyages and once again describes them as being preliminary to the permanent settlement of modern Virginia.[5] Morton, however, identifies the focus of Raleigh's efforts as being within the bounds of modern North Carolina.

It was approximately half a century after the settlement at Jamestown before there were any settlers in the region that was destined to become North Carolina. Nevertheless, during that time a handful of publications appeared that took notice of this special area.[6] The earliest of these was merely the text of a lengthy sermon preached by Patrick Copland in London and published as *Virginia's God be Thanked*.[7] It consisted in part of a report of an exploratory expedition made in February 1622 by John Pory to the Chowan River region. His description of a vast region of tall pines, fertile cornfields, and friendly Indians anxious to establish trade with Englishmen hinted future

5. Richard L. Morton, *Colonial Virginia*, 2 vols. (Chapel Hill: University of North Carolina Press, 1960), 1:2–4.

6. These and others are fully described in my "Carolina in the Seventeenth Century: An Annotated Bibliography of Contemporary Publications," *NCHR* 41 (January 1964): 74–104.

7. Patrick Copland, *Virginia's God be Thanked; or, A Sermon of Thanksgiving for the happie success of the affayres in Virginia this last yeare* (London: William Sheffard and John Bellamie, 1622).

benefits to England, especially in the production of naval stores that might free her from dependence upon the Scandinavian countries.

The English Civil War lasting from 1642 to 1649, as well as the establishment of the commonwealth following the beheading of Charles I in 1649, are reflected in a new interest in the North Carolina region. The Virginia assembly in 1643 authorized the discovery of new land west and south of the Appomattox River, while in 1646 two military expeditions made their way to the Chowan River. English refugees may have been interested in escaping to the New World, and Governor Sir William Berkeley stood ready to welcome them. A series of publications, three of which appeared in the fateful year of 1649, seem to have been designed to lure English colonists to North Carolina.[8]

One of these was William Bullock's *Virginia Impartially examined, and left to publick view* in which he dealt with Maryland, Virginia, and Roanoke.[9] This sixty-six-page tract was based on materials from the author's own library as well as on information furnished to him by men who had lived in Virginia or had engaged in trade with the colony. He cited Thomas Hariot, Ralph Lane, and John Smith among the authors consulted and Samuel Vassell, his own contemporary who had had an interest in the colonization of Carolana under the 1629 grant to Sir Robert Heath, as one from whom he had personal information.

A newspaper of the same year, the *Moderate Intelligencer*, in its issue for 26 April described Carolana in glowing terms. The weather and climate, natural resources, and the Indians were described and the relation of Carolana to Virginia explained. This article clearly was designed as an appeal to colonists as it explained that a governor for the region was about

8. William S. Powell, ed., *Ye Countie of Albemarle in Carolina* (Raleigh: State Department of Archives and History, 1958), pp. 81–82.
9. William Bullock, *Virginia Impartially examined, and left to publick view, to be considered by all Iudicious and honest men* (London: John Hammond, 1649).

to depart and prospective colonists were given directions for getting additional information.[10] We have no further evidence of any such plans.

Finally, published anonymously, was *A Perfect Description of Virginia* presenting information about the people there, natural resources, and the produce of the land.[11] It also contained "A Narration of the Countrey, within a few dayes journey of Virginia, West and by South, where people come to trade." This publication repeated Pory's 1622 report, but it also related that Governor Sir George Yeardley at that time had intended, before such movements from Jamestown were halted by the Indian massacre in the early spring, to send a larger expedition to that southerly region.

These three publications of 1649 touched more or less incidentally on the North Carolina region, but in 1650 a little book appeared that deserves to be classed as the first history of North Carolina. Edward Williams, Gentleman, the author, was probably a resident of London who never visited either Virginia or Carolina. Typical of other seventeenth-century works, his little book bore a rather long title: *Virgo Triumphans, or, Virginia richly and truly valued; more especially the South part thereof: viz. The fertile Carolana, and no lesse excellent Isle of Roanoke, of Latitude from 31 to 37 Degr. . . .*[12] Like its predecessors it was a promotional tract designed to lure adventurers and planters; yet it presented something of a chronological account of the region. Williams cited Ralph Lane, Thomas Hariot, John Pory, and Sir William Berkeley as sources for the facts that he related. The work was dedicated to Parliament, recent victor in the Civil War, and it promised that visitors to the region

10. This article was transcribed and edited by Hugh T. Lefler in the *NCHR* 32 (January 1955): 102–5, although there are minor discrepancies in the transcription.

11. *A Perfect Description of Virginia* (London: Printed for Richard Wodenoth, 1649).

12. Edward Williams, *Virgo Triumphans* . . . (London: Printed by Thomas Harper for John Stephenson, 1650).

described "shall discover the beauties of a long neglected Virgin, the incomparable Roanoke, and the adjacent excellencies of Carolana, a Country whom God and nature has indulged with blessings incommunicable to any other Region."[13]

The two earliest publications concerning North Carolina following the granting of the Carolina Charter of 1663 both dealt with the abortive settlement on the Cape Fear River. William Hilton, English-born Massachusetts sea captain, led an expedition late in 1663 to Cape Fear under the sponsorship of several gentlemen and merchants of the island of Barbados. The following year he published *A Relation of A Discovery Lately Made on the Coast of Florida* (as he termed the locale), in which he recounted what he and his companions had discovered.[14] His observations on the land, plants, and wildlife, as well as on the Indians, are reminiscent of those of the Roanoke explorers nearly a century earlier. A number of place-names, notably Stag Park and Rocky Point, assigned by members of this expedition are still in use. In 1662 Hilton had led a group of New Englanders to the same place and the two voyages have often been confused. Louise Hall separated them and discussed at some length the earlier and less well known visit in an article published in the *New England Historical and Genealogical Register* in 1970.[15] The immediate results of Hilton's voyages and his report were the announcement of generous inducements to settlers by the Lords Proprietors, the establishment on the Cape Fear River of the County of Clarendon, and the development of Charles Town, which flourished there for a few years.

The second publication to grow out of the interest here was issued anonymously as *A Brief Description of the Province of Carolina on the Coasts of Floreda. And More perticularly of a*

13. Ibid., "To the Reader," [c3, recto].
14. William Hilton, *A Relation of a Discovery Lately Made on the Coast of Florida* (London: Printed by J. C. for Simon Miller, 1664).
15. Louise Hall, "New Englanders at Sea: Cape Fear before the Royal Charter of 24 March 1662/3," *New England Historical and Genealogical Register* 124 (April 1970):88–108.

New-Plantation began by the English at Cape-Feare, on the River now by them called Charles-River.[16] In this work a concise description of the geography of Carolina is followed by an account of the settlement mentioned in the title. It had quickly grown to a community of 800 persons with good houses and forts. Natural features were described in words clearly designed to attract still more families. Features of the government were stressed because they too were attractive. Six specific "privileges" enjoyed by the colonists were set forth. Among these were "full and free Liberty of Conscience," "freedom from Custom for all *Wine, Silk, Raisins, Currance, Oyl, Olives*, and *Almonds*," and the authority "to choose annually from among themselves a certain Number of Men, according to their divisions, which constitute the General Assembly." The little book also contained an appeal to certain craftsmen and others to remove to the colony. Reminiscent of pleas made on behalf of Virginia a few decades earlier, the author also noted, "If any Maid or single Woman have a desire to go over, they will think themselves in the Golden Age, when Men paid a Dowry for their Wives; for if they be but Civil, and under 50 years of Age, some honest Man or other, will purchase them for their Wives."[17]

This 1666 publication was the apparent source for at least some of the information about Carolina that appeared in one of the earliest general works on America. John Ogilby, printer and king's cosmographer, issued a 674-page book in 1671 entitled *America: Being the Latest, and most Accurate Description; of the New World; Containing The Original of the Inhabitants, and Remarkable Voyages thither.*[18] A double-page map of the province of North Carolina preceded an eight-page account of current conditions in the colony. Information for the map and perhaps

16. *A Brief Description of the Province of Carolina* . . . (London: Printed for Robert Horne, 1666).

17. Ibid., pp. 9–10.

18. John Ogilby, *America* . . . (London: Printed by the Author, 1671).

also for some of the text was furnished to Ogilby by John Locke
while some came from *A Brief Description of the Province of
Carolina*. The map was the first to be issued following the
proprietary grant, and it contained a great many new place-
names.[19] Most of the text appears to have been freshly composed
for this book and bears no relation to any of the previously
published works on Carolina. As was true of its predecessors,
however, this was another highly flattering piece, and Carolina
was described in glowing terms. Tall trees suitable for masts;
woods well stocked with deer, rabbits, birds, and other game;
rivers "stor'd with plenty of excellent Fish of several sorts,
which are taken with great ease in abundance"; and a "happy
Climate" all combined, the author stressed, to make Carolina
"promising in its very infancy." Terms offered by the Lords
Proprietors to settlers were explained and the Fundamental
Constitutions summarized.[20]

In 1669 and 1670 a young German physician, John
Lederer, who was visiting in Virginia, made three journeys
of exploration to the west and the south. An account of these
was published two years later as *The Discoveries of John Lederer*,
a publication of interest in part because it was not a promotional
tract in the sense that most of the earlier pieces had been.[21]
The second journey, in the spring of 1670, took him across
Piedmont North Carolina and to within sight of the mountains.
Lederer's description of the country, the Indians, and the
natural products of the region furnish the earliest account of

19. William P. Cumming, *The Southeast in Early Maps* (Princeton, N.J.:
Princeton University Press, 1958), pp. 32–33.

20. Ogilby, *America*, pp. 207–12.

21. John Lederer, *The Discoveries of John Lederer* (London: Printed by J. C.
for Samuel Heyrick, 1672). The printer probably was the same one who issued
William Hilton's *Relation* in 1664. In 1958 the Wachovia Historical Society,
Winston-Salem, sponsored publication of Lederer's book with notes by William P.
Cumming. Professor Cumming also included transcripts of a number of previously unpublished letters by and about Lederer to Governor John Winthrop, Jr.,
of Connecticut.

that area. His trailblazing expedition was intended to open the great Indian Trading Path, and it soon was being traversed by fur traders between Virginia and the southwest. The text of his book supplied information on the Piedmont section of North Carolina for geographers and historians for many years.

Before the end of the seventeenth century several more purely promotional tracts appeared, each of which contained some new facts about the growing colony. *Carolina; or, A Description Of the Present State of that Country*, by T. A., Gentleman, who was perhaps Thomas Ash or more likely Thomas Amy, contains a summary of the history of the colony and by way of current information notes that wheat was beginning to be grown as an export crop.[22] The author also related that in Carolina men had lately discovered that from corn, with the help of a still, they could produce a strong drink like brandy. Robert Ferguson in the same year produced a slim volume entitled *The Present State of Carolina*, which included a fresh report on the Indians, including some population estimates and comments on birth control among them. His reference to Negro slaves in the colony is perhaps the earliest notice of that class of people in Carolina.[23]

The text of most of these tracts was included in Alexander S. Salley's *Narratives of Early Carolina, 1650–1708* but with inadequate bibliographical description and only moderate annotation.[24] The time is ripe for the preparation of a new edition of this valuable work, which should be expanded to include a number of additional tracts, more careful study of the authors and printers, and above all else a thorough and analytical index. Such a work would bring to the attention

22. *Carolina; or, a Description of the Present State of that Country* (London: Printed for W. C., 1682).
23. Robert Ferguson, *The Present State of Carolina* (London: Printed by John Bringhurst, 1682).
24. Alexander S. Salley, *Narratives of Early Carolina, 1650–1708* (New York: Charles Scribner's Sons, 1911).

of interested readers a vast amount of contemporary information on exploration and settlement; relations with the Indians, especially the trade with them; and government, agriculture, transportation, and wildlife.

The eighteenth century produced several works dealing exclusively or almost so with North Carolina, and in two cases these have come to be recognized as American classics. The earlier one is John Lawson's *A New Voyage to Carolina*, from which generations of American historians, anthropologists, and others have drawn fascinating descriptions of Indians and colonists. Lawson's book included a journal of an expedition begun in December 1700 at a point on the Atlantic north of Charleston, South Carolina, and continued through the backcountry, across Piedmont North Carolina, and to the site of the new town of Bath. His book is valuable for its description of the land and for its account of the state of the colony at that time, but especially for the unusual as well as the ordinary information that he recorded about the Indians. His close observation and his sympathetic understanding of the natives enabled Lawson to write of them as few of his contemporaries did. The care with which he recorded the routine as well as the extraordinary customs of the Indians makes *A New Voyage to Carolina* unique.[25]

Equally fascinating and more highly regarded as an

25. John Lawson, *A New Voyage to Carolina* (London, 1709). Although this work has been reprinted a number of times, perhaps the most useful edition is *A New Voyage to Carolina by John Lawson*, edited with an introduction and notes by Hugh T. Lefler (Chapel Hill: University of North Carolina Press, 1967). Based in a large measure on Lawson, John Brickell, *The Natural History of North-Carolina* (Dublin: Printed by James Carson, 1737), has been both praised and condemned, but the consensus seems to be that it has little value in its own right because of its plagiarism. See Percy G. Adams, "John Lawson's Alter-Ego—Dr. John Brickell," *NCHR* 24 (July 1957): 313–25; and Marcus B. Simpson, Jr., and Sallie W. Simpson, "The Reverend John Clayton's Letters to the Royal Society of London, 1693–1694: An Important Source for Dr. John Brickell's *Natural History of North-Carolina*, 1737," *NCHR* 54 (January 1977): 1–16. There are also certain portions of Brickell's text that suggest that he may have read William Byrd's manuscript.

example of early American literature is William Byrd's *History of the Dividing Line betwixt Virginia and North Carolina* and his "Secret History of the Line." Both were the product of Byrd's role in surveying the line between the two colonies in 1728. Byrd was a fastidious author who was always rewriting and polishing; so he refused during his lifetime to publish his work. He did, however, permit Thomas Jefferson, Mark Catesby, and other close friends to examine it.[26] The *History* was not published until 1841, and the "Secret History" remained in manuscript until 1929.[27] Byrd's delineation of North Carolinians as indolent ne'er-do-wells was compatible with the attitude of Virginians toward their Carolina neighbors for over half a century, and with the publication in 1841 of his journal the description was regarded as still applicable. Extracts eventually found their way into anthologies, and the author came to be appreciated for his humor, for his frank comments on his personal habits, and for his keen observation of Indian and pioneer life. The "Secret History" remained relatively unknown until 1929 when the North Carolina Historical Commission published both of Byrd's works on facing pages so that they could be easily compared. The "Secret History" is only about half the length of the *History*, but it contains a number of documents, letters, and addresses that are absent in the latter.

These seventeenth- and early eighteenth-century works may, in most cases, be placed in either or both of the two categories into which historians usually classify their sources: primary or secondary. There is much in them that was drawn

26. Louis B. Wright, *The Prose Works of William Byrd of Westover* (Cambridge, Mass.: Harvard University Press, 1966), pp. 1–2, 418.

27. William Byrd, *The Westover Manuscripts: Containing the History of the Dividing Line betwixt Virginia and North Carolina; A Journey to the Land of Eden*, A.D. *1733; and A Progress to the Mines. Written about 1728 to 1736, and Now First Published* (Petersburg, Va.: Printed by E. and J. C. Rufflin, 1841); and William K. Boyd, ed., *William Byrd's Histories of the Dividing Line betwixt Virginia and North Carolina* (Raleigh: North Carolina Historical Commission, 1929), pp. 13–321, recto only.

from the authors' personal knowledge, and it was these works that influenced both the thought and the action of people of the time who were instrumental in developing and settling North Carolina. On the other hand, most of them also were based in part on research into documents or on interviews with knowledgeable persons. Recent historians have made use of some of these publications, but it is apparent that better use can still be made of them. Two examples of unusual information may suffice to suggest the clues that these contemporary publications may hold. There are several references to an "engine" offered for use in Carolina by one Nathan Somers. With it he could "raise Trees up by the Roots quite out of the Earth, and throw them down near the place where they grew." Or he could "carry the fallen Trees, and lay them in order round the intended Inclosure . . . as an indifferent Boundary for Cattle; and carry the Remainder into convenient heaps within the said Inclosure."[28] This certainly sounds like a crane, and such machines may be well known to students of eighteenth-century agriculture, but to my knowledge no one has suggested that such a machine was ever used in clearing North Carolina land. A second example is seen in the fact that both Edward Williams's *Virgo Triumphans* in 1650 and Edward Blands's *Discovery of New Brittaine* the next year were "Printed by Thomas Harper for John Stephenson," while in 1682 John Bringhurst printed both Robert Ferguson's *Present State of Carolina* and Nathan Somers's *Proposals for Clearing Land in Carolina*. Why did John Stephenson and John Bringhurst have this material printed? What was their interest in Carolina? Their names do not appear in the likely places in the colonial records, but it seems apparent that they are both worth investigating.

Further clues that may lead to interesting discoveries may

28. Nathan Somers, *Proposals for Clearing Land in Carolina, East Jersey, Pensilvania, West Jersey: Or any other Parts of America* (London: Printed and sold by John Bringhurst, 1682), broadside. The same information appears in *A true Description of Carolina* (London: Printed for Joel Gascoine, 1682), p. 4.

be found in the personal names that occur in these early works. Byrd's *Journey to the Land of Eden*, for example, relates that in 1733 in the backcountry of North Carolina he found one Aaron Pinston. This was extremely early for settlement in that part of the colony. Recent research in the history of the region, however, verifies that he did, indeed, live there, and a small local stream still bears his name. As settlers crowded in around him a few years later, he pushed farther west and continued the pattern of fleeing ahead of thick settlement until he ended up across the mountains.[29]

Beginning early in the eighteenth century a number of works appeared in which the North Carolina region was discussed. The scope and purpose of the book, of course, determined the length, and often the quality as well, of the Carolina material. One of the earliest such works, and probably the one best known to most Americans for many years, was John Oldmixon's two-volume *History of the British Empire in America*, published in London in 1708. Oldmixon, a Whig historian and pamphleteer, devoted two chapters to "The History of Carolina" in which he discussed a variety of topics. Much emphasis was laid on the proprietary government, the role of dissenters in the colony, and relations with the Indians. Reference was made a number of times to people and events apparently not recorded elsewhere. For example, who was the Captain Halsted sent by the Proprietors in 1671 with a supply of provisions and stores for the colony?[30]

Oldmixon's work has been held in low regard by a number of subsequent writers. Francis L. Hawks commented in 1858 that "it contains almost as many errors as pages, and, unsupported, is not to be trusted." He believed that it was "manufactured to meet an existing demand in the market for

29. Wright, *The Prose Works of William Byrd*, p. 406. William S. Powell, *When the Past Refused to Die: A History of Caswell County, North Carolina* (Durham: Moore Publishing Co., 1977), p. 33.

30. John Oldmixon, *History of the British Empire in America*, 2 vols. (London: Printed for J. Brotherton, J. Clarke, . . . 1741), 1:464.

something about the colonies in America."[31] Robert Beverley was so concerned by the errors in Oldmixon that he was moved to write a history of Virginia in order to correct them. As a pamphleteer Oldmixon was accustomed to writing for a purpose, and he was not totally altruistic in preparing this history. His purpose was to demonstrate the value of the colonies to England and in so doing he presented the West Indies and the continental colonies together. It has been said that later American historians, "concentrating their attention on the continental colonies, forgot that more comprehensive viewpoint and thus largely missed the proper perspective of colonial history. Not until the twentieth century, particularly in the work of Charles M. Andrews, did American writers recapture that perspective."[32]

Like Captain John Smith many years earlier, William Stith opened his *History of the First Discovery and Settlement of Virginia*, printed in Williamsburg by William Parks in 1747, with the Roanoke colonies. In an initial chapter of thirty-four pages he related the facts of Sir Walter Raleigh's efforts to colonize America and also recorded some of the legends surrounding the Roanoke colonies. Writing in a clear and appealing style, Stith was careful to distinguish between fact and legend. He was, in fact, one of the founding fathers of an American scholarly tradition. With Thomas Prince and Thomas Hutchinson he developed a standard of historical research far advanced for his day. He discussed the reliability of his sources and drew upon contemporary records whenever possible. Because Stith's account ends with the year 1624, he had no occasion to pursue the history of the North Carolina region beyond Roanoke Island.[33] His account coincides with the information gathered by Hakluyt, and it was to Stith that many North Carolinians were indebted for knowledge of their state's early history.

31. Francis L. Hawks, *History of North Carolina*, 2 vols. (Fayetteville: E. J. Hale & Son, 1857–58), 2:481.

32. Kraus, *History of American History*, pp. 72–73.

33. Ibid., pp. 3–4, 92–95.

A substantial work by George Chalmers, an English lawyer who lived in Maryland for a time prior to the American Revolution, was printed in London in 1779. His *Political Annals of the Present United Colonies, From Their Settlement to the Peace of 1763* dealt with each of the colonies in turn, and the chapter on Carolina fills more than fifty pages. Chalmers, a pioneer in the use of contemporary documents in writing the history of North Carolina, had access to records of the Board of Trade, and he made effective use of them. In his narrative he incorporated extracts from the documents and in most cases provided a citation to the original. Among the citations Chalmers also reproduced many documents in their entirety. His style is interesting and extremely readable, and although he ends his narrative with the year 1693, he presents a balanced picture of Albemarle and Clarendon counties. The *Political Annals* may be consulted with profit by modern historians for its felicity of style, for the documents printed there, and for an understanding of a loyalist's point of view toward the colony at the end of the American Revolution. Insofar as the history of North Carolina in the seventeenth century is concerned, it would be difficult to recommend a more concise and direct statement than that given by Chalmers of the exploration and settlement, relations with the Proprietors, and internal upheavals. Chalmers's sympathetic comments about the Indians have a very modern tone to them.[34]

It has sometimes been said that little southern history is known outside the region because there were no southern poets and authors comparable to those of New England to record the significant events. Further comment might explain that

34. George Chalmers, *Political Annals of the Present United Colonies, From Their Settlement to the Peace of 1763, Compiled chiefly from Records, and authorised often by the Insertion of State-Papers* (London: Printed by Galabin and Baker . . . for the Author, 1779), pp. 512–66. I have worked from a copy in the University of North Carolina Library in Chapel Hill that may be unique. It bears a different imprint from that usually cited and may be the author's page proofs as there are numerous proofreader's marks throughout.

New England writers ignored or even belittled southern history. Witness Jedidiah Morse, Connecticut-born, Yale-educated Congregational clergyman, whose *American Geography; or, A View of the Present Situation of the United States of America* was first published in 1789 and afterwards issued in a variety of editions at home and abroad. While his entry pertaining to North Carolina contains a good description of the natural features, the towns, population, manners and customs, and government, his remarks on the history of the state leave much to be desired. "The history of North-Carolina is less known than that of any of the other states," he observed. "From the best accounts that history affords, the first permanent settlement in North-Carolina was made about the year 1710, by a number of Palatines from Germany." After relating extensive information about the Tuscarora Indian War and casually referring to the purchase of the proprietary rights by the crown in 1729, Morse concluded, "From this period to the revolution in 1776, the history of North-Carolina is unpublished, and of course unknown, except to those who have had access to the records of the province."[35] Admittedly North Carolinians had shown no interest in their history, but Oldmixon and Chalmers were certainly available to Morse. In addition, Morse had lived in Georgia for a time, and surely a man of his education would have heard something about events in North Carolina after it became a royal colony.

Apparently the earliest nineteenth-century publication to take note of North Carolina was John Daly Burk's *The History of Virginia from Its First Settlement to the Present Day*, published in two volumes in 1804 and 1805.[36] A chapter devoted to the various Roanoke voyages is preliminary to the history of the

35. Jedidiah Morse, *The American Geography; or, A View of the present situation of the United States of America* (London: Printed for John Stockdale, 1792), pp. 421–23.

36. John Daly Burk, *The History of Virginia from Its First Settlement to the Present Day*, 2 vols. (Petersburg, Va.: Printed for the Author, by Dickson & Pescud, 1804–5).

colony of Virginia. Sources cited include Hakluyt, Stith, Beverley, and Jeremy Belknap's "American Biography."

Benjamin Trumbull in 1810 dealt a little more justly with North Carolina than his fellow Connecticut native—Morse—had just two decades earlier. Scattered throughout Trumbull's *General History of the United States of America; from the Discovery in 1492* at appropriate places there are references to events in North Carolina such as early Spanish explorations, Sir Walter Raleigh, Albemarle County, and the German Palatines. There also is a ten-page summary review from the Roanoke Island period until 1729 (perhaps reflecting Morse's terminal date), a brief reference to the exploration and settlement of the Cape Fear section, and then an account of South Carolina and Georgia. Trumbull cited a manuscript of Benjamin Hawkins as the source for his information about white-Indian relations at Cape Fear during the years from 1661 to 1663. Hawkins, a native of what is now Warren County, was appointed Indian agent for all of the tribes south of the Ohio River by President Washington in 1796. As a student of Indian history, he compiled records of various tribes, but most of his manuscripts were destroyed by fire. Material that he gathered pertaining to the Creeks is now in the possession of the Georgia Historical Society, but the manuscript cited by Trumbull appears not to have survived.[37]

The first attempt to write a book-length history of North Carolina was that of Hugh Williamson. It resulted in the publication in Philadelphia in 1812 of two volumes entitled *The History of North Carolina.* Jared Sparks, Connecticut-born historian and editor, was not impressed with Williamson's efforts. In a belated review he commented, "We have seldom attempted to read, in the shape of history, so meagre, and so unsatisfactory a performance. It contains but few facts, and

37. Stephen B. Weeks, "Benjamin Hawkins," in Samuel A. Ashe and others, eds., *Biographical History of North Carolina*, 8 vols. (Greensboro: Charles L. Van Noppen, 1905–17), 5:152.

these, one would suppose, the author took pains to select from
the most unimportant of such as has fallen in his way. . . . It
is certainly unfortunate, that his book should be abroad
purporting to be an accurate and complete history."[38]

Williamson's reputation did not improve with time, and
later observers were equally as harsh. Half a century after the
publication of Williamson's book Francis L. Hawks observed that
"North Carolinians do not recognize Williamson's work as a
history of their State. It is inaccurate in a great many particulars;
and sometimes, as the present writer can testify, when there is
proof that the original record was lying before him." Still later,
Charles Kendall Adams, professor of history at the University of
Michigan, spoke disparagingly of the efforts of North Carolina's
first historian: "Though this work, in amplitude of margins and
generosity of type, presents an attractive appearance, it is
exceedingly unsatisfactory to the reader. The author apparently
cared nothing for historical perspective; for he selected his topics
with the most astounding disregard of their importance. But for
the position, and even fame, of the author the work would be
quite unworthy of notice."[39]

These appraisals represent contemporary and later
nineteenth-century opinions. It should be noted, however,
that Williamson's was a pioneering work, and it was he who took
note of a number of interesting and significant events in the
history of his adopted state. His account of Culpeper's Rebellion,
of the arrival of the Moravians, of the resistance to the Stamp
Act, and of the Regulators, to mention only a few, may not be
told fully, but at least they were touched upon and the basic
facts laid out. His sources were discussed in a preface, while
in an appendix he both cited and quoted from contemporary
documents. The time is at hand for a fresh reading of Williamson
and for recognition of the trail he blazed. H. G. Jones in 1966

38. *North American Review* 12 (January 1821): 37.
39. Hawks, *History of North Carolina*, 2:540. Charles K. Adams, *A Manual
of Historical Literature* (New York: Harper & Brothers, 1882), p. 558.

commented on Williamson's work and condemned it "as a travesty when judged by twentieth-century standards"; yet at the same time he termed it "significant."[40] The author's use of official and private manuscript sources was commended, and because some of these sources no longer exist it might be worthwhile to attempt to reconstruct Williamson's work habits and try to extract the information that came from lost documents.

Williamson's history was clearly recognized by his contemporaries as being inadequate. The *Raleigh Register* of 11 November 1825 considered it "scarcely a skeleton of a history" when it reported that plans were under way for what promised to be a more complete and better written one. Archibald D. Murphey, lawyer, judge, legislator, and Tar Heel visionary, proposed about 1820 to write a well-rounded history of the state, "in a style worthy of its subject."[41] He planned to secure copies of records from England, a plan in which Williamson had been rebuffed by George Chalmers, who held a position of some influence in that area in London. Murphey drew up an ambitious outline for his history, corresponded with his contemporaries concerning sources, and prepared a lengthy introduction and extensive, well organized notes. Unfortunately he was unable to complete his work, and perhaps he can best be credited with publicizing the need for a good history and with creating interest in getting copies of colonial records from England.[42]

As early as 1791 François-Xavier Martin, a printer and subsequently a lawyer and judge, who had been living in New Bern for about eight years, began to plan the writing of a history of the state. His employment to publish a revisal of the laws in 1803 strengthened this determination, and as a member of the

40. H. G. Jones, *For History's Sake* (Chapel Hill: University of North Carolina, 1966), pp. 134–37.
41. William Henry Hoyt, ed., *The Papers of Archibald D. Murphey*, 2 vols. (Raleigh: E. M. Uzzell & Co., 1914), 1:273–74.
42. Jones, *For History's Sake*, pp. 145–57, contains the best account of Murphey's ambitious plan.

General Assembly a few years later he began making copies of executive and legislative records. In 1809 Martin received a judicial appointment in Mississippi and in 1810 was named judge in New Orleans. When he left North Carolina, he took with him the material he had collected for a state history, and when he learned that Murphey contemplated writing a history, Martin rushed to press with his own work. His two-volume *History of North Carolina, From the Earliest Period* appeared in 1829.[43] Some years later a member of the University of North Carolina faculty commented that Martin made "no attempt to set forth events in the relation of cause and effect, nor to state them in such a way that this relation will become obvious. The work is thrown into the form of annals; the succession of paragraphs often seems to be determined by nothing else than the juxtaposition in time of the events they contain."[44]

Martin's history, after some preliminary remarks about the Spanish in America, begins with the Roanoke explorations, and it concludes with the Halifax Resolves. An analysis of Martin's history published in 1959 by W. Buck Yearns, although critical of the author's style in some instances, commended the work for its treatment of the early period, for the ninety-year period after 1663, and for his quotation of "flavorsome" phrases and passages from documents.[45] As Yearns noted, Martin cited some of his sources in very brief form at the end of each chapter but often employed such general terms as "records," "magazine," or "gazettes" without further identifying them. As in the case of Williamson's work, Martin's might be of use for whatever material can be identified as having come from sources that are

43. François-Xavier Martin, *History of North Carolina, From the Earliest Period*, 2 vols. (New Orleans: Printed by A. T. Penniman & Co., 1829).

44. Fordyce M. Hubbard, "An Address Delivered before the Historical Society of the University of North Carolina, June 1851," *North Carolina University Magazine* 1 (October 1852): 350.

45. W. Buck Yearns, "François X. Martin and His *History of North Carolina*," *NCHR* 36 (January 1959): 17–27.

no longer available. After all, he did take with him to Louisiana an unknown quantity of original records that were lost to the weather and vermin there. He admits this in the preface to the first volume. H. G. Jones has also reviewed the sad story of these documents in his book, *For History's Sake*.[46]

In 1851 one of the most popular history books ever to be published concerning North Carolina made its appearance. John Hill Wheeler, native of Murfreesboro and graduate of Columbian College (now George Washington University), became interested in state history when he served as state treasurer from 1842 until 1844. His *Historical Sketches of North Carolina, from 1584 to 1851* was published as two volumes bound into one.[47] The first volume contains a history in both narrative and tabular form, much of it covering a period beyond the scope of this paper. Nevertheless, there are seven brief chapters dealing with the period between 1584 and 1765, for which Wheeler cited such sources as Hakluyt, Lawson, Williamson, and Chalmers, as well as manuscripts from the Board of Trade and other documents from London made available to him by George Bancroft. The text is packed with information, most of it apparently intended merely to serve as the source of information for quick reference. Wheeler may have been responsible for originating the often quoted statement that Governor Gabriel Johnston was a physician. Recent investigation has demonstrated that this is incorrect.[48]

The second "volume" of Wheeler's work consists of information on each of the counties together with lists of members of the General Assembly and sometimes other officials from the county. Numerous errors appear in both the

46. Jones, *For History's Sake*, pp. 138–45.
47. John Hill Wheeler, *Historical Sketches of North Carolina, from 1584 to 1851*, 2 vols. in 1 (Philadelphia: Lippincott, Grambo and Co., 1851).
48. A concise biography of Johnston by Jaquelin Drane Nash prepared for the forthcoming *Dictionary of North Carolina Biography* proves that Johnston was not a physician.

text and in the lists. It was perhaps because so many names appeared in this work that it was extremely popular. Ten thousand copies were sold in one year, and it has been reprinted a number of times since.[49]

While many genealogists, local historians, and newspaper feature editors swear by Wheeler, often pulling it off the shelf to "prove" a point, others swear *at* it. A number of years ago a history professor described this work as "a jumble of ill-digested material; indeed, [it] is rather a collection of tables, lists, and facts than a history."[50] Wheeler, however, deserves at least some modest recognition for his landmark index; his book was the first history of the state to contain one.

Francis L. Hawks, native of New Bern, University of North Carolina alumnus, lawyer, clergyman, and historian, who was long interested in the collection of documentary material for the state and who visited England in search of source materials, published a two-volume history of North Carolina in the late 1850s.[51] In a prefatory statement Hawks explained that he planned to publish several volumes and that the first would consist primarily of documents concerning the very earliest history of North Carolina. Nevertheless, he noted, "we shall endeavor to enliven the dullness and relieve the quaintness of these worthy old chroniclers by such notes and remarks as may serve to link pleasantly together the past with the present." Concluding that "the soul of history is TRUTH," he suggested that the reader would find

in the reprint of these old publications, all the means extant of eviscerating the truth for himself; while the writer voluntarily shuts out the possibility of his substituting invention for the sober realities of History: in his narrative of *facts* he must conform to the early testimony which he has placed in the hands of the reader; his deductions, suggestions, reflections, &c., are his own, and will pass

49. Jones, *For History's Sake*, p. 175.
50. Adams, *Manual of Historical Literature*, pp. 558–59.
51. Hawks, *History of North Carolina*, (see footnote 31 for full citation).

for what they are worth with the intelligent, without the risk of being confounded with the *facts* of early records.[52]

Hawks's first volume was composed of the text of various documents concerning Raleigh's Roanoke ventures, but throughout he included full and interesting explanatory notes. There also was a biographical sketch of Sir Walter Raleigh and, by way of conclusion, a two-chapter narrative of the events of 1584 through 1590. The second volume was also heavily documentary, but it contained more narrative text and was arranged by subject. Such unexpected topics as agriculture and manufactures, religion and learning, and manners and customs are included. The author's style is engaging, clear, and precise; and the text is extensively documented. There are references to both manuscript and printed sources as well as to secondary material. A number of maps and at least one engraving enhance the usefulness of this work. Although the author's personal feelings are sometimes only thinly disguised (as in his references to northern slave traders and to the treatment of the Indians by early settlers),[53] his history is worthy of respect for the text of the documents it made available as well as for its interpretation of events by one who was closer to them by several generations than we are today.

The preface to the second volume clearly indicated that a third volume was planned. Stephen B. Weeks once pointed out that Joseph Sabin reported that a third volume was printed and shipped south about 1861.[54] Such a volume, if printed, was surely a victim of the Civil War, for none was known to Weeks, nor has one been recorded since.

John Wheeler Moore, University of North Carolina alumnus and lawyer, was the author of a two-volume *History of*

52. Ibid., 1:ix.
53. Ibid., 2:227–28, 557–58.
54. Stephen B. Weeks, *A Bibliography of the Historical Literature of North Carolina* (Cambridge, Mass.: The Library of Harvard University, 1895), p. 26.

North Carolina; From the Earliest Discoveries to the Present Time.[55]
It was drawn almost entirely from secondary sources, but the
early material is interesting for the undocumented notes
supplied by the author probably from local tradition. In this work
for the first time something akin to "interpretation" begins to
appear as opposed to a mere recitation of fact. For example,
Moore observes that "Carolina and Virginia were the fruits of
English patriotism and adventure. No discomfort at home sent
abroad the bold men who first came to Roanoke and Jamestown.
They were neither soured by religious persecution nor yet hostile
to a reigning family. They emigrated in all loyalty and submission
to enlarge in another hemisphere, the power and glory of the
land they still loved though no longer their home." Moore also
displays a sympathetic attitude toward Governor William
Tryon's role in the province during the Stamp Act Resistance.[56]
It was a rare North Carolinian who found it possible to speak favorably of Tryon before Marshall DeLancey Haywood's *Governor
William Tryon* appeared in 1903.[57] Stephen B. Weeks regarded
Moore's as "probably the best of all books dealing with the
history of the State as a whole."[58]

   As the result of an act of the legislature in 1881, the year
following the publication of Moore's history, work began on the
collecting, editing, and publishing of the colonial and state
records of North Carolina. The first volume of the *Colonial
Records of North Carolina* appeared in 1886 and the last of the ten
in that series was published in 1890.[59] At last the resources

   55. John Wheeler Moore, *History of North Carolina; From the Earliest
Discoveries to the Present Time*, 2 vols. (Raleigh: Alfred Williams & Co., 1880).
   56. Ibid., 1:xii, 95.
   57. Marshall DeLancey Haywood, *Governor William Tryon, and His Administration in the Province of North Carolina, 1765–1771* (Raleigh: W. M. Uzzell, Printer,
1903).
   58. Weeks, *A Bibliography of Historical Literature*, p. 37.
   59. For an account of the collection and publication of the colonial and
state records of North Carolina, see H. G. Jones, *For History's Sake*, pp. 211–36.

necessary for a full relation of the history of North Carolina as an English colony were available.

Samuel A. Ashe was the first to publish a study based on these volumes of documentary material. His *History of North Carolina*, the first volume of which covered the period from 1584 to 1783, appeared in 1908.[60] Based on careful research, this history divided events into "epochs" with the period that we are considering here, the years 1584 through 1764, forming four epochs. These were all logical divisions that have generally been followed by Ashe's successors in the field. The first dealt with the Raleigh colonies, the second with charters and early settlement between 1629 and 1663, the third with the proprietary period, and the fourth with North Carolina as a royal province. Ashe wrote well, expressed himself clearly, and led his reader easily through the course of the colony's history. For the curious or the scholarly he listed his sources in marginal notes while in footnotes he provided explanatory information or additional facts that did not fit easily into the narrative of the text. Extensive illustrations, contemporary maps, and maps especially prepared for his history enhanced the volume's usefulness and its appeal to the popular audience.

While a large portion of the text dealt with political and military matters, such topics as trade and agriculture, religion, the daily life of the people, and other aspects of social history were not ignored. The physical setting was adequately portrayed, and individuals who played significant roles in the events of the time were usually characterized.

Ashe brought order to the mass of facts available to him. He used his sources well and reported objectively. He did not view North Carolina as in a vacuum but from time to time took note of events outside the province. Although he was not a "professional" historian (he was a newspaper editor, public

60. Samuel A. Ashe, *History of North Carolina* (Greensboro: Charles L. Van Noppen, Publisher, 1908). In 1925 a second volume was published bringing the history up to that very year.

official, legislator, and lawyer), he provided the organization of North Carolina history that has been widely followed.

Just eleven years after Ashe's first volume appeared, the first of two works on the colonial period by R. D. W. Connor was published. The earlier of these was the first in a three-volume cooperative series in which William K. Boyd and J. G. de Roulhac Hamilton collaborated to cover later periods. Connor's contribution to the *History of North Carolina* was confined to the colonial and revolutionary periods, 1584 to 1783.[61] Connor was a professional historian and came to his task with a broader perspective than any of his predecessors. In many instances, however, he could add little to what Ashe had already recorded. Nevertheless, he enlarged on many things that Ashe had touched upon only lightly. Connor, for example, devoted an entire chapter to society, religion, and education and another to the coming of the Scotch-Irish and Germans, while in others he was able to expand upon topics covered by Ashe, particularly in those dealing with intercolonial and imperial relations.

Just ten years after the appearance of his first colonial history, Connor was the author of a two-volume account of the state's history covering the years from 1584 to 1925, which dealt with the same period as Ashe's two volumes. *North Carolina: Rebuilding an Ancient Commonwealth* was, in many respects, almost identical to the author's former history. A comparison of some sentences will demonstrate this:

> In colonial times, class distinctions were sharply drawn.[62]

> In colonial times social distinctions were carefully drawn.[63]

61. R. D. W. Connor et al., *History of North Carolina*, 3 vols. (Chicago and New York: Lewis Publishing Co., 1919), vol. 1, *The Colonial and Revolutionary Periods, 1584–1783*, by R. D. W. Connor.

62. Connor, *Colonial and Revolutionary Periods*, p. 180.

63. R. D. W. Connor, *North Carolina: Rebuilding an Ancient Commonwealth, 1584–1925*, 2 vols. (Chicago and New York: American Historical Society, Inc., 1929), 1:164.

The transfer of Carolina from the Lords Proprietors to the Crown worked no important changes in the outward form of the machinery of government.[64]

The transfer of Carolina to the Crown worked no important changes in the outward form of the machinery of the government of the colony.[65]

The next history in sequence was *North Carolina: The Old North State and the New* by Archibald Henderson, published in 1941 in two volumes.[66] The author, professor of mathematics at the University of North Carolina, was also noted as a biographer, drama critic, and historian. In a foreword Henderson explained that he had been interested in the history of his native state for many years, that he had done research in depositories at home and abroad, and that he had published some of his findings in journals, newspapers, and in pamphlets. The time had come, he felt, to put his work into a more solid form. He announced that his primary purpose in so doing was

to tell forthrightly, simply, and lucidly, within the given framework, the true story of the life of the people in all its aspects: social, sociological, intellectual, literary, scientific, cultural, industrial, political, military, economic, religious. The writer may confess, however naïvely, that he has cherished the hope of writing a more than merely readable, indeed if that be possible of achievement, an absorbingly interesting story of the evolving genius of a people, from the pioneer and crude state of 1584 to the enlightened civilization of today.[67]

Henderson was not a historian by training even though he practiced the historian's craft with skill and understanding. He was, nevertheless, the subject of some unpublished criticism for what was sometimes regarded as undue attention paid to his own ancestors. His ancestors were distinguished and to have

64. Connor, *Colonial and Revolutionary Periods*, p. 210.
65. Connor, *Rebuilding an Ancient Commonwealth*, 1:219.
66. Archibald Henderson, *North Carolina: The Old North State and the New*, 2 vols. (Chicago: Lewis Historical Publishing Co., 1941).
67. Ibid., 1:vi.

omitted reference to them would have been a disservice to his readers. Samuel A. Ashe was likewise a descendant of distinguished ancestors, but so far as is known he was not criticized for his references to them.

Henderson's history of North Carolina prior to 1765 was a fresh retelling of a familiar story into which he worked a considerable amount of British and British colonial history. Contemporary material drawn from local records also enlivened his account while his illustrations were well chosen and appropriate. Photographs of some of the John White watercolors were better than the de Bry engravings used so often by earlier historians. In addition his history was also illustrated with portraits of many of the men about whom he wrote. His chapters on cultural growth and development brought to light a new aspect of North Carolina history on such topics as literature, libraries, printing, newspapers, cartography, science, and other subjects.

The current classic North Carolina history now in its third edition is *North Carolina: The History of a Southern State*, by Hugh T. Lefler and Albert Ray Newsome.[68] For the early period, in many respects, it is quite similar in organization to the volumes by Connor and is, in fact, often a close paraphrase of the works of that author. A few examples will demonstrate this:

Connor: Reports of the survey were made not to the Lords Proprietors but to the Crown for when it was completed North Carolina had ceased to be a proprietary colony.[69]

Lefler-Newsome: The official report of the boundary line commissioners was made to the King, not to the Proprietors, because meantime

68. Hugh T. Lefler and Albert Ray Newsome, *North Carolina: The History of a Southern State* (Chapel Hill: University of North Carolina Press, 1954). Later editions were issued in 1963 and 1973. The 1963 edition represented a moderately thorough revision, but the 1973 edition was merely an extension of the second one. In 1976 there was a second printing of the third edition in which a few minor errors, primarily typographical, were corrected.

69. Connor, *Rebuilding an Ancient Commonwealth*, 1:145.

the sale of Carolina to the Crown had been consummated, and
North Carolina became a royal colony, July 25, 1729.[70]

Connor: The term Scotch-Irish is a misnomer, and does not, as
one would naturally suppose, signify a mixed race of Scotch
and Irish ancestry.[71]

Lefler-Newsome: The term Scotch-Irish is a misnomer. It is geographical
and not racial and does not imply a mixture of the two national
stocks.[72]

Connor: The transfer of Carolina to the Crown worked no important
changes in the outward form of the machinery of the
Government of the colony. Governor, council, assembly, and
courts, as well as the various administrative agencies, remained
as they were.[73]

Lefler-Newsome: The transfer of the colony to the Crown in 1729
marked no significant change in the structure of government, on
either the provincial or local level. The powers and duties of
governor, council, assembly, courts and local officials were
unchanged.[74]

Lefler followed this cooperative work with a two-volume
History of North Carolina, of which he alone was the author.[75]
The first twelve chapters of the first volume, the only portion
of the work dealing with the colony of North Carolina prior
to 1765, represent only modest changes from the 1954 history,
and some parts are identical. The advantage of this work is that
it contains some documentation whereas the earlier work did
not. This new work was not without its flaws, however, and a
number of them were cited by H. G. Jones in a critical appraisal
in the *North Carolina Historical Review*.[76]

70. Lefler and Newsome, *North Carolina* (1954 ed.), p. 67.
71. Connor, *Rebuilding an Ancient Commonwealth*, 1:153.
72. Lefler and Newsome, *North Carolina*, p. 74.
73. Connor, *Rebuilding an Ancient Commonwealth*, 1:219.
74. Lefler and Newsome, *North Carolina*, p. 138.
75. Hugh T. Lefler, *History of North Carolina*, 2 vols. (New York: Lewis
Historical Publishing Co., 1956).
76. *NCHR* 35 (January 1957): 105–8.

Lefler and William S. Powell collaborated to produce a volume in the series History of the American Colonies published by Scribners. *Colonial North Carolina* appeared in 1973.[77] One reviewer described this work as "a major synthesis,"[78] while another found it to be "impressive in its scope, its clarity, and its conciseness." The second reviewer, however, was highly critical of the book for its lack of detail concerning slavery and the status of women in the colony. "In the face of the detailed demographic work being done on New England towns," he found it intolerable that a work on colonial North Carolina should have so little to say about women, marriage, and children.[79] He clearly was unaware that sources for such information are not as readily available for North Carolina as for the New England colonies.

A new trend in writing of the colonial period in North Carolina as well as of later periods requires the use of local records. The availability of court minutes, land records, estate papers, and other primary sources on microfilm for most of the counties has encouraged the use of such records by many more scholars. No longer is it necessary to travel from county to county. Two pioneer works appeared in 1964. Harry Roy Merrens's *Colonial North Carolina in the Eighteenth Century*, a study in historical geography, dealt with the settlement of the colony, the increase in population, and the changing economic geography particularly with respect to the use of forest resources and the production of commercial crops. Robert W. Ramsey in *Carolina Cradle: Settlement of the Northwest Carolina Frontier, 1747–1762*, focused attention on a small area west of the Yadkin River that was settled by people largely from New Jersey, Pennsylvania, and Maryland. He examined the causes of the

77. Hugh T. Lefler and William S. Powell, *Colonial North Carolina* (New York: Charles Scribner's Sons, 1973).

78. James LaVerne Anderson of the University of Georgia in the *Journal of Southern History* 40 (August 1974): 458–59.

79. Jerome J. Nadelhaft of the University of Maine, Orono, in the *William and Mary Quarterly*, 3d ser., 31 (July 1974): 507–9.

southward migration as revealed by local records in the colonies from which the people came and their life in the newly opened frontier region as recorded in North Carolina records. Published in the following year, Lawrence Lee's *The Lower Cape Fear in Colonial Days* is an in-depth look at a coastal region from the earliest days of settlement until the American Revolution.[80]

The most impressive recent work in the colonial period perhaps had its inspiration in the Carolina Charter Tercentenary Commission's series of monographs. John V. Allcott wrote on colonial homes in North Carolina; E. Lawrence Lee on the Indian wars in North Carolina, from 1663 to 1764; William S. Powell on the Proprietors of Carolina; Hugh F. Rankin on Culpeper's Rebellion, 1675 to 1689; and Blackwell P. Robinson on the royal governors. Following in the same tradition is Alan D. Watson's recent *Society in Colonial North Carolina*, published in 1975 by the Division of Archives and History. Watson has published articles on related subjects in the *North Carolina Historical Review*. That interest in the colonial period is alive and well is reflected in the variety of subjects investigated in recent years by scholars. Lindley S. Butler wrote "Early Settlement of Carolina: Virginia's Southern Frontier," in the January 1971 *Virginia Magazine of History and Biography*; William S. Price wrote " 'Men of Good Estates': Wealth Among North Carolina's Royal Councillors" in the January 1972 *North Carolina Historical Review*; Herbert R. Paschal wrote "Charles Griffin: Schoolmaster to the Southern Frontier," in *East Carolina College Publications in History*; Mattie Erma Edwards Parker wrote "Legal Aspects of Culpeper's Rebellion" in the *North Carolina Historical Review* for the spring of 1968; and Elizabeth G. McPherson wrote "Nathaniel Batts, Landholder on Pasquotank River, 1660" in the Winter 1966 issue

80. Harry Roy Merrens, *Colonial North Carolina in the Eighteenth Century: A Study in Historical Geography* (Chapel Hill: University of North Carolina Press, 1964); Robert W. Ramsey, *Carolina Cradle: Settlement of the Northwest Carolina Frontier, 1747–1762* (Chapel Hill: University of North Carolina Press, 1964); Lawrence Lee, *The Lower Cape Fear in Colonial Days* (Chapel Hill: University of North Carolina Press, 1965).

of the *North Carolina Historical Review*. Theses and dissertations on a variety of colonial subjects appear regularly as do honors essays and term papers.

More such studies may be anticipated as the work of the Colonial Records Project, a program initiated by the Carolina Charter Tercentenary Commission, continues. Five volumes in a new series of *Colonial Records* have been published and are beginning to be cited in footnotes of scholarly articles. Xerox and microfilm copies of records from the Public Record Office, the British Library, and elsewhere in England are now available in the state archives and the collection grows almost daily.

What further remains to be done? First, I suppose, we might encourage the preparation of a history of colonial North Carolina to stand beside Richard Morton's work on Virginia and Eugene Sirmans's on South Carolina. Biographies are always worthwhile both to serve the needs of scholars and students and to entertain as well as instruct the general reader. This list of special topics might be extended indefinitely, but historical work is best undertaken because of personal inspiration and not from artificial stimulation. Few North Carolina historians have yet been sufficiently inspired to study this period, but with the growing number of articles being published and the expanding collections of sources, this situation is bound to change.

2

Revolutionary North Carolina, 1765–1789

by Alan D. Watson

Writing upon the immediate close of the bicentennial celebration of America's independence, with its heady slogans, gushy panegyrics, and eventual apathy in the face of rampant commercialism, it is sobering to remember that 1776 was but the midpoint of the revolutionary era. Although the revolutionary movement in North Carolina failed to receive the publicity accorded the activities of its neighboring colonies, the province chafed under the new directions of Britain's colonial policy and was not slow in opting for independence. Yet the march toward revolution and formal separation from England proved more exhilarating than the tasks of winning the war and establishing a viable government. The tribulations of the war and the political factionalism of the Confederation years yielded to a reluctant decision in 1789 to join the new Union, but almost immediately the state regretted this forward step and retreated to its time-honored agrarian insularity.

The revolutionary era has been the subject of historical investigation for more than a century and a half as North Carolina has benefited from a full complement of histories dating from the second decade of the nineteenth century. However, with one exception the early works generally evidenced perfunctory research, an obsessive concern with politics and war, a stylistic dullness, and a patriotic desire to present North

Carolina as a repository of republican virtue.[1] The exception,
of course, was the *History of North Carolina* by Francis L. Hawks,
who, unfortunately for historians of the Revolution, concluded
his study with the downfall of the Proprietary in 1729.[2] Thus the
state depended upon the superficial narratives of professional
men and politicians for its histories and awaited the twentieth
century for accounts of the Revolution that could match the
work of David Ramsay.[3]

The first published histories of North Carolina derived
from the efforts of Hugh Williamson and François X. Martin,
immigrants to the state and participants in the public affairs of
the late revolutionary and early national years. Appearing in
1812, *The History of North Carolina* in two volumes by Williamson
proved a mass of impertinent data and not a few factual blunders
connected by a graceless style. Most disappointing was the
termination of the work with the outbreak of the Revolution,
thereby omitting the war years and Confederation era whose
history Williamson had helped to shape.[4] Among Martin's
voluminous literary and legal output was a two-volume *History*

1. See Stephen B. Weeks, "The North Carolina Historians," *Proceedings
and Addresses of the Fifteenth Annual Session of the State Literary and Historical
Association* [1–2 December 1914] (Raleigh: North Carolina Historical Commission,
1915), pp. 71–86; Guion Griffis Johnson, *Ante-Bellum North Carolina: A Social
History* (Chapel Hill: University of North Carolina Press, 1937), pp. 817–23; H. G.
Jones, *For History's Sake: The Preservation and Publication of North Carolina History,
1663–1903* (Chapel Hill: University of North Carolina Press, 1966).

2. Francis L. Hawks, *History of North Carolina*, 2 vols. (Fayetteville: E. J.
Hale & Son, 1857–58).

3. For the work of Ramsay see Charles G. Sellers, "The American
Revolution: Southern Founders of a National Tradition," in Arthur S. Link and
Rembert W. Patrick, eds., *Writing Southern History: Essays in Historiography in
Honor of Fletcher M. Green* (Baton Rouge: Louisiana State University Press, 1965),
pp. 38–43.

4. Hugh Williamson, *The History of North Carolina*, 2 vols. (Philadelphia:
Thomas Dobson, 1812). See also Stephen B. Weeks, "Hugh Williamson," in
Samuel A. Ashe, ed., *Biographical History of North Carolina from Colonial Times to
the Present*, 8 vols. (Greensboro: C. L. Van Noppen, 1905–17), 5:458–66. Actually

of North Carolina that was published in 1829.[5] Influenced by the temperament or legal training of its author, the narrative was a dull, laborious affair in which the author "presented his dry and factual account without defending, accusing, or ext[ra]polating." Ending in 1776, the material of the second volume was "merely dumped . . . on the printed page, the result sometimes resembling an almanac as much as a history."[6]

When Joseph S. Jones took up his pen to defend the integrity of the Mecklenburg Declaration of Independence and the patriotism of William Hooper, both of which had been impugned by Thomas Jefferson, he produced the state's first major study dealing solely with the Revolution. In *A Defence of the Revolutionary History of North Carolina*, Jones wrote to reveal "the proud historic deeds" of North Carolinians, which in turn would hopefully bring a modicum of respect to the state and rescue it from the baleful influence of its overbearing neighbor to the north.[7] Jones was successful by his standards in recounting the virtues of North Carolina's revolutionaries and exposing Jefferson as a man whose name deserved "the execration of every native citizen of North Carolina," but it was a tortuous, sentimental, and blindly partisan effort, wholly lacking in the generosity exhibited by Jefferson toward North Carolina.[8]

Although John H. Wheeler had ample opportunity to advance these early studies, his *Historical Sketches of North*

---

the narrative concluded with the defeat of the Regulators at the Battle of Alamance in 1771; a few pages briefly carried the discussion to the outbreak of the Revolution (Williamson, *History of North Carolina*, 2:162–72).

5. François-Xavier Martin, *The History of North Carolina, from the Earliest Period*, 2 vols. (New Orleans: A. T. Penniman & Co., 1829).

6. W. B. Yearns, "François X. Martin and His *History of North Carolina*," *North Carolina Historical Review* (hereafter cited as *NCHR*) 36 (1959): 25, 23.

7. Jo[seph] Seawell Jones, *A Defence of the Revolutionary History of North Carolina from the Aspersions of Mr. Jefferson* (Boston: Charles Bowen, and Raleigh: Turner and Hughes, 1834), p. viii.

8. Ibid., p. vii. See also Edwin A. Miles, "Joseph Seawell Jones— Historian and Humbug," *NCHR* 34 (1957): 483–506.

Carolina, published as two volumes in one in 1851, failed to meet the challenge.[9] In fact, the title is misleading because most of the work comprised collections of data, county histories, and biographical sketches. It did, however, in halting fashion extend the coverage of the state's past beyond 1776. Fittingly, perhaps, some improvement flowed from the labors of John Wheeler Moore, nephew and namesake of Wheeler. Reared in a Jeffersonian Democratic tradition and serving ably in the Confederacy, Moore in his *History of North Carolina* provided a useful antidote to Jones's diatribe against Virginia and extended appreciative understanding to the efforts of the radicals, later Antifederalists, during the Revolution. Still, this was not a people's history as Moore apprised his readers that "a good history . . . must give prominence and light to certain figures."[10] While improving upon the flat and lifeless narrative of Martin, Moore failed to approach the eloquence of Jones and lacked the trained historian's appreciation of the proportionate importance of the materials with which he worked.

Although the patrician historians of the nineteenth century usually produced uncritical, romantic history, admittedly they worked with limited source materials, a handicap that was partially corrected by the publication of *The Colonial Records* and *The State Records of North Carolina* at the end of the century.[11] By that time the early professional historians, best exemplified by

9. John H. Wheeler, *Historical Sketches of North Carolina. . .* , 2 vols. in 1 (Philadelphia: Lippincott, Grambo, and Co., 1851). For other works written at approximately that time see William H. Foote, *Sketches of North Carolina, Historical and Biographical* (New York: Robert Carter, 1846) and E. W. Caruthers, *Revolutionary Incidents: and Sketches of Character, Chiefly in the "Old North State"* (Philadelphia: Hayes & Zell, 1854).

10. John Wheeler Moore, *History of North Carolina from the Earliest Discoveries to the Present Time*, 2 vols. (Raleigh: Alfred Williams & Co., 1880), p. iv. See also S. A. Ashe, "John Wheeler Moore," *Biographical History of North Carolina*, 8:359–64.

11. William L. Saunders, ed., *The Colonial Records of North Carolina*, 10 vols. (Raleigh: State of North Carolina, 1886–1890); Walter Clark, ed., *The State*

Enoch W. Sikes and Charles L. Raper, had begun to investigate North Carolina's past. In *The Transition of North Carolina from Colony to Commonwealth*, Sikes, a Johns Hopkins trained scholar, combined Herbert Baxter Adams's concern with institutional history and J. C. Ballagh's interest in southern history to produce a fairly dispassionate account of the prerevolutionary years.[12] Sikes manifestly sympathized with the aims of the revolutionaries but was no devotee of wholesale democracy. Raper continued that objectivity in *North Carolina: A Study in English Colonial Government*, a work that bore the impress of the imperial influence. His study ended in 1775 as opposed to that of Sikes, which carried the investigation to 1776, and together they set the tone for scholarly endeavors in the twentieth century.[13]

Samuel A. Ashe, editor, lawyer, and politician, advanced the efforts of Sikes and Raper in his two-volume *History of North Carolina*, which carried the history of the state to the twentieth century.[14] Although Ashe was not a trained historian, his thorough research and sound judgment combined to produce a solid history. Its principal defect is a strict adherence to a chronological approach that sometimes obscures significant events and ideological considerations in a maze of unrelated data. The three-volume *History of North Carolina*, which appeared

---

Records of North Carolina, 16 vols. [numbered 11–26] (Winston, Goldsboro, and Raleigh: State of North Carolina, 1895–1907). Note the romantic history of the state as found in the editors' introductions to the volumes. See also Jones, *For History's Sake*, pp. 211–36.

12. Enoch W. Sikes, *The Transition of North Carolina from Colony to Commonwealth*, Johns Hopkins University Studies in Historical and Political Science, vol. 16, nos. 10–11 (Baltimore: Johns Hopkins Press, 1898).

13. Charles L. Raper, *North Carolina: A Study in English Colonial Government* (New York: Macmillan Company, and London: McMillan Co., 1904). The Imperial School of historians appeared in the 1890s, in part as a reaction to the excessively nationalistic history of the nineteenth century. The imperialists tended to be more objective in their assessment of British-colonial relations and consequently showed more sympathy for the British position.

14. Samuel A. Ashe, *History of North Carolina*, 2 vols. (Greensboro: C. L.

in 1919, attempted to rectify that weakness by emphasizing "movements rather than events, ideals rather than men, orderly development rather than the phenomena of antiquarian interest."[15] William K. Boyd, in *The Federal Period, 1783–1860*, added little to Ashe's coverage of the Confederation, but R. D. W. Connor, in *The Colonial and Revolutionary Periods, 1584–1783*, improved substantially upon earlier considerations of the revolutionary years. Connor corrected many of Ashe's factual errors and produced a highly readable history. In addition to his compelling style, Connor was the first to grant serious consideration to the social history of the era.[16]

Indeed, subsequent histories have generally been grounded on Connor's efforts. In a two-volume work published in 1941, Archibald Henderson's informed discussion of the west added luster to an otherwise mediocre recounting of the events of the revolutionary years. In 1956 Hugh T. Lefler brought his expertise in colonial and North Carolina history to his two-volume history of the state. Disappointingly, it did little to advance the discussion of the Revolution found in his standard textbook history that was published two years earlier. Moreover, virtually the same account appeared in Lefler's later collaborative production with William S. Powell, *Colonial North Carolina*, which concludes with the outbreak of the Revolution. However, this work is designed for the general reader as well as the scholar and constitutes a particularly well-written introduction to North Carolina's early history.[17]

Van Noppen, 1908–25). See also R. D. W. Connor, "Samuel A'Court Ashe: Historian of North Carolina," *NCHR* 3 (1926): 132–35.

15. R. D. W. Connor et al., *History of North Carolina*, 3 vols. (Chicago and New York: Lewis Publishing Co., 1919), vol. 2, William K. Boyd, *The Federal Period, 1783–1860*, p. v. (Vol. 1, R. D. W. Connor, *The Colonial and Revolutionary Periods, 1584–1783*; vol. 3, J. G. de Roulhac Hamilton, *North Carolina since 1860*.)

16. In *North Carolina: Rebuilding an Ancient Commonwealth, 1584–1925*, 2 vols. (Chicago and New York: American Historical Society, Inc., 1929), R. D. W. Connor adds little to his previous work.

17. Archibald Henderson, *North Carolina: The Old North State and the New,*

In addition to the general surveys, the revolutionary era has received specific treatment by way of numerous short monographs and essays, which is due primarily to the opportunities for publication provided by the James Sprunt Studies in History and Political Science, the Trinity College Historical Society *Papers*, the *North Carolina Booklet*, and the *North Carolina Historical Review*.[18] Nevertheless, North Carolina has only one incisive political analysis of the means by which the colony was drawn into the effort to oppose Great Britain. Published in 1957, Charles G. Sellers's trenchant discussion of the purposive efforts of the Whigs to effect the separation of North Carolina from the empire has yet to be surpassed. Lindley S. Butler, in *North Carolina and the Coming of the Revolution, 1763–1776*, one of several short works sponsored by the North Carolina Bicentennial Commission, incorporates the latest scholarly endeavors in a sprightly survey of the period but does not intend to examine in detail the politics of the independence movement. The best sectional treatment of the onset of the Revolution is found in Lawrence Lee, *The Lower Cape Fear in Colonial Days*.[19]

As Butler realizes, history cannot be neatly divided into disparate segments. Thus the momentum toward revolution in North Carolina can be traced most easily and obviously from the Stamp Act crisis of 1765. The circumstances contributing

---

2 vols. (Chicago: Lewis Publishing Company, 1941); Hugh T. Lefler, *History of North Carolina*, 2 vols. (New York: Lewis Historical Publishing Company, 1956); Hugh T. Lefler and Albert Ray Newsome, *North Carolina: The History of a Southern State* (Chapel Hill: University of North Carolina Press, 1954); Hugh T. Lefler and William S. Powell, *Colonial North Carolina: A History* (New York: Charles Scribner's Sons, 1973).

18. See Paul Murray, "Thirty Years of the New History: A Study of *The North Carolina Historical Review*, 1924–1953," *NCHR* 32 (1955): 174–93; Thomas C. Parramore, "Forging the Tremulous Link: The First Half-Century of the *North Carolina Historical Review*," *NCHR* 51 (1974): 361–78.

19. Charles Grier Sellers, Jr., "Making a Revolution: The North Carolina Whigs, 1765–1775," in J. Carlyle Sitterson, ed., *Studies in Southern History*, James Sprunt Studies in History and Political Science, vol. 39 (Chapel Hill: University of North Carolina Press, 1957), pp. 23–46; Lindley S. Butler, *North Carolina and the*

to the rift in Anglo-American relations, however, and the
development of a revolutionary mentality can be discerned in the
preceding two decades. The representation controversy of 1746,
the reorganization of the Board of Trade in 1752, the dispute
over the tenure of judges, and British deviation from basic
mercantilist principles impressed North Carolinians with their
dependence upon the mother country and created among many
colonials a fear of English encroachment upon provincial
autonomy.[20] Allegations that events preceding the passage of the
Stamp Act were inconsequential are misleading. Hence the
proposition that the "Currency Act of 1764 . . . caused little
difficulty in North Carolina" has been contradicted by Robert M.
Weir, who shows that British currency restrictions burdened the
provincials and constituted one of the grievances impelling
North Carolina toward independence.[21]

    Nonetheless, it was the Stamp Act that brought the
colonies to the brink of revolt a decade before war began.
Opposition to the Stamp Act in the lower Cape Fear, the center
of ferment at that time in North Carolina, has been well

Coming of the Revolution, 1763–1776 (Raleigh: North Carolina Department of
Cultural Resources, 1976); Lawrence Lee, *The Lower Cape Fear in Colonial Days*
(Chapel Hill: University of North Carolina Press, 1965).

    20. See Jack P. Greene, "An Uneasy Connection: An Analysis of the
Preconditions of the American Revolution," in Stephen G. Kurtz and James H.
Hutson, eds., *Essays on the American Revolution* (Chapel Hill: University of North
Carolina Press, 1973), pp. 32–80; Lawrence F. London, "The Representation
Controversy in Colonial North Carolina," *NCHR* 11 (1934): 255–70; Bernhard
Knollenberg, *Origin of the American Revolution, 1759–1766* (New York: Macmillan
Company, 1960); J. M. Bumsted, " 'Things in the Womb of Time': Ideas of
American Independence, 1633–1763," *William and Mary Quarterly* (hereafter cited
as *WMQ*), 3d ser., 31 (1974): 533–64; and the suggestive comments in C. Robert
Haywood, "The Mind of the North Carolina Advocates of Mercantilism," *NCHR*
33 (1956): 139–165, esp. 164–65.

    21. Lefler and Newsome, *North Carolina: The History of a Southern State*, 3d
ed. (Chapel Hill: University of North Carolina Press, 1973), p. 193; Robert M.
Weir, "North Carolina's Reaction to the Currency Act of 1764," *NCHR* 40 (1963):
183–99. See, however, E. James Ferguson, "Currency Finance: An Interpretation
of Colonial Monetary Practices," *WMQ*, 3d ser., 10 (1953): 153–80.

documented by Lawrence Lee in "Days of Defiance."[22] C. Robert
Haywood examines "The Mind of the North Carolina Opponents
of the Stamp Act" and finds that the primary importance of the
resistance "was to release the mind of the North Carolinians
from the unthinking acceptance of the 'Old Colonial System,'"
resulting in "a demand for local control of North Carolina with
equal status with every other unit of the Empire." Further
insight into the North Carolina mentality regarding British
taxation can be gained from *Not a Conquered People*, edited by
William S. Price, Jr., which contains pamphlets on the subject
by Martin Howard and Maurice Moore, who ably supported the
British and colonial approaches to taxation respectively.[23]

Although the colonial agents have received the highest
commendation for their cooperative efforts in securing the
repeal of the Stamp Act legislation, North Carolina's agency had
fallen into abeyance at that time. S. J. Ervin, Jr., provides a brief
survey of the agency but effectively ends his discussion with the
appointment of Henry E. McCulloh in 1768. The standard
treatment of the southern agents by Ella Lonn and the more
recent, insightful analysis by Michael Kammen give a better
perspective of the agency but still leave the role of North
Carolina's representatives obscure.[24]

As Ervin notes, the ineffectiveness of the North Carolina
agency was at least partially attributable to the "constant

22. Lawrence Lee, "Days of Defiance: Resistance to the Stamp Act in the
Lower Cape Fear," *NCHR* 43 (1966): 186–202.

23. C. Robert Haywood, "The Mind of the North Carolina Opponents of
the Stamp Act," *NCHR* 29 (1952): 317–43; William S. Price, Jr., ed., *Not a
Conquered People* (Raleigh: North Carolina Department of Cultural Resources,
1975). Of course Edmund S. Morgan and Helen W. Morgan, *The Stamp Act Crisis:
Prologue to Revolution* (Chapel Hill: University of North Carolina Press, 1953),
must not be overlooked.

24. Samuel J. Ervin, Jr., "The Provincial Agents of North Carolina," *James
Sprunt Studies in History and Political Science* 16 (1919): 63–77; Ella Lonn, *The
Colonial Agents of the Southern Colonies* (Chapel Hill: University of North Carolina
Press, 1945); Michael G. Kammen, *A Rope of Sand: The Colonial Agents, British
Politics, and the American Revolution* (Ithaca, N.Y.: Cornell University Press, 1968).

bickering between the lower house and the governor and
between the house and the council."[25] Charles S. Cooke offers
an easy entree to the relationship of the governor, council, and
assembly despite his conclusion that the Revolution would
"usher in the Golden Era of Humanity and the Universal
Monarchy of Man."[26] Florence Cook's investigation entitled
"Procedure in the North Carolina Colonial Assembly, 1731–
1770" reveals that "relations between the [assembly and council]
were exceptionally close." Yet, throughout the colonial era, and
particularly after 1760, there was "a steady growth in the dignity
and consciousness" of the lower house as increasing thought
was "given to the place of the assembly as a body representing
the colony in opposition to the governor and the council, who
maintained the prerogative of the crown."[27] Jack P. Greene not
only places the North Carolina assembly's "quest for power"
within the context of the southern colonies but also provides the
most lucid explanation of the power struggle between the lower
house and the governor and council. In "Political Mimesis"
Greene enlarges upon Cook's observation that the assembly
often looked to the House of Commons as a model of conduct by
showing that the parliamentary model served all the colonies in
providing a rationale for ideological opposition to British rule.[28]

In addition to an understanding of the confrontation in
the political arena, an awareness of the general institutional
context of the revolutionary era is helpful in comprehending the

25. Ervin, "Provincial Agents," p. 77.
26. Charles S. Cooke, "The Governor, Council, and Assembly in Royal
North Carolina," *James Sprunt Studies in History and Political Science* 12 (1912): 7–40.
27. Florence Cook, "Procedure in the North Carolina Colonial Assembly,
1731–1770," *NCHR* 8 (1931): 258–83.
28. Jack P. Greene, *The Quest for Power: The Lower Houses of Assembly in the
Southern Royal Colonies, 1689–1776* (Chapel Hill: University of North Carolina
Press, 1963); "Political Mimesis: A Consideration of the Historical and Cultural
Roots of Legislative Behavior in the British Colonies in the Eighteenth Century,"
American Historical Review (hereafter cited as *AHR*) 75 (1969): 337–60. See also
Greene, "The North Carolina Lower House and the Power to Appoint Public
Treasurers, 1711–1775," *NCHR* 40 (1963): 37–53.

thrust toward independence. Coralie Parker's examination of taxation in North Carolina is basic, but M. L. M. Kay's discussion of the subject in the late colonial period is mandatory, particularly for his contention that North Carolina was onerously taxed by comparison with England.[29] For a treatment of the king's dues, Beverley W. Bond's investigation of the quitrents remains unsurpassed.[30] Ernest H. Alderman and R. W. Herring treat the North Carolina bar and judicial system respectively; David L. Corbitt delineates the judicial districts of the colony.[31] Mary P. Smith's "Borough Representation in North Carolina" supersedes Francis Nash's study of that often controversial matter in colonial and early state politics.[32] At the lower echelon of government, Julian P. Boyd, in "The Sheriff in Colonial North Carolina," demonstrates the power and corruption in that office as well as the influence of the "courthouse ring," which often caused the restiveness found by Nannie May Tilley among the local populace of Granville County.[33]

The unrest at the local level also stemmed from

29. Coralie Parker, *The History of Taxation in North Carolina during the Colonial Period* (New York: Columbia University Press, 1928); M. L. M. Kay, "Provincial Taxes in North Carolina during the Administrations of Dobbs and Tryon," *NCHR* 42 (1965): 440–53; Kay, "The Payment of Provincial and Local Taxes in North Carolina, 1748–1771," *WMQ*, 3d ser., 26 (1969): 218–39.

30. Beverley W. Bond, Jr., *The Quit-Rent System in the American Colonies* (New Haven: Yale University Press, 1919). See also the earlier, inadequate work by Edwin W. Kennedy, *Quit Rents and Currency in North Carolina, 1663–1776* (Baltimore: J. W. Bond Co., 1902).

31. Ernest H. Alderman, "The North Carolina Bar," *James Sprunt Studies in History and Political Science* 13 (1913): 5–31; R. W. Herring, "The Judicial System of the Proprietary and Royal Governments in North Carolina," *North Carolina Journal of Law* 1 (1904): 84–93, 359–64; David L. Corbitt, "Judicial Districts of North Carolina, 1746–1934," *NCHR* 12 (1935): 45–61.

32. Mary Phlegar Smith, "Borough Representation in North Carolina," *NCHR* 7 (1930): 177–91; Francis Nash, "The Borough Towns of North Carolina," *North Carolina Booklet* (hereafter cited as *NCB*) 6 (1906): 83–102.

33. Julian P. Boyd, "The Sheriff in Colonial North Carolina," *NCHR* 5 (1928): 151–80; Nannie May Tilley, "Political Disturbances in Granville County," *NCHR* 18 (1941): 339–59. See also Alan D. Watson, "The Appointment of Sheriffs in Colonial North Carolina: A Reexamination," *NCHR* 53 (1976): 385–98.

disenchantment over land matters. The political repercussions arising from North Carolina's dissatisfaction with the 1764 and 1772 surveys of the South Carolina boundary can be followed in the comprehensive *North Carolina Boundary Disputes Involving Her Southern Line* by Marvin L. Skaggs, a detailed treatment that is overly sympathetic toward the northern colony. The Granville District, comprising approximately the northern half of the province, received its only sustained consideration in 1913 by E. Merton Coulter; three years later Archibald Henderson suggested that the strife generated by Granville's agents and the closing of the land office contributed in small measure to the Regulator unrest.[34]

The Regulator uprising has been one of the most provocative subjects of the prewar years. The Whig historians of the nineteenth century, beginning with Jones and Wheeler, viewed the Regulation as a prelude to the Revolution, or, in Wheeler's words, the Battle of Alamance represented "the first blood spilled in these United States, in resistance to exactions of English rulers, and oppressions by the English government."[35] Although the Whig position was abandoned in the twentieth century, a corollary view, suggested by John S. Bassett in his pioneering work in 1894 and followed by William S. Powell in *The War of the Regulation*, holds that the Regulation was an object lesson to later revolutionaries in the use of armed resistance to authority.[36]

34. Marvin L. Skaggs, *North Carolina Boundary Disputes Involving Her Southern Line*, James Sprunt Studies in History and Political Science, vol. 25 (Chapel Hill: University of North Carolina Press, 1941); E. Merton Coulter, "The Granville District," *James Sprunt Studies in History and Political Science* 13 (1913): 35–56; Archibald Henderson, "Origin of the Regulation," *AHR* 21 (1916): 320–32.

35. Jones, *Defence*, p. 48; Wheeler, *Historical Sketches*, 1:59.

36. John S. Bassett, "The Regulators of North Carolina (1765–1771)," *Annual Report of the American Historical Association for 1894* (Washington, D.C.: American Historical Association, 1895), pp. 141–212; William S. Powell, *The War of the Regulation and the Battle of Alamance, May 16, 1771* (Raleigh: State Department of Archives and History, 1949). See also Sikes, *Transition of North Carolina*, p. 9, and Raper, *North Carolina*, p. 238. Sellers significantly alters the argument by

Led by Bassett, who observed that the Regulators sought redress for specific grievances rather than to topple the prevailing government, historians of the twentieth century consider the Regulation as an internal conflict within the province. Those writing in the Progressive vein feel that the Regulators represented the essence of the class struggle in North Carolina and symbolized the internal revolution that occurred throughout the colonies in conjunction with the move for independence from Great Britain. As Elisha P. Douglass states in *Rebels and Democrats*, events in North Carolina constituted the "most articulate, comprehensive, and violent" of all the colonial democratic protests against aristocratic domination of government.[37]

Currently the prevailing assessment of the Regulation, best represented by Lefler in his collaborative efforts with Wager and Powell, and in his text on North Carolina, sees the movement as a sectional confrontation pitting western farmers against eastern politicos. The sources of sectional conflict emanated from divergent racial stocks; religious affiliations; economies; and, most explosively, politics.[38] Lending further credence to the sectional approach are the biographers of Governor Tryon and the editors of *The Regulators in North Carolina: A Documentary History, 1759–1776*, an outstanding set of documents relating to the dissension in the province.[39]

---

contending that provincial leaders gained experience "in techniques for imposing their policies on a divided populace" ("Making a Revolution," p. 25).

37. Elisha P. Douglass, *Rebels and Democrats: The Struggle for Equal Political Rights and Majority Rule during the American Revolution* (Chapel Hill: University of North Carolina Press, 1955), p. 71.

38. Hugh T. Lefler and Paul W. Wager, eds., *Orange County, 1752–1952* (Chapel Hill: Orange Printshop, 1953); Lefler and Powell, *Colonial North Carolina*, pp. 217–39; Lefler and Newsome, *North Carolina*, 3d ed., pp. 173–90.

39. Marshall DeLancey Haywood, *Governor William Tryon and His Administration in the Province of North Carolina, 1765–1771* (Raleigh: E. M. Uzzell, 1903); Alonzo T. Dill, *Governor Tryon and His Palace* (Chapel Hill: University of North Carolina Press, 1955); William S. Powell, James K. Huhta, and Thomas J. Farnham, eds., *The Regulators in North Carolina: A Documentary History, 1759–1776* (Raleigh: State Department of Archives and History, 1971), p. xxvi. Although they

49   Revolutionary North Carolina, 1765–1789

Reacting vigorously to the sectional interpretation and refining the Progressive conception of the Regulation is Michael Kay, whose work to date embodies some of the most sophisticated and elucidating of the current investigations of eighteenth-century North Carolina. In 1965 Kay denied the Lockean conceptual framework of a liberal America by contending that the Regulation was a movement of "class conscious agriculturalists, hop[ing] to bring into being a society that protected their interests and promoted the well being of productive and non-exploitive men." Subsequent articles provided support for this thesis until in 1976 Kay, in "The North Carolina Regulation, 1766–1776," adduced sufficient proof of class divisions in colonial North Carolina to permit him to declare that "historians who argue that class consciousness and class conflict were denied in the colonies by the equitable distribution of wealth and social mobility, as compared with England, are merely prescribing shibboleths to replace hard analysis."[40] Kay is persuasive. Recently his position has been adopted by Rowland Berthoff and John M. Murrin as well as Lindley S. Butler.[41]

---

embrace the east-west sectional interpretation, Powell et al. accept the validity of other approaches as well, eventually asserting that "it was outside the province of North Carolina . . . that the Regulator movement had one of its greatest effects." It "aroused [the] sympathy and common feelings of discontent [that] contributed to the growing movement toward the American Revolution" (*The Regulators in North Carolina*, p. xxvi).

40. M. L. M. Kay, "An Analysis of a British Colony in Late Eighteenth Century America in the Light of Current American Historiographical Controversy," *Australian Journal of Politics and History* 11 (1965): 170–84; Kay, "The North Carolina Regulation, 1766–1776: A Class Conflict," in Alfred F. Young, ed., *The American Revolution: Explorations in the History of American Radicalism* (DeKalb, Ill.: Northern Illinois University Press, 1976), pp. 71–123.

41. Rowland Berthoff and John M. Murrin, "Feudalism, Communalism, and the Yeoman Freeholder: The American Revolution Considered as a Social Accident," in *Essays on the American Revolution*, pp. 256–88; Butler, *North Carolina and the Coming of the Revolution*, p. 44. The historiographical survey by George R. Adams, "The Carolina Regulators: A Note on Changing Interpretations," *NCHR* 44 (1972): 345–52, is seriously deficient on two counts: it omits any mention of the work of Kay and it attempts a correlative discussion of the Regulator movements

While the arguments of Lefler, Kay, and others are meritorious, James P. Whittenburg believes that "neither a class nor a sectional interpretation explains why so many western planters risked treason by joining the insurrection." He feels that the Regulation constituted a violent reaction by planters to the increased domination of the backcountry economy and politics by merchants and lawyers. The decline of the planter elite stemmed from the rapid economic development of the west, a disruptive force that tended to promote political instability and proffered opportunities for enrichment and advancement. Moving to take advantage of the situation, merchants and lawyers challenged the hegemony of the planters.[42]

The debate over the impact of the Regulation on the coming of the Revolution has sometimes detracted from a proper appreciation of the controversy over the foreign attachment law. Jack Greene feels that foreign attachment was the most important issue besides taxation "in promoting the rise of Revolutionary sentiment in [the] colony," and the matter has finally received intensive analysis from H. Braughn Taylor.[43] Although Don Higginbotham notes the economic importance of foreign attachment for contemporaries and Sellers agrees that there were incidental economic benefits accruing to some North Carolinians from attachment, Taylor claims that its importance was primarily symbolic. Denying foreign attachment represented another in a long series of "rights" of which Parliament in conspiratorial fashion was attempting to deprive the colonials.[44]

---

of North and South Carolina when the two differed so basically as to make such an integration impractical. See Richard M. Brown, *The South Carolina Regulators* (Cambridge, Mass.: The Belknap Press of Harvard University Press, 1963).

42. James P. Whittenburg, "Planters, Merchants, and Lawyers: Social Change and the Origins of the North Carolina Regulation," *WMQ*, 3d ser., 34 (1977): 215–38.

43. Greene, *Quest for Power*, p. 424; H. Braughn Taylor, "The Foreign Attachment Law and the Coming of the Revolution in North Carolina," *NCHR* 52 (1975): 20–36.

44. Don Higginbotham, ed., *The Papers of James Iredell*, 2 vols. (Raleigh:

The controversy over the authenticity of the Mecklenburg
Declaration of Independence of 20 May 1775 has absorbed an
inordinate amount of historians' energy. Although no one
doubts the validity of the resolutions of 31 May 1775, Whig
historians of the nineteenth century, again led by Jones,
also stoutly upheld the verity of the earlier document. The
declaration continues to claim support in the twentieth century,[45]
but disclaimers, especially the devastating critiques of William
Henry Hoyt and A. S. Salley, Jr., have set the tone of opinion for
historians in this century.[46] Nevertheless, as late as 1969,
Chalmers Davidson refused to offend the sensitivities of those
who defend the declaration by nicely skirting the issue of
authenticity.[47] On the whole, however, R. D. W. Connor best
approached the argument by asserting that "North Carolina's
Priority in the Demand for Independence" rested upon the
Halifax Resolves rather than either of the Mecklenburg papers.[48]

The Halifax Resolves were the product of the fourth of
five provincial congresses, which, in conjunction with the

Division of Archives and History, Department of Cultural Resources, 1976), 1:lxi,
n. 30. See also Bernard Bailyn, *The Ideological Origins of the American Revolution*
(Cambridge, Mass.: The Belknap Press of Harvard University Press, 1967).

45. Jones, *Defence*, pp. 294–308. See also Bruce Craven, "The Mecklen-
burg Declaration of Independence," *NCB* 8 (1909): 203–48, and V. V. McNitt,
Chain of Error and the Mecklenburg Declaration of Independence (Palmer, Mass., and
New York: Hampden Hills Press, 1960).

46. William Henry Hoyt, *The Mecklenburg Declaration of Independence* (New
York and London: G. P. Putnam's Sons, 1907); A. S. Salley, Jr., "The Mecklenburg
Declaration of Independence," *NCB* 8 (1909): 155–202. Hoyt caused Samuel A.
Ashe to alter his attitude toward the Mecklenburg Declaration from the first to the
second volume of his *History of North Carolina*. See Connor, "Samuel A'Court
Ashe," p. 135. For a thorough discussion of the historiography of the Mecklen-
burg Declaration see Richard M. Current, "That Other Declaration: May 20,
1775–May 20, 1975," *NCHR* 54 (1977): 169–91.

47. Chalmers G. Davidson, "Independent Mecklenburg," *NCHR* 46
(1969): 122–29.

48. R. D. W. Connor, "North Carolina's Priority in the Demand for
Independence," *South Atlantic Quarterly* (hereafter cited as *SAQ*) 8 (1909): 234–54.

committees of safety, instigated the revolutionary break and directed the transition to statehood.[49] The Fifth Provincial Congress meeting at Halifax in November 1776 has been the most controversial of the conventions. Historians have contended that the October 1776 election for delegates to the congress was characterized by violence occasioned by a bitter struggle between "radicals" and "conservatives." The result was a triumph for a strong, well organized radical movement that championed government dominated by the common people. Recently, however, Robert L. Ganyard has denied the existence of a concerted radical drive and attendant electoral strife, concluding that "the evidence suggests that in North Carolina, as in most other states, the proponents of democracy, while active and not without influence, were nevertheless insufficiently powerful and too poorly organized to be at the center of the Revolutionary movement or to represent its principal thrust."[50]

The controversy centering on the election of October 1776 has extended to the constitution that emanated from the congress. Historians have attributed the authorship of the document to Willie Jones, Thomas Jones, Richard Caswell, and Thomas Burke.[51] The nature of the constitution is also a moot question. Most agree that a spirit of moderation and compromise prevailed in the Fifth Provincial Congress. Ganyard follows Frank Nash, Fletcher Green, B. P. Robinson, and a reluctant E. P. Douglass in emphasizing the conservative nature of the

49. See Thomas W. Pittman, "The Revolutionary Congresses of North Carolina," *NCB* 2 (1902): 3–18; Bessie Lewis Whitaker, *The Provincial Council and Committees of Safety in North Carolina*, James Sprunt Studies in History and Political Science, vol. 8 (Chapel Hill: University of North Carolina Press, 1908).

50. Robert L. Ganyard, "Radicals and Conservatives in Revolutionary North Carolina: A Point at Issue, the October Election, 1776," *WMQ*, 3d ser., 24 (1967): 568–87, esp. pp. 570–71, n. 3. See also Ganyard's concise, yet detailed, description of the transition of North Carolina from colony to statehood in *The Emergence of North Carolina's Revolutionary State Government* (Raleigh: North Carolina Department of Cultural Resources, 1978).

51. Blackwell P. Robinson, "Willie Jones of Halifax," *NCHR* 18 (1941): 24.

constitution.[52] Yet D. H. Gilpatrick observes that the constitution
may not have been democratic by later standards, but it permitted a more democratic government. Moreover, government
functioned as a democracy after 1776, "militant and assertive,
if not always enlightened and judicious."[53] Improving upon the
work of E. W. Sikes and Frank Nash, Earle H. Ketcham, in
"The Sources of the North Carolina Constitution of 1776," finds
that the framers of the document drew upon the colonial
experience of North Carolina, the constitutions of neighboring
states, such basic written guarantees of English liberties as the
Magna Charta and Bill of Rights, and various English and
American liberal philosophers.[54]

From the standpoint of the dominant British personalities
involved in the onset of the Revolution, North Carolina has
benefited from several studies of the governors of the province.
Blackwell P. Robinson briefly surveys their careers in *The Five
Royal Governors of North Carolina*, and Desmond Clarke's
objective biography of Arthur Dobbs is indispensable for the
proper setting of the prerevolutionary era. Less objective than
Clarke but just as readable is Marshall DeLancey Haywood,
Governor William Tryon, which serves as a useful corrective to
previous descriptions of Tryon as the minion of a tyrannical
monarch. Alonzo T. Dill, in *Governor Tryon and His Palace*, evinces
the readability of a successful journalist in his general history
of Tryon's tenure but does not advance beyond Haywood's

52. Frank Nash, "The North Carolina Constitution of 1776 and Its
Makers," *James Sprunt Studies in History and Political Science* 11 (1912): 7–23;
Fletcher Green, *Constitutional Development of the South Atlantic States, 1776–1860*
(Chapel Hill: University of North Carolina Press, 1930), p. 98; Douglass, *Rebels
and Democrats*, pp. 121–29. Robinson agrees with R. D. W. Connor that the
constitution produced a democratic government in form but an oligarchical
one in fact (Robinson, "Willie Jones," p. 25; R. D. W. Connor, *Ante-Bellum Builders
of North Carolina*, North Carolina State Normal & Industrial College Historical
Publications, no. 3 [Greensboro, N.C.: Published by the College, 1914], p. 23).
53. Delbert H. Gilpatrick, *Jeffersonian Democracy in North Carolina, 1789–
1816* (New York: Columbia University Press, 1931), p. 26.
54. E. W. Sikes, "Our First Constitution, 1776," *NCB* 7 (1907): 131–37;

analysis of the governor's administration.[55] Vernon O. Stumpf's
description of Josiah Martin's early career concludes with the
observation that if the governor "had had time, it is quite
possible that Martin might have had an opportunity to reconcile"
some of the problems bequeathed by Tryon, "but the growing
revolutionary ferment blocked any peaceful solution." The
statement rings true as Stumpf subsequently depicts Martin's
stormy administration and the collapse of royal government
in North Carolina.[56]

North Carolina's patriots, of course, received earlier
and more appreciative recognition, and in the biographical
investigations of those who led the cause for separation from
Great Britain can be seen the rush of events that ended in
independence. Jones hastened to the defense of William Hooper
when Jefferson had the audacity to doubt Hooper's support
of the Revolution. In 1894 Edwin A. Alderman's effusive
plaudits added to Hooper's stature as a patriot of the first rank,
but, following Allan J. McCurry's "Suggestion" regarding
Joseph Hewes's revolutionary sentiment, David T. Morgan and
William J. Schmidt have shown that neither Hewes, Penn,
nor Hooper, North Carolina's signers of the Declaration of
Independence, readily endorsed separation from England, and

Nash, "Constitution of 1776"; Earle H. Ketcham, "The Sources of the North
Carolina Constitution of 1776," *NCHR* 6 (1929): 215–36.

55. Blackwell P. Robinson, *The Five Royal Governors of North Carolina,
1729–1775* (Raleigh: Carolina Charter Tercentenary Commission, 1963); Desmond
Clarke, *Arthur Dobbs Esquire, 1689–1765* (Chapel Hill: University of North
Carolina Press, 1957); Haywood, *Governor William Tryon*; Dill, *Governor Tryon and
His Palace*.

56. Vernon O. Stumpf, "Josiah Martin and His Search for Success: The
Road to North Carolina," *NCHR* 53 (1976): 55–79; Stumpf, "Governor Josiah
Martin: The Road to the Cape Fear," Lower Cape Fear Historical Society *Bulletin*
18 (October 1975). See also Dill, "Tryon's Palace: A Neglected Niche of North
Carolina History," *NCHR* 19 (1942): 119–67; Dill, "Eighteenth Century New Bern:
A History of the Town and Craven County, 1700–1800, Parts V–VIII," *NCHR* 23
(1946): 47–78, 142–71, 325–59, 495–535; and Richard B. Sheridan, "The West
Indian Antecedents of Josiah Martin, Last Royal Governor of North Carolina,"
NCHR 54 (1977): 253–70.

that Hooper, at least, subsequently entertained reservations about the forces that he had helped to unleash.[57]

The careers of John Harvey, Samuel Johnston, Cornelius Harnett, and Richard Caswell received their first serious attention from R. D. W. Connor in various articles, a biography of Harnett, and *Revolutionary Leaders of North Carolina*.[58] John G. Coyle's essay adds little to Connor's biography of Harnett, but David T. Morgan contends that Connor was "misled by Harnett's relatively quiet approach in the performance of his duty" in the Continental Congress and that Harnett made "valuable contributions which give him a reasonable claim to the title of minor American statesman."[59] Of the remaining subjects of Connor's *Revolutionary Leaders*, only Caswell has received satisfactory consideration. C. B. Alexander's essay on his early years is unimpressive, but two subsequent articles examining Caswell's career after 1774 are superb.[60] Harvey remains

57. Edwin A. Alderman, *William Hooper: The Prophet of American Independence* (Chapel Hill: Guilford Battle Ground Co., 1894); Allen J. McCurry, "Joseph Hewes and Independence: A Suggestion," *NCHR* 40 (1963): 455–64: David T. Morgan and William J. Schmidt, "From Economic Sanctions to Political Separation: The North Carolina Delegation to the Continental Congress, 1774–1776," *NCHR* 52 (1975): 215–34. For a sound discussion of North Carolina's seventeen delegates to the Continental Congress see Morgan and Schmidt, *North Carolinians in the Continental Congress* (Winston-Salem, N.C.: John F. Blair, 1976). Note also Thomas M. Pittman, "John Penn," *NCB* 4 (September 1904): 5–23; Walter Sikes, "Joseph Hewes," *NCB* 4 (September 1904): 25–36; and Archibald Maclaine Hooper, "Life of William Hooper," *NCB* 5 (1905): 39–71.

58. R. D. W. Connor, "Cornelius Harnett: The Pride of the Cape Fear," *NCB* 5 (1906): 171–201; "John Harvey," *NCB* 8 (1908): 3–42; "Governor Samuel Johnston," *NCB* 11 (1912): 259–85; *Cornelius Harnett: An Essay in North Carolina History* (Raleigh: Edwards & Broughton Printing Company, 1909); *Revolutionary Leaders of North Carolina*, North Carolina State Normal & Industrial College Historical Publications, no. 2 (Greensboro, N.C.: Published by the College, 1910).

59. John G. Coyle, "Cornelius Harnett," *Journal of the American Irish Historical Society* 29 (1930–31): 148–56; David T. Morgan, "Cornelius Harnett: Revolutionary Leader and Delegate to the Continental Congress," *NCHR* 44 (1972): 229–41.

60. C. B. Alexander, "The Training of Richard Caswell"; "Richard Caswell: Versatile Leader of the Revolution"; "Richard Caswell's Military and Later Public Services," *NCHR* 23 (1946): 13–31, 119–41, 287–312.

neglected and Johnston appears indirectly through treatments of Iredell.[61] Although poorly received at the outset in southern literary circles, Griffith J. McRee's *Life and Correspondence of James Iredell*, supplemented only by a long essay from Henry Groves Connor in 1912, proved to be the authoritative account of the jurist's career for more than a century.[62] McRee treated the Antifederalists as fairly as any historian of the nineteenth century and evidenced a "surprisingly critical spirit" of historical scholarship,[63] but his Victorian sentiments, prosouthern bias, and often superficial account of the Revolution demanded an updated work that appeared in 1976 with Don Higginbotham's excellent edition of *The Papers of James Iredell*. It is unfortunate that the two volumes terminate in 1783, but the introductory essay and Higginbotham's article, "James Iredell's Efforts to Preserve the First British Empire,"[64] constitute the best available commentary on the intellectual origins of the Revolution from the vantage point of the Albemarle and the conservative Whigs.[65]

North Carolina's radicals, Willie Jones and Thomas Burke, have also been recognized. No one has improved upon

61. See the brief essay by T. Murray Allen, "Samuel Johnston in Revolutionary Times," Trinity College Historical Society *Papers* 5 (1905): 39–49.

62. Griffith J. McRee, ed., *Life and Correspondence of James Iredell, One of the Associate Justices of the Supreme Court of the United States*, 2 vols. (New York: D. Appleton and Co., 1857–58); H. G. Connor, "James Iredell," *NCB* 11 (1912): 201–50.

63. See Clyde Wilson, "Griffith John McRee: An Unromantic Historian of the Old South," *NCHR* 47 (1970): 1–23.

64. Higginbotham, ed., *Papers of James Iredell*; "James Iredell's Efforts to Preserve the First British Empire," *NCHR* 49 (1972): 127–45.

65. For a prosopographical approach to revolutionary leadership see James Kirby Martin, *Men in Rebellion: Higher Governmental Leaders and the Coming of the American Revolution* (New Brunswick, N.J.: Rutgers University Press, 1973). For the activities of the Masons in North Carolina see Marshall DeLancey Haywood, "The Masonic Revolutionary Patriots of North Carolina," *NCB* 12 (1912): 21–40; and Thomas C. Parramore, *Launching the Craft: The First Half-Century of Freemasonry in North Carolina* (Raleigh: Grand Lodge of North Carolina A. F. and A. M., 1975).

Blackwell P. Robinson's sketches of Jones, the aristocratic democrat, who was "cut from the same pattern as Jefferson."[66] While Jones remained faithful to his political convictions, Burke's transition from democrat to aristocrat has been described by Elisha P. Douglass. Jennings P. Sanders investigates Burke's checkered years in the Continental Congress and finds that Burke was an able delegate, respected even by the enemies he made, and moderately attracted by the principles of a unified national government. Finally, the tragic gubernatorial tenure and untimely death of the young politician have been outlined in sympathetic but scholarly fashion by J. G. de Roulhac Hamilton and John S. Watterson.[67]

Although Archibald Henderson exaggerated that "no American colony . . . surpassed North Carolina in the number and variety of instrumentalities by which women aided the American patriots and fostered the spirit of opposition," writings on the activities of the distaff patriots corroborate Joan Hoff Wilson's caveat that concentration on outstanding personalities may well result in the misrepresentation or misunderstanding of the group.[68] The sometimes doubtful accounts of the revolutionary heroines have been ably summarized by Lida T. Rodman and Mary Hilliard Hinton; the falsity of one, the ride of Polly Slocumb to the Battle of Moore's Creek Bridge, has been shown by John B. Flowers.[69] The most cherished episode of

66. Robinson, "Willie Jones, Parts I and II," p. 170.
67. Elisha P. Douglass, "Thomas Burke, Disillusioned Democrat," *NCHR* 26 (1949): 150–86; Jennings B. Sanders, "Thomas Burke in the Continental Congress," *NCHR* 9 (1932): 22–37; J. G. de Roulhac Hamilton, "Governor Thomas Burke," *NCB* 6 (1906): 103–22; John S. Watterson III, "The Ordeal of Governor Burke," *NCHR* 48 (1971): 95–117.
68. Archibald Henderson, "Elizabeth Maxwell Steel: Patriot," *NCB* 12 (1912): 65–103; Joan Hoff Wilson, "The Illusion of Change: Women and the American Revolution," *The American Revolution*, pp. 385–445.
69. Lida T. Rodman, "Patriotic Women of North Carolina in the Revolution," *D.A.R. Magazine*, 45 (1914): 145–52; Mary Hilliard Hinton, "Other North Carolina Heroines of the Revolution," *NCB* 18 (1918): 64–75; John Baxton Flowers III, "Did Polly Slocumb Ride to the Battle of Moore's Creek Bridge?" Lower Cape

feminine revolutionary ardor was the Edenton Tea Party, recounted inaccurately by Richard C. Dillard and most concisely and objectively by Don Higginbotham.[70] Tory sympathizer Flora Macdonald receives brief biographical treatment, confined principally to her North Carolina years, by J. P. MacLean in *Flora Macdonald in America*, which Elizabeth Gray Vining updates and expands in her exhaustively researched and well written *Flora: A Biography*.[71]

The standard account and fullest consideration of the Tory element is Robert O. DeMond, *The Loyalists in North Carolina during the Revolution*, which vividly portrays the character of the civil war in the state and the dispersion of the loyalists after the winning of independence.[72] Although historians have generally felt that the Moore's Creek episode represented the peak of loyalist opposition in the state, Carole W. Troxler shows that resistance to the government heightened in the years between 1777 and 1780. Moreover, she improves on DeMond's study by attempting to explain in more than superficial fashion the reasons for the attachment to the British cause by large numbers of North Carolinians. Her efforts lead in part to a social interpretation of loyalism, centering on the loyalists' affiliation in many cases with the Anglican church. Jeffrey J. Crow substantiates this view in his investigation of the Llewelyn

---

Fear Historical Society *Bulletin* 19 (February 1976). See also Richard Dillard, "Some North Carolina Heroines of the Revolution," *NCB* 8 (1909): 325–33; William Carson Ervin, "Grace Greenlee, A Revolutionary Heroine," *NCB* 15 (1915): 12–27.

70. Richard Dillard, *The Historic Tea-Party of Edenton, October 25th, 1774: An Incident in North Carolina Connected with British Taxation* (Edenton, N.C., 1925); Higginbotham, ed., *Papers of James Iredell*, 1:285–86n. See also Fred A. Olds, "The Celebrated Edenton, N.C., Tea Party," *D.A.R. Magazine*, 56 (1922): 327–33.

71. J. P. MacLean, *Flora Macdonald in America with a Brief Sketch of Her Life and Adventures* (Lumberton, N.C.: A. W. MacLean, 1909); Elizabeth Gray Vining, *Flora: A Biography* (Philadelphia: J. B. Lippincott Company, 1966). See also Dorothy Mackay Quynn, "Flora Macdonald in History," *NCHR* 18 (1941):236–58.

72. Robert O. DeMond, *The Loyalists in North Carolina during the Revolution* (Durham, N.C.: Duke University Press, 1940).

Conspiracy of 1777. The most exact determination of the nature and motives of the loyalists is found in Wallace Brown, *The King's Friends*, a revealing study based on an examination of the American loyalist claims but subject to the limitations described by Eugene R. Fingerhut.[73]

The nature and number of the loyalists in North Carolina have long been the subject of debate. William E. Dodd attributed "the almost shameful lethargy of North Carolina during the long period of 1777 to 1780" in support of the war effort to the opposition of the former Regulators and Scots, whom he virtually equated with Tories, as well as to the reluctance of conservative Whigs to press forward too rapidly.[74] Sallie J. Davis agrees and concludes "that the war of independence in North Carolina was not a struggle of the people, but rather of a patriotic faction scattered throughout the State."[75] Although exact figures are virtually impossible to obtain, Isaac Harrell's observation that the "number of active loyalists was probably smaller than generally conceded" fails to help. Certainly the number exceeded the average for the states calculated by Paul H. Smith to be at about 20 percent of the population.[76]

The war effort rested principally upon the exertions of the militia and Continentals.[77] E. Merton Wheeler feels that the

73. Carole W. Troxler, *The Loyalist Experience in North Carolina* (Raleigh: North Carolina Department of Cultural Resources, 1976); Jeffrey J. Crow, "Tory Plots and Anglican Loyalty: The Llewelyn Conspiracy of 1777," *NCHR* 55 (1978): 1–17; Wallace Brown, *The King's Friends: The Composition and Motives of the American Loyalist Claimants* (Providence, R.I.: Brown University Press, 1965); Eugene R. Fingerhut, "Uses and Abuses of the American Loyalists' Claims: A Critique of Quantitative Analyses," *WMQ*, 3d ser., 25 (1968): 245–58.

74. William E. Dodd, "North Carolina in the Revolution," *SAQ* 1 (1902): 156–61; see also Duane Meyer, *The Highland Scots of North Carolina, 1732–1776* (Chapel Hill: University of North Carolina Press, 1961).

75. Sallie Joyner Davis, "North Carolina's Part in the Revolution, III," *SAQ* 3 (1904): 154–65.

76. Isaac S. Harrell, "North Carolina Loyalists," *NCHR* 3 (1926): 575–90; Paul H. Smith, "The American Loyalists: Notes on Their Organization and Numerical Strength," *WMQ*, 3d ser., 25 (1968): 259–77.

77. The activities of the "partisans" or "irregulars" can be followed in

quality of the North Carolina militia organization was at least comparable to that of the other colonies on the eve of the Revolution. After stressing the flexibility and adaptability brought to militia matters throughout the course of the eighteenth century, he concludes that "whatever blame or praise that the militia's performance in the Revolution deserves must be heaped upon those individuals who led and served it, not upon the organization."[78] Luther L. Gobbel is not reluctant to castigate the field performance of the militia, but recently scholars such as Robert C. Pugh and John Shy have noted the usefulness of the militia in suppressing loyalists, harassing British regulars, cutting supply lines, and even serving ably in pitched battle when used wisely in conjunction with the Continentals.[79] According to Pugh, "the American militia deserves recognition as a necessary element of final victory."[80]

   In *The North Carolina Continentals*, Hugh F. Rankin, one of the best narrative historians working in the revolutionary era, has combined extensive research, graceful style, and meticulous scholarship to produce the standard treatise on that aspect of the state's military endeavor.[81] He generally supports

---

Chalmers G. Davidson, *Piedmont Partisan: The Life and Times of Brigadier-General William Lee Davidson* (Davidson, N.C.: Davidson College, 1951); and Blackwell P. Robinson, *William R. Davie* (Chapel Hill: University of North Carolina Press, 1957), chap. 4. See also Fordyce M. Hubbard, *Life of William Richardson Davie, Governor of North Carolina*, in Jared Sparks, ed., *The Library of American Biography*, 2d ser., vol. 15, (Boston: Charles C. Little and James Brown, 1848).

   78. E. Merton Wheeler, "Development and Organization of the North Carolina Militia," *NCHR* 41 (1964): 307–23.

   79. Luther L. Gobbel, "The Militia of North Carolina in Colonial and Revolutionary Times," Trinity College Historical Society *Papers* 13 (1919): 35–61; Robert C. Pugh, "The Revolutionary Militia in the Southern Campaign, 1780–1781," *WMQ*, 3d ser., 14 (1957): 154–75; John Shy, "The American Revolution: The Military Conflict Considered as a Revolutionary War," *Essays on the American Revolution*, pp. 121–56. For the importance of the militia even in defeat see J. O. Carr, "The Battle of Rockfish Creek in Duplin County," *NCB* 6 (1907): 177–84.

   80. Pugh, "The Revolutionary Militia," p. 175.

   81. Hugh F. Rankin, *The North Carolina Continentals* (Chapel Hill: University of North Carolina Press, 1971). See also Frank Nash, "The Continental Line of North Carolina," *NCB* 17 (1918): 105–34.

Clyde L. King's assertion that North Carolina exercised control
over all its military units, including the Continentals, and
expands Paul V. Lutz's brief summarization of North Carolina's
concern for its troops. The need to supply the troops with such
necessities as salt gives rise to R. L. Hilldrup's contention
that the state subjected its inhabitants to far more detailed and
burdensome regulations than had been imposed by the British,
but these measures were excused as the price of winning the war
and securing a free government.[82]

The military conflict in North Carolina is given needed
perspective by the general histories of Willard Wallace and
John R. Alden and best surveyed in the many studies of
Rankin.[83] Of particular importance is "The Moore's Creek Bridge
Campaign," in which Rankin claims that the patriot victory
contributed to North Carolina's decision for independence at
Halifax, quelled potential unrest among the slaves, permitted the
confiscation of loyalist property, and, by way of the excellent
showing of the militia, prevented North Carolina from filling
the state's quota for Continental troops. The response of
the Wilmington Committee of Public Safety to the loyalist
threat in 1776 has been shown by Laura P. Frech and may be
followed in the *Wilmington-New Hanover Safety Committee
Minutes, 1774–1776*.[84]

82. Clyde L. King, "Military Organizations of North Carolina during the
American Revolution," *NCB* 8 (1908): 43–55; Paul V. Lutz, "A State's Concern for
the Soldiers' Welfare: How North Carolina Provided for Her Troops during the
Revolution," *NCHR* 43 (1965): 315–18; R. L. Hilldrup, "The Salt Supply of North
Carolina during the American Revolution," *NCHR* 22 (1945): 393–417.

83. Willard W. Wallace, *Appeal to Arms: A Military History of the American
Revolution* (New York: Harper and Brothers, 1951); John R. Alden, *The American
Revolution, 1775–1783* (New York: Harper & Row, 1954); Hugh F. Rankin, *North
Carolina Continentals*; Rankin, *North Carolina in the American Revolution* (Raleigh:
State Department of Archives and History, 1959); Rankin, *Greene and Cornwallis:
The Campaign in the Carolinas* (Raleigh: North Carolina Department of Cultural
Resources, 1976).

84. Hugh F. Rankin, "The Moore's Creek Bridge Campaign," *NCHR* 30
(1953): 23–60; Laura P. Frech, "The Wilmington Committee of Public Safety and
the Loyalist Rising of February 1776," *NCHR* 41 (1964): 21–35; Leora H. McEach-

The war returned in earnest to North Carolina in 1780.
David Schenck, who "determined to write [a] book in defence
of his native state, and in vindication of the honor and
patriotism of her people," exemplified the approach of the early
historians to the revolutionary conflict.[85] Within the past quarter
century, however, sound biographies of William Lee Davidson,
William R. Davie, Daniel Morgan, and Charles, Lord Cornwallis,
have added to the large and growing body of literature dealing
with Nathanael Greene and the southern campaign.[86] Burke
Davis, in *The Cowpens-Guilford Courthouse Campaign*, provides a
factually and interpretatively reliable introduction, but the
studies of M. F. Treacy and Theodore Thayer hold more interest
for scholars. In referring to Greene as one of the finest strategists
on either side, George W. Kyte fairly sums up the assessment
of the general's contribution to the war effort in the South.[87]

---

ern and Isabel M. Williams, eds., *Wilmington-New Hanover Safety Committee Minutes, 1774–1776* (Wilmington, N.C.: Wilmington-New Hanover American Revolution Bi-centennial Association, 1974).

85. David Schenck, *North Carolina, 1780–1781* . . . (Raleigh: Edwards & Broughton, 1889), p. 12.

86. Davidson, *Piedmont Partisan*; Robinson, *William R. Davie*; Don Higginbotham, *Daniel Morgan: Revolutionary Rifleman* (Chapel Hill: University of North Carolina Press, 1961); Franklin Wickwire and Mary Wickwire, *Cornwallis: The American Adventure* (Boston: Houghton Mifflin Company, 1970). See also W. A. Graham, "General William Lee Davidson," *NCB* 13 (1913): 11–39; Blackwell P. Robinson, ed., *The Revolutionary War Sketches of William R. Davie* (Raleigh: North Carolina Department of Cultural Resources, 1976); William Alexander Graham, *General Joseph Graham and His Papers on North Carolina Revolutionary History* . . . (Raleigh: Edwards & Broughton, 1904); Kemp P. Battle, "The Life and Services of Brigadier General Jethro Sumner," *NCB* 8 (1908): 111–40; Archibald Henderson, "Isaac Shelby, Revolutionary Patriot and Border Hero," *NCB* 16 (1917): 109–44; "Isaac Shelby, Part II, 1780–1783," ibid., 18 (1918): 3–56.

87. Burke Davis, *The Cowpens-Guilford Courthouse Campaign* (New York: J. P. Lippincott Company, 1962); M. F. Treacy, *Prelude to Yorktown: The Southern Campaign of Nathanael Greene, 1780–1781* (Chapel Hill: University of North Carolina Press, 1963); Theodore Thayer, *Nathanael Greene: Strategist of the American Revolution* (New York: Twayne Publishers, 1960); George W. Kyte, "Victory in the South: An Appraisal of General Greene's Strategy in the Carolinas," *NCHR* 37 (1960): 321–47. For the literature dealing with Greene, see Sellers, "The American Revolution," *Writing Southern History*, pp. 46–47.

The North Carolina navy has been an inconspicuous
factor in the revolutionary struggle. That Marshall DeLancey
Haywood's inaccurate and incomplete treatment of that aspect of
the war stood unchallenged for sixty years attests to the
insignificance of the navy.[88] William N. Still, Jr., has finally
rescued the navy from oblivion in a well researched, compact
work that corrects and extends Haywood's consideration. Still
admits that the British blockade of North Carolina was
ineffective, but not because of the armed naval protection
provided by the state. "Rather it was because the British
government was slow to recognize the importance of those
waters to the American cause, and when it finally did so, it was
too late."[89] A partial explanation of the British dilatoriness is
found in Norman C. Delaney, "The Outer Banks of North
Carolina during the Revolutionary War," which emphasizes the
dangers of those treacherous shoals, particularly for the British.[90]

The role of the Indians in revolutionary North Carolina
has yet to receive satisfactory consideration. However, general
coverage provided by the recent works of Jack P. Sosin and
James H. O'Donnell shows that settlement in the west, followed
by white disregard for territorial boundaries and British
overtures, brought the wrath of the Indians, particularly the
Cherokees, to the North Carolina frontier by 1776.[91] For the

88. Marshall DeLancey Haywood, "The State Navy of North Carolina in
the War of the Revolution," *NCB* 17 (1917): 48–56.

89. William N. Still, Jr., *North Carolina's Revolutionary War Navy* (Raleigh:
North Carolina Department of Cultural Resources, 1976), p. 29. For an interesting
episode involving North Carolina privateersmen see Thomas C. Parramore, "The
Great Escape from Forten Gaol: An Incident of the Revolution," *NCHR* 45 (1968):
349–56, which reinforces Jesse Lemisch's view of the loyalties of the American
seamen in "Listening to the 'Inarticulate,' " *Journal of Social History* 3 (1969): 1–29.

90. Norman C. Delaney, "The Outer Banks of North Carolina during the
Revolutionary War," *NCHR* 36 (1959): 1–16.

91. Jack P. Sosin, *The Revolutionary Frontier, 1763–1783* (New York: Holt,
Rinehart and Winston, 1967); James H. O'Donnell, *Southern Indians in the
American Revolution* (Knoxville, Tenn.: University of Tennessee Press, 1973). See
also William K. Boyd, "Early Relations of North Carolina and the West," *NCB* 7
(1908): 193–209.

state, O'Donnell's emotional account, *The Cherokees of North Carolina in the American Revolution*, with its vitriolic attacks on white iniquities, contrasts sharply with Robert L. Ganyard's dispassionate narrative, "The Threat from the West," in which Ganyard finds that the Griffith Rutherford expedition "had quashed a potential Indian rising of serious proportions at a very critical period and reduced substantially the danger of a large-scale Indian threat for the duration of the Revolution."[92] The Treaty of Long Island of Holston, conveniently reprinted with a brief comment by Archibald Henderson, temporarily brought peace to the frontier.[93] Randolph Downes shows that in the 1780s continued westward expansion by whites combined with the speculative machinations of men like William Blount and John Sevier to make the Cherokees mere pawns in state and national politics.[94] O'Donnell concludes that the whites would never be satisfied until they had taken the land of the Indians. He continues, "In many ways, the Cherokee Trail of Tears had its beginning during the period of the American Revolution," surely a tragic commentary on the origins of the country.[95]

The history of the Revolution remains compartmentalized, and rare is the work that relates the impact of the military effort

92. James H. O'Donnell, *The Cherokees of North Carolina in the American Revolution* (Raleigh: North Carolina Department of Cultural Resources, 1976); Robert L. Ganyard, "Threat from the West: North Carolina and the Cherokee, 1776–1778," *NCHR* 45 (1968): 47–66. See also the detailed accounts of S. A. Ashe, "Rutherford's Expedition Against the Indians, 1776," *NCB* 4 (December 1904): 3–28, and Philip M. Hamer, "The Wataugans and the Cherokee Indians in 1776," East Tennessee Historical Society *Publications* 3 (1931): 108–26.

93. Archibald Henderson, "The Treaty of Long Island of Holston, July, 1777," *NCHR* 8 (1931): 55–116.

94. Randolph C. Downes, "Cherokee-American Relations in the Upper Tennessee Valley, 1776–1791," East Tennessee Historical Society *Publications* 8 (1936): 35–53; William H. Masterson, *William Blount* (Baton Rouge: Louisiana State University Press, 1954); Carl Driver, *John Sevier: Pioneer of the Old Southwest* (Chapel Hill: University of North Carolina Press, 1932).

95. O'Donnell, *Cherokees of North Carolina*, p. 34.

to the society in which the conflict occurred.[96] The exception is Jeffrey J. Crow, *The Black Experience in Revolutionary North Carolina*, which not only constitutes the first comprehensive effort to understand the black population of early North Carolina but also shows the impact of the struggle for independence upon the slaves of the state.[97] For other aspects of the social scene, Alice E. Mathews, *Society in Revolutionary North Carolina*, is excellent. However, Mathews should be read in conjunction with Lee's chapters on life and religion in the lower Cape Fear and followed by Guion G. Johnson's monumental *Ante-Bellum North Carolina: A Social History*.[98]

Certainly the revolutionary years provided the crucible for the development of education in North Carolina, and no institution was more justly famous than the Log College of the Reverend David Caldwell. Eli Caruthers's nineteenth-century biography of Caldwell is still useful but must be supplemented by Aubrey Brooks, "David Caldwell and His Log College."[99] The origins of the University of North Carolina can be found in R. D. W. Connor, "The Genesis of Higher Education in North Carolina." Still, consideration would not be complete without

96. For excellent forays into this area see Don Higginbotham, *The War of American Independence: Military Attitudes, Policies, and Practice, 1763–1789* (New York: Macmillan Company, 1971); Shy, "The American Revolution Considered as a Revolutionary War," *Essays on the American Revolution*, pp. 121–56; and Ronald Hoffman, "The 'Disaffected' in the Revolutionary South," *The American Revolution*, pp. 275–316.

97. Jeffrey J. Crow, *The Black Experience in Revolutionary North Carolina* (Raleigh: North Carolina Department of Cultural Resources, 1977).

98. Alice E. Mathews, *Society in Revolutionary North Carolina* (Raleigh: North Carolina Department of Cultural Resources, 1976); Lee, *The Lower Cape Fear in Colonial Days*, chaps. 14–15; Johnson, *Ante-Bellum North Carolina*. See also Samuel A. Ashe, "Social Conditions in North Carolina in 1783," *NCB* 10 (1911): 200–222.

99. Eli W. Caruthers, *A Sketch of the Life and Character of the Reverend David Caldwell, D. D.* (Greensboro, N.C.: Printed by Swaim and Sherwood, 1842); Aubrey Lee Brooks, "David Caldwell and His Log College," *NCHR* 28 (1951): 399–407. See also Charles Lee Smith, "David Caldwell—Teacher, Preacher, Patriot," *NCB* 11 (1912): 251–58.

consulting Blackwell P. Robinson, *William R. Davie*; and Kemp P. Battle, *History of the University of North Carolina*.[100]

Education comprised more than institutional instruction, however, as Lawrence A. Cremin has ably demonstrated in *American Education: The Colonial Experience, 1607–1783*.[101] For example, developing transportation and communication facilities described by C. C. Crittenden fostered new ideas and loosened the grip of parochialism on North Carolinians.[102] Another liberating force and potent element in the formation of the revolutionary circumstance as described by Arthur M. Schlesinger, Sr., was the newspaper.[103] Crittenden adequately surveys journalism in *North Carolina Newspapers Before 1790*; Robert N. Elliott, Jr., and Durward T. Stokes add depth to the careers of James Davis and Adam Boyd respectively, two of the earliest publishers in the province. From newspaper advertisements, Wesley H. Wallace has produced illuminating insights into the nature of the society and economy of North Carolina before 1778.[104]

100. R. D. W. Connor, "The Genesis of Higher Education in North Carolina," *NCHR* 27 (1950): 1–14; Robinson, *William R. Davie*, chap. 8; Kemp P. Battle, *History of the University of North Carolina*, 2 vols. (Raleigh: Edwards & Broughton, 1907–12). See also the brief consideration of Queen's College by Marshall DeLancey Haywood, "The Story of Queen's College or Liberty Hall in the Province of North Carolina," *NCB* 11 (1912): 169–75, and the disappointing treatment by William Earle Drake, *Higher Education in North Carolina Before 1860* (New York: Carlton Press, 1964).

101. Lawrence A. Cremin, *American Education: The Colonial Experience, 1607–1783* (New York: Harper & Row, 1970).

102. Charles C. Crittenden, "Inland Navigation in North Carolina, 1763–1789"; "Overland Travel and Transportation in North Carolina, 1763–1789"; "Means of Communication in North Carolina, 1763–1789," *NCHR* 8 (1931): 145–54, 239–57, 373–83.

103. Arthur M. Schlesinger, *Prelude to Independence: The Newspaper War on Britain, 1764–1776* (New York: Alfred A. Knopf, 1965).

104. Charles C. Crittenden, *North Carolina Newspapers Before 1790*, James Sprunt Studies in History and Political Science, vol. 20 (Chapel Hill: University of North Carolina Press, 1928); Robert N. Elliott, Jr., "James Davis and the Beginning of the Newspaper in North Carolina," *NCHR* 43 (1965): 1–20; Durward T. Stokes, "Adam Boyd, Publisher, Preacher, and Patriot," *NCHR* 49 (1972): 1–21; Wesley H. Wallace, "Property and Trade: Main Themes of Early North Carolina

Any investigation of religion in the revolutionary era must necessarily account for the disestablishment of the Anglican church. A consideration of the disreputable activities of such Anglican clergymen as Michael Smith leads David T. Morgan to state, "No wonder the Anglican church never won the respect of North Carolinians; no wonder it was disestablished with hardly a murmur in 1776." But Paul Conkin finds that the church was gaining strength as the war approached and that disestablishment was the result of a desire for greater "local religious autonomy, coupled with the steady growth of dissenters and the unpopular role played by the Anglican clergy in the Revolution."[105] The birth and travail of the Protestant Episcopal church, especially the efforts of such notables as Thomas Blount and Charles Pettigrew, are portrayed by Sarah M. Lemmon in several articles and a biography of Pettigrew.[106]

The role of the dissenters can be followed in the older survey by Stephen B. Weeks and in *Religion and the American Revolution in North Carolina* by Robert M. Calhoon but must be reinforced by the standard histories of the various denominations.[107] The exceptionally rich *Records of the Moravians in North*

Newspaper Advertisements," *NCHR* 32 (1955): 451–82; Wallace, "Cultural and Social Advertising in Early North Carolina Newspapers," *NCHR* 33 (1956): 281–309. See also Stephen B. Weeks, "Pre-Revolutionary Printers in North Carolina: Davis, Steuart, and Boyd," *NCB* 15 (1915): 104–22.

105. David T. Morgan, "Scandal in Carolina: The Story of a Capricious Missionary," *NCHR* 47 (1970):233–43. For support of Morgan's view of the Anglican ministry see Thomas C. Parramore, "John Alexander, Anglican Missionary," *NCHR* 43 (1966): 305–15; Paul Conkin, "The Church Establishment in North Carolina, 1765–1776," *NCHR* 32 (1955): 30.

106. Sarah McCulloh Lemmon, "The Genesis of the Protestant Episcopal Diocese in North Carolina, 1701–1823," *NCHR* 28 (1951): 426–62; Lemmon, "Nathaniel Blount: Last Clergyman of the 'Old Church,'" *NCHR* 50 (1973): 351–64; Lemmon, *Parson Pettigrew of the "Old Church": 1744–1807*, James Sprunt Studies in History and Political Science, vol. 52 (Chapel Hill: University of North Carolina Press, 1970). See also Bennett H. Wall, "Charles Pettigrew, First Bishop-Elect of the North Carolina Episcopal Church," *NCHR* 28 (1951): 15–46.

107. Stephen B. Weeks, *The Religious Development in the Province of North Carolina*, Johns Hopkins University Studies in Historical and Political Science, vol.

Carolina have permitted many detailed studies of that group including Ruth Blackwelder's "The Attitude of North Carolina Moravians toward the American Revolution" and Hunter James's *The Quiet People of the Land: A Story of the North Carolina Moravians in Revolutionary Times.*[108] Dorothy Gilbert Thorne follows the efforts of the North Carolina Quakers to cope with wartime pressures.[109]

Many aspects of the economy of the revolutionary period have been treated by Crittenden in *The Commerce of North Carolina, 1763–1789*, which adds depth to a number of his previously published articles. Far broader than the title indicates, the study shows that by 1763 North Carolina had developed an economy independent of the overarching influence of Virginia and South Carolina, agrees with Justin Williams that British mercantilist restrictions were not burdensome, and finds that difficulties in communication between east and west encouraged misinterpretation of British actions and then impeded British efforts to crush the Revolution.[110] Supplementing Crittenden is

10, nos. 5–6 (Baltimore: Johns Hopkins Press, 1892); Robert M. Calhoon, *Religion and the American Revolution in North Carolina* (Raleigh: North Carolina Department of Cultural Resources, 1976). Detailed studies of various aspects of religion in the period include James R. Caldwell, "The Church of Granville County, North Carolina, in the Eighteenth Century," *Studies in Southern History*, pp. 1–22; Durward T. Stokes, "North Carolina and the Great Revival of 1800," *NCHR* 43 (1966): 401–12; "Henry Patillo in North Carolina," *NCHR* 44 (1967): 373–91; David T. Morgan, "The Great Awakening in North Carolina, 1740–1775: The Baptist Phase," *NCHR* 45 (1968): 264–83.

108. Adelaide L. Fries et al., eds., *Records of the Moravians in North Carolina*, 11 vols. (Raleigh: North Carolina Historical Commission, 1922–69); Ruth Blackwelder, "The Attitude of North Carolina Moravians toward the American Revolution," *NCHR* 9 (1932): 1–21; Hunter James, *The Quiet People of the Land: A Story of the North Carolina Moravians in Revolutionary Times* (Chapel Hill: University of North Carolina Press, 1976).

109. Dorothy Gilbert Thorne, "North Carolina Friends and the Revolution," *NCHR* 38 (1961): 323–40.

110. Charles C. Crittenden, *The Commerce of North Carolina, 1763–1789* (New Haven: Yale University Press, 1936); Crittenden, "The Seacoast in North Carolina History, 1763–1789," *NCHR* 7 (1930): 433–42; Crittenden, "Ships and Shipbuilding in North Carolina, 1763–1789," *NCHR* 8 (1931): 1–13; Justin Wil-

the detailed description entitled "Economic Conditions in North
Carolina About 1780" by F. G. and P. M. Morris and the
insights into the mercantile operations of the 1780s provided by
Alice B. Keith and William Masterson in their work on John Gray
Blount and William Blount. No consideration of the economy
would be complete, however, without the consultation of H. Roy
Merrens, *Colonial North Carolina in the Eighteenth Century*, a
masterful work that relates to virtually every field of historical
endeavor in colonial North Carolina.[111]

Any investigation of the economy as well as the politics
of the period would be incomplete without reference to the
west. Archibald Henderson and Thomas P. Abernethy catalog
in detail the provincial interest in the transmontane region
before the Revolution, including the speculative ventures of
Richard Henderson and the organization of the Transylvania
Company.[112] Generating more interest among historians is
Franklin, the first western "state." Among the voluminous
writings of Samuel C. Williams is the *History of the Lost State
of Franklin*, which remains the standard study. Williams and
Carl Driver, principal biographer of John Sevier, agree that
"grievances against the mother State, [the settlers'] fear of

liams, "English Mercantilism and Carolina Naval Stores, 1705–1776," *Journal of
Southern History* 1 (1935): 168–85.

111. Francis G. Morris and Phyllis M. Morris, "Economic Conditions in
North Carolina About 1780, Parts I–II," *NCHR* 16 (1939): 107–33, 296–327; Alice B.
Keith, "John Gray and Thomas Blount, Merchants, 1783–1800," *NCHR* 25 (1948):
194–205; "William Blount in North Carolina Politics, 1781–1789," *Studies in
Southern History*, pp. 47–61; Masterson, *William Blount*; H. Roy Merrens, *Colonial
North Carolina in the Eighteenth Century: A Study in Historical Geography* (Chapel
Hill: University of North Carolina Press, 1964).

112. Archibald Henderson, *The Conquest of the Old Southwest . . . 1740–
1790* (New York: Century Company, 1920); "Richard Henderson and the Occupa-
tion of Kentucky, 1775," *Mississippi Valley Historical Review* 1 (1914): 341–63;
Henderson, "The Creative Forces in Westward Expansion: Henderson and
Boone," *NCB* 14 (1915): 111–39; Henderson, "The Transylvania Company: A
Study in Personnel," *Filson Club History Quarterly* 21 (1947): 229–42; Thomas P.
Abernethy, *From Frontier to Plantation in Tennessee: A Study in Frontier Democracy*
(Chapel Hill: University of North Carolina Press, 1932).

continued domination, the subordination of their interests to
those of the eastern part of North Carolina, their apparent
abandonment by that government, and their resentment against
real and fancied wrongs led them to embark upon a new
experiment in self-government."[113] Walter F. Cannon concurs in
this "separatist" rationale to account for the founding of
Franklin. But in canvassing the debate over the establishment
of the state he finds three other explanations for its appearance:
the "democratic," which sees Franklin as the epitome of the
individualistic spirit of a frontier people; the "ingrate," which
views Franklin as the result of the "lawless thirst for power" by
Sevier and others working against the "patriotic and self-
sacrificing" impulses of North Carolina; and the "speculative,"
best exemplified by Abernethy, which concludes that the North
Carolina cession of 1784 and its repeal resulted from "a game
played between two rival goups of land speculators."[114] St.
George L. Sioussat puts the matter in national perspective when
arguing that North Carolina's decision to retain the western
lands involved "the adjustment of State and Federal relations
in regard to two fundamental and correlated powers, the control
of the purse and the control of the land system."[115]

Regarding the politics of the Confederation era, Ganyard
declares that the "proponents of democracy" failed to represent
the "principal thrust" of the Revolution, but W. E. Dodd and
D. H. Gilpatrick, who assert that the radicals dominated politics

113. Samuel C. Williams, *History of the Lost State of Franklin* (Johnson City,
Tenn.: Watauga Press, 1924); Driver, *John Sevier*; Driver, introduction to Williams,
History of the Lost State of Franklin, rev. ed. (New York: Press of the Pioneers, 1933),
p. xvii. For concurrence see Frederick Jackson Turner, *The Significance of Sections in
American History* (New York: H. Holt and Company, 1932), pp. 136–38.

114. Walter F. Cannon, "Four Interpretations of the History of the State of
Franklin," East Tennessee Historical Society *Publications* 22 (1950): 3–18; Aber-
nethy, *From Frontier to Plantation*, p. 89. For agreement with Abernethy see Paul
M. Fink, "Some Phases of the History of the State of Franklin," *Tennessee Historical
Quarterly* 16 (1957): 195–213.

115. St. George L. Sioussat, "The North Carolina Cession of 1784 in its
Federal Aspects," Organization of American Historians *Proceedings* 2 (1908):
35–62.

from 1776 to 1789, reflect the prevailing consensus.[116] The superior position of the radicals might well have stemmed from the general satisfaction of the populace with the prevailing state of affairs. Crittenden, in *The Commerce of North Carolina*, denies the "critical period" interpretation of the decade by showing that the economy recovered rapidly from the ravages of the war. An article entitled "North Carolina Tariff Policies, 1775–1789," by William F. Zornow buttresses Merrill Jensen's contention that state tariffs were fairly uniform with little discrimination against other states.[117]

The most impressive denial of the "critical period" thesis comes from James R. Morrill, *The Practice and Politics of Fiat Finance*. Following the methodology of E. James Ferguson in *The Power of the Purse* and arriving at conclusions similar to those of Jensen and Ferguson, Morrill feels that the disruption of North Carolina's preindustrial economy by the war followed by the exigencies of retiring its war debt and providing a circulating medium of exchange necessitated as well as justified fiat emissions and an attendant antifederalism.[118] His detailed examination of the liquidation of the North Carolina debt to Martinique generally supports the conclusion of an earlier study by B. U. Ratchford, though the latter overstates the case when he declares that "the success finally achieved reflects credit upon the state and upon the officials responsible for maintaining the integrity of its financial obligations."[119]

116. William E. Dodd, *The Life of Nathaniel Macon* (Raleigh: Edwards & Broughton, 1903), chap. 7; Gilpatrick, *Jeffersonian Democracy*, pp. 24–36.

117. William F. Zornow, "North Carolina Tariff Practices, 1775–1789," *NCHR* 32 (1955): 151–64; Merrill Jensen, *The New Nation: A History of the United States during the Confederation, 1781–1789* (New York: Alfred A. Knopf, 1950).

118. James R. Morrill, *The Practice and Politics of Fiat Finance: North Carolina in the Confederation, 1783–1789* (Chapel Hill: University of North Carolina Press, 1969); E. James Ferguson, *The Power of the Purse: A History of American Public Finance, 1776–1790* (Chapel Hill: University of North Carolina Press, 1961). See also Adelaide L. Fries, "North Carolina Certificates of the Revolutionary War Period," *NCHR* 9 (1932): 229–41.

119. B. U. Ratchford, "An International Debt Settlement: The North

That North Carolina did not experience "critical" times during the Confederation tends to support Forrest McDonald's contention that "those states that had done well on their own were inclined to desire to continue on their own."[120] Led by Willie Jones, the Antifederalists soundly defeated the proposed adoption of the federal Constitution in 1788, but the Federalists launched a massive educational campaign to alter the political climate of the state.[121] The efforts of such Federalist worthies as Iredell, Johnston, Davie, and Williamson have been described at length;[122] their labors were rewarded at the Fayetteville Convention in 1789 when North Carolina voted to join the Union.

Although no satisfactory analysis of Confederation politics exists, Louise I. Trenholme's *The Ratification of the Federal Constitution in North Carolina*, which builds upon the earlier studies of Dodd and Wagstaff, suffices. Reflecting the dominant Progressive influence of the times, Trenholme sees the division between conservatives and radicals (translated to Federalists and Antifederalists) based on sectional, socioeconomic differences with certain religious denominations and the parochialism of the majority of North Carolinians adding to the strength of the

---

Carolina Debt to France," *AHR* 40 (1934): 63–69. For another aspect of the debt question see Whitney K. Bates, "Northern Speculators and Southern State Debts," *WMQ*, 3d ser., 19 (1962): 30–48.

120. Forrest McDonald, *We the People: The Economic Origins of the Constitution* (Chicago: University of Chicago Press, 1958), p. 416.

121. For eyewitness views of the campaigning of 1788 and 1789, see Julian P. Boyd, ed., "A North Carolina Citizen on the Federal Constitution, 1788," *NCHR* 16 (1939): 36–53; Thomas C. Parramore, "A Year in Hertford County with Elkanah Watson," *NCHR* 41 (1964): 448–63.

122. In addition to works cited previously see John W. Neal, "Life and Public Services of Hugh Williamson, 1735–1819," Trinity College Historical Society *Papers* 13 (1919): 62–111; Delbert H. Gilpatrick, "Contemporary Opinion of Hugh Williamson," *NCHR* 17 (1940): 26–36; Alice B. Keith, "William Blount in North Carolina Politics, 1781–1789," *Studies in Southern History*, pp. 47–61, in which she rationalizes Blount's earlier negative statements regarding the Constitution; and Merritt B. Pound, *Benjamin Hawkins, Indian Agent* (Athens: University of Georgia Press, 1951).

latter group.[123] Although William C. Pool's analysis of the
economic interests of the members of the Hillsborough and
Fayetteville conventions specifically refutes the Beardian thesis
by showing that the ownership of property among the
representatives was evenly distributed,[124] Morrill reformulates
Beardian concepts along the lines of more sophisticated
interpretations such as those posited by McDonald, Main, and
Ferguson.[125] However, Morrill's own dichotomous cleavage
between the "idealism" of the Federalists and the "realism"
of the Antifederalists to explain the politics of the late 1780s lacks
the rigorous corroborative support generally found throughout
his work.

The sudden, and overwhelming, decision of North
Carolina to accept the Constitution has long intrigued historians.
H. M. Wagstaff feels that the pressure of ratification by eleven
states prompted North Carolina to join the Union.[126] Stephen B.
Weeks, in his sketch of Thomas Person, denies Dodd's earlier
assertion that the Antifederalists were thwarted in their attempt
to establish "a free and absolutely independent State" and
returns to the position of Raper, who felt that Jones, Person,
and their adherents merely sought to pressure the United States
into adding desirable amendments to the Constitution.[127]

123. Louise I. Trenholme, *The Ratification of the Federal Constitution in North Carolina* (New York: Columbia University Press, 1932), chaps. 3–4.

124. William C. Pool, "An Economic Interpretation of the Ratification of the Federal Constitution in North Carolina, Parts I–III," *NCHR* 27 (1950): 119–41, 289–313, 437–61.

125. Forrest McDonald, *E Pluribus Unum: The Formation of the American Republic, 1776–1790* (Boston: Houghton Mifflin Company, 1965); Jackson T. Main, *The Antifederalists: Critics of the Constitution, 1781–1788* (Chapel Hill: University of North Carolina Press, 1961); Ferguson, *Power of the Purse*.

126. H. M. Wagstaff, *Federalism in North Carolina*, James Sprunt Studies in History and Political Science, vol. 9 (Chapel Hill: University of North Carolina, 1910), pp. 17–18. See also H. M. Wagstaff, *States Rights and Political Parties in North Carolina, 1776–1861*, Johns Hopkins Studies in Historical and Political Science, vol. 24, nos. 7–8 (Baltimore: Johns Hopkins Press, 1906).

127. Dodd, *Life of Nathaniel Macon*, p. 51; Stephen B. Weeks, "Thomas Person," *NCB* 9 (1909): 29; Charles L. Raper, "Why North Carolina at First

Trenholme, incorporating much of the earlier work on the question, decides that the Federalist victory resulted from economic pressures imposed by the first national Congress, the state's need for protection from the Indians, confidence in the national government resulting from Washington's election, and Madison's early efforts to secure amendments to the Constitution. Eight years later A. R. Newsome generally agreed but seemed to stress the importance of economic factors as paramount. More recently, however, J. Edwin Hendricks, in his study of one Antifederalist who changed his vote to favor ratification, finds that there "was no Anti-Federalism, no rejection of the principles of the new federal union." The promise of amendments "is the only explanation which seems to fit the rapid shift of votes from the 1788 to the 1789 convention where . . . Anti-Federalists voted to approve the new Constitution."[128] But subsequently Morrill harks back to H. M. Wagstaff when he says that "the triumph of Federalism in other states and the events that flowed therefrom" gave a reluctant North Carolina "no realistic alternative to joining the Union."[129]

Any attempt to determine the direction of the revolutionary historiography of North Carolina is indeed speculative. Despite some excellent dissertations, historians appear content generally to approach the revolutionary years in piecemeal fashion by way of article or short monographic publications. The bicentennial commemoration tends to reinforce the post–World

Refused to Ratify the Federal Constitution," *Annual Report of the American Historical Association for 1905* (Washington, D.C.: Government Printing Office, 1906), 1:101–7. For an assertion of North Carolina's brief period of independence see W. W. Pierson, Jr., "The Sovereign State of North Carolina, 1787–1789," *Proceedings of the Seventeenth Annual Session of the State Literary and Historical Association*, 5–6 December 1916 (Raleigh: North Carolina Historical Commission, 1917), pp. 58–69.

128. Trenholme, *Ratification of the Federal Constitution*, pp. 242–43; Albert Ray Newsome, "North Carolina's Ratification of the Federal Constitution," *NCHR* 17 (1940): 287–301; J. Edwin Hendricks, "Joseph Winston: North Carolina Jeffersonian," *NCHR* 45 (1968): 290.

129. Morrill, *Practice and Politics of Fiat Finance*, pp. 218–19.

War II emphasis on the importance of ideological considerations to explain the nature of the separation from Great Britain and the political decisions that followed. Yet, some of the best recent work in the period, exemplified by Kay and Morrill, refines and updates the Progressive concern with a socioeconomic, class interpretation of the past and reflects the continuing reaction to consensus history.

Regardless of the direction of revolutionary historiography, its needs are manifold. For introductory purposes the era would be well served by a comprehensive, detailed treatment of the colonial years comparable to that of Richard L. Morton for Virginia and M. Eugene Sirmans for South Carolina.[130] The politics of the revolutionary period are imperfectly understood at best: Sellers's study requires modernization and extension through the war years; North Carolina's relationship with the central government during the war years and Confederation needs more careful consideration; and the full story of the debate over the Constitution must be told. Although the military history of the war has been treated in detail, an investigation of the home front and the relation of the war to the society in which it occurred would be invaluable, particularly for North Carolina with its devastating civil conflict. At present, satisfactory biographical studies of individuals involved in the Revolution are few. Maurice Moore, Samuel Johnston, and James Iredell have been slighted or ignored; John Sevier and Willie Jones exemplify those who might benefit from more modern treatments. But these are only some of the more obvious gaps in the presentation of North Carolina's revolutionary history. Further reflection would quickly add to the list of potential subject matter. Clearly the revolutionary era in North Carolina's past is an open and promising field to those who would avail themselves of its opportunities.

130. Richard L. Morton, *Colonial Virginia*, 2 vols. (Chapel Hill: University of North Carolina Press, 1960); M. Eugene Sirmans, *Colonial South Carolina: A Political History, 1663–1763* (Chapel Hill: University of North Carolina Press, 1966).

3

A Troubled Culture: North Carolina in the New Nation, 1790–1834

by Robert M. Calhoon

The traditional history of North Carolina from ratification of the federal Constitution in 1789 until the eve of the second state constitutional convention in 1835 is a story of progress, but progress impeded time and again by capricious fate. This forty-five-year period has disappointed chroniclers of the Old North State. Conditioned by events at the national level to consider 1815 as a dividing line between the early national period and the so-called Era of Good Feelings, North Carolina historians have depicted 1790 to 1815 as a period when the great energies mobilized and released by the Revolution played themselves out and dissipated. After 1815 a languishing economy and torpid political and social life earned North Carolina the name Rip Van Winkle State—a pastoral, lethargic entity within a buoyant, restless new nation.

      Hugh Lefler and the late Albert Ray Newsome demonstrated the vitality and persuasiveness of this framework in

I am grateful to Blackwell P. Robinson and Donald G. Mathews for answering many questions about North Carolina and southern religion. Alice Cotten of the North Carolina Collection and Richard A. Shrader of the Southern Historical Collection, University of North Carolina at Chapel Hill Library, were most helpful. Loren Schweninger, Jeffrey B. Allen, Robert M. Weir, Jeffrey J. Crow, and Karl A. Schleunes read and discussed the paper with me and made valuable suggestions. Most of all I appreciate the critical guidance of Robert Polk Thomson, who wrote a bracing yet understanding critique of the paper and who introduced me, in a memorable seminar at Western Reserve University some years ago, to the study of early American cultural history.

their textbook, *North Carolina: The History of a Southern State*.[1] As
their bibliography attests, Lefler and Newsome's interpretation
of these years rested substantially on the work of Samuel A.
Ashe, William K. Boyd, and R. D. W. Connor.[2] The theme of the
early nineteenth century, Connor stressed, was the "blight of
sectionalism," by which he meant a virtually nonexistent
educational system, the lack of roads and navigable rivers,
sleepy, indolent towns that provided no incentive for investment
and so crippled the state's banking system, the domination of the
state by eastern planters, the insensitivity of the legislature
to the needs of the Piedmont and the west, and the consequent
migration of 200,000 of the state's most energetic citizens to
the west and southwest.[3] Boyd's *History of North Carolina:
The Federal Period* remains the best financial history of the state
in this period, and he found both in the state's handling of
financial affairs and the banking system a record of "inexperience
and incompetence, . . . disorder, inefficiency, and corruption."[4]
Connor's hero, of course, was state senator Archibald D.
Murphey whose reports to the General Assembly between 1815
and 1818 on education, public finance, road building and other
internal improvements, and constitutional reform "brought a
more thorough comprehension of the natural and human
resources of the state, a clearer understanding of her conditions
and needs, a bolder and more abiding confidence in her future
than any other man of his generation."[5] Imbued with these

1. Hugh T. Lefler and Albert R. Newsome, *North Carolina: The History of a
Southern State*, 3d ed. (Chapel Hill: University of North Carolina Press, 1973),
chaps. 17–22.
2. Samuel A'Court Ashe, *History of North Carolina*, 2 vols. (Raleigh:
Edwards and Broughton, 1908–25), 2:chaps. 8–23; William K. Boyd, *History of
North Carolina: The Federal Period, 1783–1860* (Chicago and New York: Lewis
Publishing Co., 1919), chaps. 3–11 (hereafter cited as *Federal Period*); R. D. W.
Connor, *North Carolina: Rebuilding an Ancient Commonwealth, 1584–1925*, 2 vols.
(Chicago and New York: American Historical Society, 1929), 1:401–517.
3. Connor, *North Carolina*, 1:chaps. 20–21.
4. Boyd, *Federal Period*, pp. 150, 109, and chaps. 6 and 7 passim.
5. Connor, *North Carolina*, 1:497.

sympathies, Fletcher M. Green traced the movement for
legislative reapportionment and more equitable taxation from the
early 1800s to the constitutional convention of 1835.[6] Delbert H.
Gilpatrick and Henry M. Wagstaff described the mobilization in
the state of agrarian opposition to Hamiltonian, pro-British
national policy.[7] Albert Ray Newsome identified the expanding
interests and political ambitions that could no longer be
accommodated by the eastern, Republican, planter leadership
of the state.[8]

Boyd, Connor, Green, and J. G. de Roulhac Hamilton
(Green's mentor) represented the first generation of professional
academic historians in North Carolina. They were "southern
progressives"[9] who found in early nineteenth-century North
Carolina a conservative, rural society dominated by a powerful,
unenlightened elite who detested change and mindlessly
ignored the social cost of poverty, economic stagnation, and
unresponsive government. They saw slavery not so much as an
evil but as a blight on the lives of poor whites and free blacks and
a buttress of aristocracy and privilege.[10] They yearned in their
own time for educated, scientific, public-spirited, enterprising
political leadership drawn from the professional middle class and

6. Fletcher M. Green, *Constitutional Development in the South Atlantic
States, 1776–1860* (Chapel Hill: University of North Carolina Press, 1930); and
"Democracy in the Old South," in J. Isaac Copeland, ed., *Democracy in the Old
South and Other Essays* (Nashville: Vanderbilt University Press, 1969), pp. 65–86.

7. Delbert H. Gilpatrick, *Jeffersonian Democracy in North Carolina, 1789–
1816* (New York: Columbia University Press, 1931); Henry M. Wagstaff, *States
Rights and Political Parties in North Carolina, 1776–1861* (Baltimore: Johns Hopkins
University Press, 1906), chap. 2.

8. Albert R. Newsome, *The Presidential Election of 1824 in North Carolina*
(Chapel Hill: University of North Carolina Press, 1939).

9. On J. G. de Roulhac Hamilton in the Progressive movement, see
Joseph F. Steelman, "Origins of the Campaign for Constitutional Reform in North
Carolina, 1912–1913," presidential address to the Historical Society of North
Carolina, 22 October 1976, Elon College. A thorough study of Progressive
historiography in North Carolina, based on the scholarly writings and personal
papers of historians in the state from 1910 through 1940, and on the writings of
their students, would be an excellent subject for a doctoral dissertation.

10. See, for example, Connor, *North Carolina*, 1:452–55.

imbued with Protestant social responsibility and moral integrity. The early nineteenth century was a vivid example, for these scholars, of the difficulty of mobilizing opinion in a rural, decentralized society.

Cast in these terms, the history of the state did not fit very well into the larger pattern of southern history. North Carolina's east-west political divisions, its slavery, and its rural backwardness more or less resembled conditions elsewhere in the region, but the lack of a cultural focus in the state as well as its Quaker and Moravian minorities and the low profile of its politicians on the national level partially insulated North Carolina from the rise of southern nationalism. Elgiva D. Watson has analyzed this aloofness from southern sectionalism in her dissertation on North Carolina's antebellum cultural critics.[11] North Carolina material occupies an extremely limited portion of Charles S. Sydnor, *The Development of Southern Sectionalism, 1819–1848*, in part, one suspects, because Sydnor knew the history of North Carolina too well to fit it into his analysis of sectionalism awakened.[12]

By placing North Carolina within the framework of the Progressive interpretation of history, by relating North Carolina political development to the rise and fall of the first party system and the advent of Jacksonian politics, and by identifying a tension between Tar Heel particularism and southern nationalism, the traditional interpretation of early national and early antebellum North Carolina has answered most of the questions that it has raised. Like the Whig interpre-

11. Elgiva D. Watson, "The Pursuit of Pride: Cultural Attitudes in North Carolina, 1830–1861," Ph.D. diss., University of North Carolina at Chapel Hill, 1972.

12. Charles S. Sydnor, *The Development of Southern Sectionalism, 1819–1848* (Baton Rouge: Louisiana State University Press, 1948). Sydnor makes some penetrating remarks on local government in North Carolina on pp. 39–49. The other book in the History of the South series covering this period, Thomas P. Abernethy, *The South in the New Nation, 1789–1819* (Baton Rouge: Louisiana State University Press, 1961), devotes most of its attention to the new southern frontier and notes only North Carolina's reaction to major national political issues.

tation of history, of which it is a variant, the Connor-Hamilton-Newsome-Lefler tradition of North Carolina historiography produced a factually accurate, engrossing narrative of the development of the state flawed only by its unexamined assumptions about the nature of social change and the malleability of human nature. The substantial achievements of this school have now cleared the way for historians to ask new questions, explore new modes of understanding, and construct a new model or paradigm of the possibilities of the historical situation.[13]

In numerous recent studies, as well as in several prescient passages in older works, we can now see the shape of a new understanding of late eighteenth- and early nineteenth-century North Carolina. First, as it did for Americans everywhere, the postrevolutionary period filled North Carolinians with a sense of limitless possibility. Awed by their new destiny as an independent, virtuous, capable people, North Carolinians turned inward in search of the abilities and values needed to meet this vast, indeterminate challenge. This new preoccupation with their own character as individuals and as a people, secondly, unleashed emotions and energies that had previously been dormant. North Carolina society acquired during the first quarter of the nineteenth century a passionate culture in which hostilities, fears, and mercurial feelings of hope and despair permeated politics, education, and social intercourse. By tapping the best resources available, their own emotions and aspirations, the people of the early nineteenth century sought to make their lives and their society whole and satisfying. Third, North Carolinians, like other southerners, sought to impose order and predictability on this fluid milieu by developing fierce loyalties

13. See Michael McGiffert, "American Puritan Studies in the 1960s," *William and Mary Quarterly*, 3d ser., 27 (1970): 64–65; David A. Hollinger, "T. S. Kuhn's Theory of Science and Its Implications for History," *American Historical Review* 78 (1973): 373–74; and Robert E. Shalhope, "Thomas Jefferson's Republicanism and Antebellum Southern Thought," *Journal of Southern History* 42 (1976): 529–30.

to family, church, and local community; and by regarding local social rivals, outsiders, racial subordinates, and powerful institutions generally as the enemy. Finally, this newly impassioned culture, still hungry for stability and security, sanctioned volatile assertions of social control by the strong over the weak, the many over the few, and especially whites over blacks.

While these four sets of human impulses were not unique to North Carolina nor to the years from 1790 to 1834, their peculiar configuration and collective function within society enable historians to make sense of a great mass of otherwise unrelated data. To this extent this cluster of cultural dynamics can be weighed and distinguished from those operating in other periods and places. There is the risk in this sort of broad gauge historiographical analysis of viewing concrete historical realities from the lofty perspective of modern interpretation and thereby regarding individuals as mere pawns of powerful cultural forces. It is important to emphasize that culture consists of broadly recognized constraints on human individualism, and only as it reflects, expresses, and interacts with the personalities, values, and beliefs of individuals and groups can culture acquire objective reality. Every example in this paper, and practically every page of historical writing here considered, focuses attention on the interplay of cultural imperative and individual volition. "Believing . . . that man is an animal suspended in webs of significance he himself has spun," Clifford Geertz has written, "I take culture to be those webs and the analysis of it to be therefore not an experimental one in search of law but an interpretive one in search of meaning."[14] Embedded within the writings of North Carolina historians on the early national period, themes of introspection, celebration, constraint, and aggression indicate the structure of experience, the "webs" of cultural consciousness during this period.

The soaring hopes of the early national period generated

14. Clifford Geertz, *The Interpretation of Cultures: Selected Essays* (New York: Basic Books, 1973), p. 5.

a strong undercurrent of uncertainty and apprehension in North Carolina. Both Richard V. Buel and Roger H. Brown find America, including North Carolina, preoccupied with the fragility of republican government and convinced that honest mistakes or deliberate abuse of the public interest in foreign or fiscal policy could destroy republicanism.[15] Historians of the first party system have not satisfactorily integrated North Carolina into their story, but available studies underscore the inhibitions against partisanship in the young state. In their respective monographs on the Federalist party in the South, Lisle A. Rose and James H. Broussard show that the Federalists, while a distinct minority, had durable sources of support in North Carolina among the commercial elite in both the east and the west. The party benefited from the drive and prominence of men like William R. Davie, William Gaston, and James Iredell, who had been thrust into public life by the Revolution and whose reputations rested on their ability to help fill the vacuum of national leadership during the 1790s. The Federalists' dependence on identifiable and capable leaders in the 1790s proved its undoing in the years after 1800. Iredell died; Davie became disgusted with politics and left the state; and their most able protégé, John Steele, became a Republican. Republican ascendancy after 1800 cut North Carolina Federalists' access to national power. With amazing adaptability, however, the party remained a viable political entity until after 1815. Broussard suggests that fear of French revolutionary turmoil and international power kept the southern Federalists alive until the end of the Napoleonic wars. The party's failure to organize and publicize its cause aggressively, he contends, cost the North Carolina Federalists a substantial share of political

---

15. Richard V. Buel, Jr., *Securing the Republic: Ideology in American Politics, 1789–1815* (Ithaca: Cornell University Press, 1972), pp. 81–90, 235–40; Roger H. Brown, *The Republic in Peril: 1812* (New York: Columbia University Press, 1964), pp. 52–57, 155–57.

influence in the state.[16] David H. Fischer finds in North Carolina
Federalists a strong sensitivity to Jeffersonian belief in the
sovereignty of the people and the accountability of legislators
to their constituents.[17]

The Federalists were not merely moderating their partisanship in deference to a Jeffersonian electorate. On the contrary,
North Carolina politics demanded that leaders adopt public
stances broadly representative of the opinions and sentiments
within the state but deprecated any unbridled pursuit of power.
Sarah M. Lemmon's *Frustrated Patriots: North Carolina and the
War of 1812* is the most thoroughly researched and meticulous
study of these inhibitions. North Carolinians, as her title
suggests, were frustrated by the failure of diplomacy to ward off
British incursions on American trade, by the inadequacy of
American military preparations, and by their state's inability to
play a significant role in the military conflict. At a deeper level,
she finds the aspirations of North Carolina patriots, as children
of the Revolution, thwarted by European violations of American
neutrality and tarnished by the nation's diplomatic and military
weakness, which reflected badly on the country's manhood and
virtue. These frustrations, these apprehensions about the
permanence of revolutionary achievement, underlaid the first
party system in North Carolina. While a majority of the state's
congressional delegation were relatively obscure Republican
party regulars, the state's most talented representatives, Fed-

16. Lisle A. Rose, *Prologue to Democracy: The Federalists in the South,
1789–1800* (Lexington: University of Kentucky Press, 1968), pp. 128–30, 165–66,
260–61, 297–99; James H. Broussard, "The Federalist Party in the South Atlantic
States, 1800–1812," Ph.D. diss., Duke University, 1968, pp. 370, 376–77, 412–18.
Also see Broussard, "Party and Partisanship in American Legislatures: The South
Atlantic States, 1800–1812," *Journal of Southern History* 43 (1977): 39–58; and "The
North Carolina Federalists, 1800–1816," *North Carolina Historical Review* (hereafter
cited as *NCHR*) 55 (January 1978): 18–41.
17. David Hackett Fischer, *The Revolution in American Conservatism: The
Federalist Party in the Era of Jeffersonian Democracy* (New York: Harper and Row,
1965), pp. 387–97.

eralist William Gaston and Old Republican Richard Stanford, opposed the war. Gaston considered Madison's foreign policy disastrously inept and pro-French, while Nathaniel Macon (though he voted reluctantly for the declaration of war) and Stanford detested the role of money, office, and influence in politics and saw the war as final proof of Madison's betrayal of limited government, agrarianism, and state rights. In North Carolina, Madison's Republican supporters, as well as his Old Republican castigators and Federalist opposition, represented different understandings of the moral legacy of the Revolution.[18] The decentralization of power in the state; the backward looking, defensive posture of the sons of the Revolution; and the unwillingness of political parties to grasp openly for power therefore insulated the state from party politics. Leonard L. Richards's article on early national politics in the Cape Fear valley provides dramatic corroboration of this view. He shows that Scottish farmers in the Fayetteville district supported Federalist candidates with a high degree of regularity from the late 1790s through 1815, because they were a tightly knit community bound together by strong, patriarchal leadership; by their pro-British sympathies during the Revolution; and by their distaste for anti-Tory zealots among the Republicans in the 1790s.[19]

The more politics provided an outlet for human energies and ambitions the more North Carolinians resisted politicization. In his pioneering study of political rhetoric in North Carolina, Harry L. Watson finds a deep and pervasive fear of organized political conflict over the policies of state and local government. The rhetoric of Republicans and Federalists alike oscillated between inspiring appeals to the principles of the American Revolution, such as limited constitutional government, personal

18. Sarah M. Lemmon, *Frustrated Patriots: North Carolina and the War of 1812* (Chapel Hill: University of North Carolina Press, 1973), chaps. 8–10.
19. Leonard L. Richards, "John Adams and the Moderate Federalists: The Cape Fear Valley as a Test Case," *NCHR* 43 (Winter 1966): 14–30.

liberty, and a glorious national destiny, and entirely personal
slanders against the moral characters of rival candidates. The
prevalence of "prolonged, . . . intense campaigns of personal
vilification, slander, and abuse" by individual candidates
only proved the danger of organized party politics—the capacity
of personal remarks to "rouse" what William Gaston called
"the furious passions of party." North Carolina politicians
during the early nineteenth century, Watson concludes, were
premodern men, unable to "separate public and private roles."
Political leadership in the first generation of democratic self-
government seemed to require heroic qualities; public officials
and even candidates for office risked losing their reputations
for honesty and patriotism. The issues which mattered,
therefore, were not questions of public policy but were rather
ones of reputation, character, and support on the national scene
of the forces of light over those of darkness. Still bound to the
idea that the code of the gentleman was a way of preserving
virtue, the political culture of the period did not tolerate political
competition between competing interest groups.[20]

In higher education, as in foreign policy and party
politics, the high-minded exercise of power generated corrosive
hostilities and tensions. Southern state legislatures chartered
sixteen colleges and universities during the postrevolutionary
period, and nearly all suffered crippling financial weakness and
were wracked by internal disorder. The history of these
institutions was more than one of educational finance and
student discipline. Postrevolutionary higher education, Robert
Polk Thomson argues, ignited furious controversy over the
role of the state in the promotion of virtue and leadership.
The early history of the University of North Carolina (the first
such public institution in America) is a prime example of a clash

20. Harry L. Watson, "The Antipragmatic Consensus: Prepartisan Political Ideology in North Carolina, 1800–1835," paper read to the Historical Society of
North Carolina, 22 April 1977, Greenville.

of educational values. William R. Davie, like Jefferson and
Bishop James Madison in Virginia, wanted his university to
instill into a rising generation of aristocratic youth the full
riches of the Enlightenment: a critical appreciation of moral and
natural philosophy and the legacy of Western history, literature,
and science.[21] His rival in shaping the early curriculum at Chapel
Hill, the Reverend Samuel McCorkle, wanted to give prime
attention to Greek and Latin and to inculcating strict Protestant
orthodoxy and pious personal conduct. Davie persuaded the
trustees to adopt his liberal curriculum in 1795, but the
philosophy of the university remained an explosive issue.
Davie's vision was a university "designed to form useful and
respectful members of society—citizens capable of comprehending, improving, and defending the principles of government, citizens, who from the highest possible impulse, a just
sense of their own and the general happiness would be induced
to practice the duties of social morality."[22] That classical
republican creed and Davie's highly visible leadership, as his

21. Robert Polk Thomson, "Colleges in the Revolutionary South: The
Shaping of a Tradition," *History of Education Quarterly* 10 (Winter 1970): 399–412;
see also Alma Pauline Foerster, "The State University in the Old South: A Study
of Social and Intellectual Influences in State University Education," Ph.D. diss.,
Duke University, 1939, pp. 46–49, 59–63, 86–96. Serious scholarship on the
university trails off after 1800, reflecting in part the terminal date of R. D. W.
Connor, ed., *A Documentary History of the University of North Carolina, 1776–1799*,
2 vols. (Chapel Hill: University of North Carolina Press, 1953). Badly needed is a
second generation of studies of higher education in North Carolina building
upon Kemp Plummer Battle, *History of the University of North Carolina*, 2 vols.
(Raleigh: Edwards and Broughton, 1907–12), and George W. Paschal, *History of
Wake Forest College*, 3 vols. (Wake Forest: Wake Forest College, 1935–43). Even
more neglected is the history of academies. Alice E. Mathews, "Academia and
Res Publica: An Attempted Dialogue in Revolutionary North Carolina," a paper
read to the Historical Society of North Carolina, 22 April 1977, Greenville, is an
excellent introduction; and Charles L. Coon, ed., *The Beginnings of Public
Education in North Carolina: A Documentary History, 1790–1840*, 2 vols., and *North
Carolina Schools and Academies* (Raleigh: Edwards and Broughton, 1908 and 1915
respectively) contain a wealth of relatively unutilized data.

22. Quoted in Blackwell P. Robinson, *William R. Davie: A Biography*
(Chapel Hill: University of North Carolina Press, 1957), p. 248.

biographer Blackwell P. Robinson shows, had a disturbing, destabilizing impact on the state. Adept and resourceful, his strength lay in his reputation, ability, and cosmopolitanism. Those very qualities thrust him into power and also mobilized opposition to "high toned, . . . aristocratic principles" of education. The vitriolic attack on Davie's Federalism by Willis Alston in 1803 in a race for Congress, which drove Davie into retirement and out of the state, was a measure of the collapse of support for enlightened education as a bulwark of classical republican idealism.[23] A student riot in 1799 saw the president of the university horsewhipped, but more ominously it confronted and nearly destroyed the presumptive authority that Davie believed ought to belong to properly constituted, socially useful public institutions.[24] "Colleges had always been envisioned as corporate societies serving the corporate needs of the community," Thomson concludes; "the Revolution dissolved the supposed unity of existence and left exposed multiple factions and interests now capable of exerting political influence." As a result, "a college could be viewed as an institution serving the special needs of a particular denomination" or "as an agency promoting the political well-being of the state" or "as a place where the sons of the gentry could receive a liberal or professional education. It could no longer be all those things."[25]

The most telling evidence of expanding horizons of awareness and deepening introspection in North Carolina during the late eighteenth and early nineteenth centuries appears in the most recent scholarship on the Second Great Awakening in the South. The sudden self-scrutiny accompanying the republican experiment, when channeled into new kinds of religious experience, had an electrifying effect on all of society. John B. Boles paints a vivid portrait of the lethargy, drift, and

23. Ibid., chap. 8 and Appendix C.
24. Steven J. Novak, *The Rights of Youth: American Colleges and Student Revolt, 1798–1815* (Cambridge: Harvard University Press, 1977), pp. 106–15.
25. Thomson, "Colleges in the Revolutionary South," p. 405.

spiritual numbness in the 1790s that filled clergymen with apocalyptic fears of the moral and spiritual collapse of society. Mobilized by this danger, they enunciated a "theory of providential deliverance" by which fervent prayer and an abiding faith in the power of God to awaken men to their need of salvation could effect the needed miracle.[26] Durward T. Stokes's painstaking historical detective work on the Reverend James O'Kelly and his North Carolina and Virginia followers identifies a deep yearning among rural folk for a Christocentric religion of direct personal access of each believer to his Savior. O'Kelly's followers, first known as O'Kellians, then Republican Methodists, and finally simply as Christians, "renounced all human institutions in the churches as a species of popery and not fit to govern souls," which was a rejection of all forms of ecclesiastical authority. "The blessed Jesus was proclaimed King and Head of the People," Kelly exulted, "without one dissenting voice."[27]

26. John B. Boles, *The Great Revival, 1787–1805: The Origins of the Southern Evangelical Mind* (Lexington: University of Kentucky Press, 1972), chaps. 1–3. See also Durward T. Stokes, "North Carolina and the Great Revival of 1800," and "Adam Boyd: Publisher, Preacher, and Patriot," *NCHR* 43 (1966): 401–12, and 49 (1972): 1–21; Sarah M. Lemmon, "Nathaniel Blount: Last Clergyman of the 'Old Church,'" *NCHR* 50 (1973): 351–64; and Thomas T. Taylor, "Essays on the Career and Thought of Samuel Eusebius McCorkle," M.A. thesis, University of North Carolina at Greensboro, 1978.

27. Durward T. Stokes and William T. Scott, *A History of the Christian Church in the South* (Burlington: Southern Conference of the United Church of Christ, 1975), p. 27. Though based more on Virginia than North Carolina sources (for the most part available in the Church History Room, Elon College Library) Stokes's chapters on O'Kelly and his followers are the best evidence available on the religious consequences of cultural decentralization in the early national South. There is a great deal of unused, valuable material in the diary of Jeremiah Norman, 1793–1801, Stephen B. Weeks Collection, Southern Historical Collection, University of North Carolina at Chapel Hill Library (see Robert M. Calhoon, ed., *Religion and the American Revolution in North Carolina* [Raleigh: North Carolina Department of Cultural Resources, 1976], pp. 59–65). Denominational archives for the state contain abundant fresh sources; although these parish records and fragments of autobiographical writings by clergymen are difficult to use, these very limitations force the scholar to reconstruct in a piecemeal fashion the social composition and internal polity of the churches, and these methods hold the

The yearning for a moral order, harmony among men, and a new sense of personal worth and identity, Donald G. Mathews argues, did not simply spring from abstruse religious doctrine, nor was it merely an expression of the mobility and individualism of the frontier. Southern evangelicalism was a vital fusion of highly personal religious experience and warm protective communalism. While the traditional emphasis on their individualism, voluntarism, and subjective apprehension of truth is valid, Mathews explains, "equally characteristic of such people was their insistence on initiating the individual into a permanent, intimate relationship with other people who shared the same experience and views of the meaning of life and who were committed to the goal of converting the rest of society." The rippling effect of the Great Awakening as it spread through the rural South spasmodically during the first third of the nineteenth century; the constantly expanding scope of religious activity conducted by Methodist itinerants and congregationally autonomous Baptists; and the creation of a system of church discipline and collective responsibility for the welfare and morality of wayward individuals—taken together—brought organization and cohesion to seemingly democratic, voluntary, ungovernable religious bodies. The members of the Mattrimony Baptist Church in Rockingham County affirmed in 1794 their intention to do "the work of the lord and to set in order the

---

potential for significant interpretive results. These archives include the Historical Foundation of the Presbyterian and Reformed Churches, Montreat; North Carolina Synod, Lutheran Church in America, Archives, Salisbury; German Reformed Archives, Catawba College Library, Salisbury; Quaker Collection, Guilford College Library; [Episcopal] Church Historical Society, Austin, Texas; Baptist Collection, Wake Forest University Library, Winston-Salem; Roman Catholic Diocesan Library, Raleigh; and the World Methodist Building, Lake Junaluska. Finally, the Southern Historical Collection, University of North Carolina at Chapel Hill, contains very extensive holdings in church history. Also see Larry E. Tise, *The Yadkin Melting Pot: Methodism and the Moravians in the Yadkin Valley, 1750–1850* (Winston-Salem: Clay Publishing Co., 1967); and "North Carolina Methodism from the Revolution to the War of 1812," in O. Kelly Ingram, ed., *Methodism Alive in North Carolina: A Commemorative Volume for the Bicentennial of the First Carolina Circuit* (Durham: Duke University Divinity School, 1976), pp. 33–48.

things that are wanton." This misquotation of Titus 1:5, where
the apostle called on the church to set in order the things that are
wanting, eloquently expressed the evangelical perception of the
secular society to which they were witnesses: its "senseless"
ignorance of spiritual reality and "careless" stewardship of
life itself. "As a people at odds with a social system that
demeaned or ignored them," Mathews concludes, "Evangelicals
placed" the individual "in a community which cared for him,
for in the Evangelical view care was the one thing in which
society was most deficient."[28]

Thrust in upon themselves by the opportunity to build a
new social and political order and by their own perplexity
and limitations, North Carolinians discovered that their own
feelings and desires could be a source of insight and guidance.
In suggesting that North Carolinians acquired a passionate
culture in the early nineteenth century, historians are not
suggesting a sudden collapse of older rational restraints and
social inhibitions. The eighteenth century had its share of social
turbulence, and the basic conservatism, ideological consensus,
and backwardness of the state in the nineteenth century
were themselves powerful stabilizing forces. An increasingly
flamboyant response of people to events and problems,
however, did become an integral, dynamic feature of society.
Anger, pride, exultations, gratitude, vengeance, and enmity
became significant emotional armor protecting individuals from
the hazards of life and the terrors of the unknown. These
passions in part comprised a new culture, that is, prevailing
notions about how people ought to behave.[29]

28. Donald G. Mathews, *Religion in the Old South* (Chicago: University of
Chicago Press, 1977), pp. 40–43; and "North Carolina Methodists in the
Nineteenth Century: Church and Society," in *Methodism in North Carolina*,
pp. 59–74.

29. See, for example, Albert Ray Newsome, "Twelve North Carolina
Counties in 1810–1811," *NCHR* 5 (1928): 413–46; ibid. 6 (1929): 67–99, 171–89,
281–309; Fletcher M. Green, ed., "Electioneering 1802 Style," ibid. 20 (1943):
238–46; Fannie Memory Farmer, "Legal Education in North Carolina," ibid. 28

The foremost authority on the tone and emotionality of southern culture is Bertram Wyatt-Brown. His preliminary papers on early southern folk culture contain significant material on and raise significant questions about North Carolina. In "The Antimission Movement in the Jacksonian South," Wyatt-Brown explores the little-known controversy that erupted in the 1820s and 1830s when northern benevolent evangelical societies sent missionaries to the South to establish Sunday schools; instruct slaves in Christian faith; and raise money for an ongoing, professionally staffed program of evangelism, education, and social benevolence. In prosperous towns the missionaries found warm support from "town ministers, militia colonels, and other dignitaries who were eager to promote religious enlightenment among their surly compatriots in the outlying countryside." But in vast remote and rural parts of the region, including much of North Carolina, the missionaries encountered fierce opposition. Their promotion of temperance seemed, according to Wyatt-Brown, a "Connecticut bluenose attempt to snatch away the convivial glass—one of the few cheap pleasures available to the dirt farmer," and their belief that universal salvation would usher in a golden age of piety smacked of Arminianism and free will. Most of all, the mission movement threatened the rural farmer preacher with replacement by a professional clergy backed by centrally controlled financial resources. "I dread the tyranny of an unconverted, man-made, money-making, . . . factoried" clergy, declared Joshua Lawrence of Tar River, North Carolina, a founder of the Primitive Baptist church that broke off from older Baptist groups in the 1830s over the issue of missionaries.[30]

Wyatt-Brown stresses the strong class antagonisms at

(1951): 271–97; and James S. Purcell, "A Book Pedlar's Progress in North Carolina," ibid. 29 (1952): 8–23.

30. Bertram Wyatt-Brown, "The Antimission Movement in the Jacksonian South: A Study in Regional Folk Culture," *Journal of Southern History* 36 (1970): 516, 520.

work in the antimission controversy and the way the dispute
drew the poor, isolated, suspicious believers at the lower end
of the social scale into a posture of righteous outrage and
common purpose. In his M.A. thesis on the Primitive Baptist
schism in North Carolina, Keith R. Burich finds a narrowing
rather than widening social gap between the Primitives and their
mission-oriented opponents. Identifying the leaders of both
groups and using tax records, Burich demonstrates that both
camps were led by propertied, slave-owning, socially mobile
elites. By the 1830s both groups of clergymen had become
professionalized; they were better educated and more adept at
using the bureaucracy of the church for their own purposes. It
was in this context of professionalization that real conflict
over power developed. Representing an older generation of
Baptist clergy entrenched in local Baptist associations, the
Primitive Baptists felt jeopardized by the host of young men
seeking "a professional, salaried status in the ministry through
the expansion of the missionary crusade and the activities of the
State Baptist Convention."[31]

Burich's findings help clarify Wyatt-Brown's paradoxical
discovery that in eastern North Carolina many Primitive Baptist
laymen were successful planters who with "luck, hard work, and
an accumulation of money and slaves" had risen from poverty to
modest riches in one generation but had not yet acquired the airs
of a gentleman.[32] Folk culture was nourished not only by class
antagonisms but also by a frank acceptance by the rural elite that
the passions and boisterousness of the common folk were an
integral and even valuable feature of their society. In his essay
"Religion and the Formation of Folk Culture" Wyatt-Brown tells
a revealing anecdote set in eastern North Carolina. A Yankee
trader named Charles Fife, who had been illegally trading with

31. Keith R. Burich, "The Primitive Baptist Schism in North Carolina: A
Study of the Professionalization of the Baptist Ministry," M.A. thesis, University
of North Carolina at Chapel Hill, 1973.
32. Wyatt-Brown, "The Antimission Movement," pp. 516–17.

slaves, was twice seized by a crowd of local citizens and tarred and feathered in full view of the local sheriff. Fife hired a young, ambitious local lawyer named Charles R. Kinney and took his detractors to court. During the trial the crowd in the courtroom became incensed at Fife's aggressive lawyer and apparently roughed him up while the judge, a prominent local planter, watched indulgently. Instead of citing the courtroom rowdies with contempt or punishing the individuals who had twice assaulted Fife, the judge fined Fife $100 for commerce with slaves. "In this instance," Wyatt-Brown comments, "the poor whites and planters appeared to be united solidly even though Fife's offense, such as it was, would have easily been handled in a court without need of tar and feathers. Fife had allegedly violated state law, but two systems of law were operating—one represented by the judge, the other a public coercion which meted out punishments in the name of all rich and poor, educated and uneducated, pious and irreligious."[33]

Wyatt-Brown's penetration of the folkways of rural southern communities in the early nineteenth century invites comparison with an older work, one of the best books ever written about North Carolina: Guion Griffis Johnson's *Ante-Bellum North Carolina: A Social History*. Spanning North Carolina from the 1780s through 1860 (the ostensible starting date is 1800) and based on meticulous sifting of newspapers, letters, legislative petitions, court decisions, family papers, church records, and memoirs (her fully exploited bibliography runs 75 pages!), this book deals with every facet of North Carolina life. While she did not impose a comprehensive interpretive structure on her rich material, she did hold a light rein on several interpretive emphases: intense localism; a "chasm" between a "small educated class and the yeomanry"; a con-

33. Bertram Wyatt-Brown, "Religion and the Formation of Folk Culture: Poor Whites in the Old South," in Lucius F. Ellsworth, ed., *The Americanization of the Gulf Coast, 1803–1850* (Pensacola: Historic Pensacola Preservation Board, 1972), pp. 20–43.

temporary conviction that cultural refinements were evidences of extravagance and effeminacy; the strong role of the family as the chief agency of social control; and the increasingly complex web of laws and practices keeping slaves and free Negroes subordinate. The book is literally a portable archive of social data, and far ahead of her time Johnson treated the seven decades of social development prior to the Civil War as a single unit governed by the rhythms of a rural, decentralized society. Its greatest value today lies in its finely textured examination of ordinary behavior; and its chapters on rural and town life, courtship, marriage, and the family depict a society inhibited by its own exuberance and caught between lofty aspiration and earthy desire. When Davidson County in 1822 asked Joseph Caldwell, president of the University of North Carolina, to locate the precise geographic center of the county as site for a county seat, she notes, Caldwell urged the county to consider a wide range of factors in situating the new town so that visitors from outlying areas would return home "with improved feelings, minds enlarged, information increased, their various business in courts and stores finished to their minds, their public spirit gratified and excited by the scene of general activity and prosperity." Caldwell's vision of town planning as an exercise in enlightened education sprang, Johnson explains, from his distaste for "the wildness and rudeness, intemperance, ferocity, gaming, licentiousness, and malicious litigation" that he found in most North Carolina county seats. In her paraphrase of a letter to the *Hillsborough Recorder* in 1820 which condemned formal dances, Johnson identified the cultural tensions caused by the introduction of high style into rustic environment: "Subscription balls created class feeling between those who attended and those who did not," Johnson explains. "A ballroom lighted with many candles and filled with sixty or seventy persons was not a suitable place for exercise. Young ladies, thinly clad and overheated with dancing, rushed out into the open air and as a result caught violent colds. . . . [W]hen a girl's mind was once possessed with the vain though pleasing anticipation of a dancing party, she could no longer pursue her school work calmly or attend to domestic duties. And finally, subscription balls [now quoting her source] 'nourished and increased the disinclination to attend divine worship.' "[34]

In New Bern in 1813, as British warships threatened the North Carolina coast, an episode recorded in Ashe's history reflected the same tension between cosmopolitan and rustic cultural standards. During a dinner given by William Gaston, Thomas Stanly "playfully tossed a morsel of cake across the table which, falling in Henry's cup of tea, splashed his vest. A lady at Henry's side made a remark that aggravated in the incident." In the ensuing duel Henry's first shot killed Stanly. Ashe's handling of the topic is revealing. He suggests that the duel between two lifelong friends, each on the threshold of a promising legal career, had a devastating emotional impact on the town, one exacerbated by the military threat, and he defends Henry on the grounds that he did not issue the challenge and that "the tragedy was ever a blight on Henry's peace of mind."[35]

The North Carolinian who most fully reconciled aspirations for a noble future with adherence to rural conservative values was, of course, Nathaniel Macon. There is no greater gap in North Carolina historiography than the lack of a modern biography of Macon that interprets him fully in the context of Warren County society, Old Republican politics, Jeffersonian individualism, and proslavery thought. The best introduction to his life remains William E. Dodd's chatty, opinionated biography.

34. Guion Griffis Johnson, *Ante-Bellum North Carolina: A Social History* (Chapel Hill: University of North Carolina Press, 1937) pp. 116–17, 157–58.

35. Ashe, *History of North Carolina*, 2:224; the useful studies of dueling in North Carolina (Martin L. Wilson, "A Survey of Dueling in the United States," M.A. thesis, University of North Carolina at Greensboro, 1969, and Stephen B. Weeks, "The Code in North Carolina," *Magazine of American History* 26 [1891]: 443–55) need to be supplanted by a new study that relates dueling to concepts of death and human aggression (see footnote 59).

Because he fully internalized Macon's values—his fear of power, his incorruptibility and flinty combativeness, his belief in the purifying influence of the popular will, and his conviction that farmers and planters shared a common interest in extremely limited government—his book demonstrates the depth and staying power of this version of extreme agrarian Jeffersonianism in North Carolina society throughout the nineteenth century.[36] "The theme of the biography," Lowry Ware writes in his dissertation on Dodd, "was the development of American history as a continuous conflict between the forces and leaders who contended for and against democracy." Believing that North Carolina "was democratic by popular instinct,"[37] Dodd underscored his conviction that Macon *"actually believed in democracy."*[38] Dodd's stark treatment itself raises these significant questions: How did Macon become aware of popular yearning for pure, simple republican government? What influences and experiences crystallized this ideological position in his mind? How did he perceive the combat between the forces of darkness and light? How in his own conduct as politician and North Carolina planter did he exhibit virtue and responsibility?

The essence of Macon's leadership was his belief that government frugality and simplicity were themselves the bond holding people and rulers together. "In proportion as men live easily and comfortably," he declared, "in proportion as they were free from burdens of taxations, they will be attached to the government in which they live." Harry L. Watson delineates Macon's skepticism about the blessings of modernization. Macon lived all his adult life in a spartan two-room farmhouse in Warren County. Debt, accumulation of wealth, the rat race for internal improvements, and the feverish pursuit of speculative gain,

36. William E. Dodd, *The Life of Nathaniel Macon* (Raleigh: Edwards and Broughton, 1903).
37. Lowry Price Ware, "The Academic Career of William E. Dodd," Ph.D. diss., University of South Carolina, 1956, pp. 37–47.
38. Dodd, *Life of Macon*, p. 401.

Macon contended, all contributed nothing to human happiness or fulfillment. Economic development only spawned a contagion of dissatisfaction with the physical facilities for transportation and trade and an insatiable desire for more and more public projects. Under the aegis of government, road and canal building and other public improvements created a dangerous mirage that government could and should solve social problems by fiat. "If Congress can make canals they can with more propriety emancipate. Be not deceived; . . . let not the love of improvement or a thirst for glory blind that sound common sense with which the Lord has blessed you."[39]

As Noble Cunningham makes clear, slavery was the crucial influence in shaping Macon's pessimistic view about human progress. The presence of blacks in America, Macon said repeatedly, was "a curse." But they were here; the South could not survive economically without their labor; free Negroes would jeopardize the stability of society if they enjoyed any of the privileges of white citizens; if not agitated by Quakers and "colonizing bible and peace societies," slaves could actually have a beneficent effect on the morality and responsibility of whites. Skeptics, he declared, should "witness the meeting between the slave and the owner and see the glad faces and hearty shaking of hands." When away from his plantation, Macon could "not recollect many circumstances in my life that gave me more uneasiness" than the illness of his slaves and the fact that "their situation in life put it out of their power" to take full responsibility for their own welfare. "Why depart from the good old way" of planter paternalism, he demanded, "which has kept us in quiet, peace, and harmony?"[40]

39. Harry L. Watson, "Squire Oldway and His Friends: Opposition to Internal Improvements in Antebellum North Carolina," *NCHR* 54 (1977): 116–18. For further support of this interpretation of Macon, see Zane L. Miller, "Senator Nathaniel Macon and the Public Domain, 1815–1828," ibid. 33 (1961): 482–99.

40. Noble Cunningham, "The Politics of Nathaniel Macon," M.A. thesis, Duke University, 1949, pp. 113–20, 124–28, 140–41; and "Nathaniel Macon and the Southern Protest against National Consolidation," *NCHR* 32 (1955): 376–84.

Just as Macon deserves a modern study that takes seriously his moral indictment of the modern age and his supreme faith in the benign moral influence of agrarianism and slavery, so we need a study of the origins of the Whig party in North Carolina, from 1815 to 1830, that locates the sources of its energy and commitment to dynamic economic development. Carolyn Wallace's excellent essay and dissertation on David Lowry Swain and William S. Hoffmann's articles and book on Jacksonian politics in North Carolina provide a helpful foundation.[41] Wallace examines the role of Swain's education, marriage to the granddaughter of Richard Caswell, legal practice, judicial and legislative service, and the political opportunity he found in Buncombe County as sources of his political style, which was nonpartisan and amiable, with an eagerness to reassure eastern slave-owning planters of his sympathy and moderation. Hoffmann's work anticipated the interpretation of the 1960s that held that Jacksonian democracy unwittingly stimulated economic competition and touched off fierce conflict between new wealth and old wealth.[42] Jackson's refusal in 1835 to distribute land sales receipts to the states came at the very time that the forces in the state seeking western development had acquired significant political leverage and organization. The backlash against Jackson made North Carolina a Whig state for the next fifteen years.[43]

41. Carolyn Andrews Wallace, "David Lowry Swain," in J. Carlisle Sitterson, ed., *Studies in Southern History* (Chapel Hill: University of North Carolina Press, 1957), pp. 62–81; and Wallace, "David Lowry Swain, 1801–1835," Ph.D. diss., University of North Carolina at Chapel Hill, 1954, chap. 2; William S. Hoffmann, "The Election of 1836 in North Carolina," NCHR 32 (1955): 31–51; Hoffmann, "The Downfall of the Democrats: The Reaction of North Carolinians to Jacksonian Land Policy," ibid. 33 (1956): 166–80; Hoffmann, "John Branch and the Origins of the Whig Party in North Carolina," ibid. 35 (1958): 299–315; and Hoffmann, *Andrew Jackson and North Carolina Politics* (Chapel Hill: University of North Carolina Press, 1958).

42. Edward Pessen, *Jacksonian America: Society, Personality, and Politics* (Homewood, Ill.: Dorsey Press, 1969), chaps. 5, 6, and 10.

43. Hoffmann, "The Downfall of the Democrats," passim.

This fluid, individualistic, flamboyant, decentralized, and conservative culture, then, cried out for containment and direction—for structure.[44] And a structure of sorts took shape; a pervasive system of inhibitions and norms to an uncertain extent thwarted human aggressiveness and provided a measure of stability. Two related subjects of recent historical study illustrate the emergence of new norms of behavior, new varieties of social discipline. The first is the family and the second is race. Bertram Wyatt-Brown's article, "Ideal Typology and

44. There is no better place to examine this cultural crisis and upheaval in values than in the monumental documentary volumes published by the state and pertaining to the early national and early antebellum periods (these are, incidentally, volumes that are little used by students of southern history): William H. Hoyt, ed., *The Papers of Archibald D. Murphey*, 2 vols. (Raleigh: E. M. Uzzell, 1914); J. G. de Roulhac Hamilton, ed., *The Papers of Thomas Ruffin*, 4 vols. (Raleigh: Edwards and Broughton, 1918–20); H. M. Wagstaff, ed., *The Papers of John Steele*, 2 vols. (Raleigh: Edwards and Broughton, 1924); J. G. de Roulhac Hamilton, ed., *The Papers of William Alexander Graham*, vol. 1, 1825–1837 (Raleigh: Department of Archives and History, 1957). There is no comparable collection of the writings of William Gaston, but his main writings can be conveniently located through the notes of J. Herman Schauinger, *William Gaston: Carolinian* (Milwaukee: Bruce Publishing Co., 1949). See, for example, Thomas Ruffin to his daughter, Catherine, 10 February 1824, for a revealing statement on the psychology of self-improvement and self-discipline as armor against a hostile moral environment, *Ruffin Papers*, 1:289–91. Murphey's celebrated report on education, which, as Harry L. Watson suggests elsewhere in this volume, saw schools as instruments of social control and moral influence in a changing, modernizing environment, declared that eighteenth-century moral philosophy and early nineteenth-century European pedagogical research had "sapped the foundations of scepticism [clearly a desirable achievement] by establishing the authority of those primitive truths and intuitive principles which form the basis on all demonstration" (see *Murphey Papers*, 2:77–82). Jesse Turner's reminiscences of Thomas Ruffin in ibid., 2:426–30 are a vivid eyewitness account of courtroom rowdiness in the early nineteenth century. The *Graham Papers*, 1:160–62, 165–68, 173, 176, relate a bitter dispute over personal honor and integrity between David M. Saunders and Willis Alston. At the very least we need a complete microfilm edition of the printed and manuscript writings of William Gaston and a sensitive analysis of Gaston's peculiar perception of his society. Consider for example his stunning conclusion in *State v. Will*: "If the passions of the slave [accused of murdering his master] be excited into unlawful violence by the inhumanity of a master, . . . is it a conclusion of law that such passions must spring from diabolical malice? . . . The prisoner is a human being, degraded indeed by

Antebellum Southern History: A Testing of a New Hypothesis,"
provides a framework within which the family and slavery can
be related to the larger context of southern society during the
first half of the nineteenth century. At the heart of southern
living, Wyatt-Brown finds "a family centered, particularistic,
ascriptive culture." By "ascriptive" he refers to "those elemental
values that southerners honored, qualities related to gender, age,
racial appearance, [and] bloodlines." Within this kind of society
the white southerners learned how to reach out to others and
how to defend themselves from those who were hostile, alien, or
powerful. "Stressing oral over literate means of expression," he
explains, "southerners were quick to detect another's personal
contempt or alien manner, since face to face communication
always involves a sensitivity to gesture, body language, and
vocal intonation. Thus, although the southern way of ordering
life provided ample means of self-identification and intense
positive loyalties, they were defended in a belligerent, anxious
spirit."[45]

The Wilmington planter and physician Armand John
DeRosset wrote an "autobiographical sketch" for his children
in 1847 that, Wyatt-Brown notes, was a superb statement of
the role of family, place, and reputation as sources of identity in
the late eighteenth and early nineteenth centuries. "On attaining
his majority before commencing his professional life," DeRosset
recalled, "my father became enamored of a Miss B. who was not
deemed on a footing with him. Being dutiful and affectionate he
yielded to his father and friends and went to sea. . . . Upon
my father's return he entered into the practice of physic. Miss B.
was married. . . . You will remark that family rank and standing
in those days was not lost sight of; hence the disapprobation of
my father's friends to his union with Miss B. No objection was
raised to his connection with your grandmother [Miss Mary

slavery, but yet having organs, dimensions, senses, affections, and passions like
our own" (quoted in Schauinger, *Gaston*, pp. 168–69).
    45. Bertram Wyatt-Brown, "Ideal Typology and Antebellum Southern
History: A Testing of a New Hypothesis," *Societas* 5 (Winter 1975): 1–29.

Ivies, daughter of a "Scotch gentleman, their mother a lady of Jamaica"]; indeed I believe his attentions were directed to her by his friends."[46]

In a myriad of ways, slavery provoked and justified a volatile style of self-assertiveness among the white population. The most dramatic evidence of such aggressiveness in North Carolina surfaced in the slave scares of 1802 and 1831, both the subjects of recent preliminary studies. In his paper on the 1802 scare, read at the 1977 meeting of the Organization of American Historians, Scott Strickland examines the numerous reports of conspiracy and incipient rebellion that terrorized Camden, Currituck, Hertford, Pasquotank, and Perquimans counties in May and June of 1802. Intensified slave patrols and sharp questioning of hundreds of suspects yielded several dozen incriminating affidavits charging individual slaves with violent and insurrectionary remarks. According to Thomas Parramore's unpublished tabulation, twenty-four slaves are known to have been executed on the basis of this evidence; much of it was obtained, Strickland shows, following severe whippings. Perhaps related to news of Gabriel's abortive rebellion in Virginia in 1800, the intensity of the North Carolina fear of servile uprising, Strickland suggests, must have arisen in part at least from conditions intrinsic to local society in northeast North Carolina. Strickland makes a plausible case that it was intertwined, in some still unexplained fashion, with the revival in the region that had started in 1801 and was still a powerful force throughout 1802. The revival momentarily swept aside racial barriers as black and white converts together gathered in baptismal ceremonies, holding hands, singing, and dissolving into tears as the preacher walked through the water and shook the hand of each person. This spontaneous breaching of traditional racial barriers, which occurred in scores of revival meetings in the area, may well have made white prosecutors all the more concerned at the language of slave witnesses who

46. Kemp P. Battle, ed., "The DeRosset Papers," *James Sprunt Historical Monographs* 4 (1903): 35–40.

testified that slaves proposed "to take white women as their
wives," "to live as white people," and, especially reminiscent
of the language of the revivals, to "breath of liberty as free
for us as for themselves."[47]
Surveying the relatively untapped "slave papers" and
related county court records in the state archives from the
Revolution through the early nineteenth century, Jeffrey J. Crow
posits a different interpretation of the 1802 slave scare. Crow sees
the episode as the culmination of a pattern of "rising tensions"
between black restiveness and white racial apprehension. The
War for Independence had "left the social arrangements of
southern life in serious disarray" and had undermined the
masters' control over their slaves. The war enabled hundreds of
North Carolina slaves to escape; illegal manumissions provoked
a swift legislative and judicial crackdown on Quakers and other
humanitarian whites; rumors of slave insurrection punctuated
the 1790s. One group of slaves even attempted to elect its own
shadow government of burgesses, justices of the peace, and
sheriffs as an ominous prelude to securing "equal justice" for
black people. Crow argues plausibly that the 1802 scare may well
have uncovered actual plans for servile insurrection and that
both hysteria and rational fear among whites may have dictated
the intensified racial repression that occurred in the state
during the early years of the new century.[48]

47. Scott Strickland, "The North Carolina Slave Conspiracy Scare of
1802," paper read to the Organization of American Historians, 8 April 1977,
Atlanta, Georgia. Also see Thomas C. Parramore, "The Great Slave Conspiracy,"
The State 39 (15 August 1971): 7–10, 19; and Parramore, *Carolina Quest* (Englewood Cliffs: Prentice-Hall, 1978), pp. 181–85, 191–96. Parramore's research is a
model of historical detective work and painstaking use of court records, and his
new junior high school textbook, *Carolina Quest*, is a masterpiece of interpretation, style, and narrative sweep.
48. Jeffrey J. Crow, *The Black Experience in Revolutionary North Carolina*
(Raleigh: Department of Cultural Resources, 1977), pp. 82–94. The antislavery
movement in North Carolina provides a great opportunity for the interior study
of ideas, values, and intelligence in the style of Winthrop D. Jordan's examination
of the racial attitudes of the North Carolina scientist and politician Dr. Hugh
Williamson (see *White Over Black: American Attitudes toward the Negro, 1550–1812*

News of the Nat Turner uprising of 23 August 1831, Claude R. Tate and Derris Lea Raper have recently shown, touched off a far more extensive slave scare in North Carolina. Rumors spread throughout eastern North Carolina in late August and most of September that the insurrectionary infection had crossed the border from Virginia and inspired slaves to murder their masters and march in mass on Raleigh, New Bern, and Wilmington. A false report that seventeen white families had been "horribly massacred" along the border of Duplin and Sampson counties led to the arrest of ten to fifteen slaves and the execution of two of them. When hastily assembled defenders of Raleigh, convinced that a black hoard had burned Wilmington to the ground, discovered no avenging slave army approaching, they seized half a dozen slaves, extracted confessions of "a diabolical plot," and summarily executed four of the "ringleaders," "monsters in human shape" whose guilt had been established "beyond doubt." At least fourteen other executions are known to have occurred, three in Onslow, one in Richmond, three in Duplin County, and seven in Wilmington, before the frenzy subsided and officials released large numbers of slaves still in custody. "The whole country seems to be in a state of high excitement," Samuel W. Tillinghast of Fayetteville observed caustically, "tremble reports and *raw head and bloody bones stories* appear to be the order of the day."[49]

[Chapel Hill: University of North Carolina Press, 1968], pp. 539–41). There are several useful descriptions of North Carolina antislavery ideas and activities: Patrick Sowle, "The North Carolina Manumission Society, 1816–1834," Peter Kent Opper, "North Carolina Quakers: Reluctant Slaveholders," both in the NCHR 42 (1965): 47–69, and 52 (1975): 37–58, and John Michael Shay, "The Anti-slavery Movement in North Carolina," Ph.D. diss., Princeton University, 1971. Philip Africa, "Slaveholding in the Salem Community, 1771–1851," NCHR 44 (1977): 271–307, combines intellectual and sociological insights and demonstrates the scholarly potential of studies of urban slavery and Moravian life.

49. *Raleigh Register*, 29 September 1831, quoted in Claude R. Tate, "The North Carolina Reaction to the Nat Turner Insurrection," graduate seminar paper, University of North Carolina at Greensboro, 1976, p. 15; and Samuel W. Tillinghast to Jane Tillinghast, 14 September 1831, quoted in Derris Lea Raper,

The major works on slavery as a labor system by U. B. Phillips, Kenneth Stampp, Eugene Genovese, Lewis Gray, and Joseph Robert contain little specific material on North Carolina slavery before 1835.[50] Rosser H. Taylor, *Slaveholding in North Carolina: An Economic View*, which is a descriptive survey of the plantation economy rather than a study of slavery itself, contains one intriguing paragraph on the Ebenezer Pettigrew plantation in Washington County from 1817 to 1829. As an incentive for good behavior, Pettigrew paid some of his slaves wages, allowed them to grow corn on their own plots, and extended them credit in a plantation store. Phillips, citing Taylor, considered this evidence of Pettigrew's shrewd management of slaves, but as Taylor himself points out, "ordinarily his Negroes failed to make enough corn to pay for the articles with which they were charged and . . . seldom received any actual cash. By flagrant misconduct Pettigrew's slaves would forfeit their corn crop." Though Genovese does not cite this example in *Roll, Jordan, Roll*, he does quote Charles Pettigrew, Ebenezer's father, advising his son in 1840 to put no faith in slave reliability: "Their condition scarce admits of honesty and they will improve opportunities of getting for themselves."[51] In his massive dissertation on the operation

"The Effects of David Walker's Appeal and Nat Turner's Insurrection in North Carolina," M.A. thesis, University of North Carolina at Chapel Hill, 1969, p. 73. Robert N. Elliott, "The Nat Turner Insurrection as Reported in the North Carolina Press," *NCHR* 38 (1961): 1–18, examines only three of nine extant newspapers of the period and treats these superficially.

50. U. B. Phillips, *Life and Labor in the Old South* (Boston: Little Brown, 1927); and *American Negro Slavery* (New York: D. Appleton and Co., 1918); Eugene Genovese, *Roll, Jordan, Roll: The World the Slaves Made* (New York: Pantheon Books, 1974); Kenneth Stampp, *The Peculiar Institution: Slavery in the Antebellum South* (New York: Alfred Knopf, 1956); in Joseph Clarke Robert, *The Tobacco Kingdom: Plantation, Market, and Factory in Virginia and North Carolina, 1800–1860* (Durham: Duke University Press, 1938), chaps. 2 and 3 describe tobacco growing in both states, but nearly all the citations are to Virginia sources; Lewis Cecil Gray, *History of Agriculture in the Southern United States to 1860*, 2 vols. (Washington, D.C.: Carnegie Institution, 1933–41).

51. Phillips, *Life and Labor in the Old South*, p. 253; Rosser H. Taylor, *Slaveholding in North Carolina: An Economic View* (Chapel Hill: University of North Carolina Press, 1926), p. 84; Genovese, *Roll, Jordan, Roll*, p. 602.

of the Pettigrew plantation, Bennett H. Wall offers a thoroughly sympathetic view of Ebenezer's paternalism and shrewd understanding of his slaves. The riches of the Pettigrew plantation papers, which Wall ably organizes and describes, hold a key to the psychology of the master-slave relationship. "To manage Negroes without the exercise of too much passion is next to an impossibility," Charles counseled his sons in 1797; "I would therefore put you on your guard lest provocations should . . . transport you beyond the limits of decency and Christian morality."[52]

Herbert G. Gutman in *The Black Family in Slavery and Freedom* finds the Pettigrew papers a rich source on slave kinship patterns; his major contribution to early antebellum North Carolina is his analysis of the Bennehan-Cameron plantation in Orange County whose records from 1776 to 1842 reveal a strong family and marriage network in which typically the slave mother's first and second offspring had different fathers, but thereafter she remained monogamous through the birth of five or six or even seven children over a span of ten to twenty years. Gutman also finds in the naming of slave children on the Bennehan-Cameron plantation an extensive network of namesakes from both parents' families and across every imaginable generational and household line: father's father, mother's half brother, mother's sister, father's half sister's daughter, and so on.[53]

Gutman's fascinating, if frustratingly oblique, reconstruction of slave family life in the Pettigrew and Bennehan-Cameron

52. Bennett H. Wall, "Ebenezer Pettigrew: An Economic Study of an Antebellum Planter," Ph.D. diss., University of North Carolina at Chapel Hill, 1946, p. 105; see also Wall, "The Founding of the Pettigrew Plantation," *NCHR* 27 (1950): 395–418; and "Ebenezer Pettigrew's Efforts to Control the Marketing of His Crops," *Agricultural History* 27 (1953): 123–32. The North Carolina Division of Archives and History is publishing the Pettigrew family papers. One volume has appeared so far. See Sarah M. Lemmon, ed., *The Pettigrew Papers* (Raleigh: Department of Archives and History, 1971–).

53. Herbert G. Gutman, *The Black Family in Slavery and Freedom, 1750–1925* (New York: Pantheon Books, 1976), pp. 262–63, 169–84.

plantations invites an extensive search through wills, estate settlements, and other sources for evidence of the family structure and kinship patterns of slaves throughout the state. Along with Genovese and Donald Mathews, Gutman makes a strong case that slaves in North Carolina, as elsewhere, created a culture of their own, centered in the family, in religion, and in their work, that resembled and paralleled the white folk culture described by Wyatt-Brown but also had an intense inner spirit of community all its own.

Several important studies clarify the relationship of black culture to the larger society of the state. Though John Hope Franklin's *The Free Negro in North Carolina, 1790–1860* is not a book about slavery per se, it is a study of the reactions of society to slavery, the impact on that society of former slaves who managed to obtain their freedom, and "the profound conviction" that racial subordination was not only unavoidable and inevitable but also "desirable."[54] In reconstructing the experience of the large group of free blacks in North Carolina across seven decades prior to 1860, Franklin—and more recently Ira Berlin—is able to probe the otherwise shadowy world where racial domination of whites over blacks actually took hold. The free black population weakened the use of race as a mechanism of social control. Berlin describes North Carolina's system of registering free Negroes when they entered towns and requiring them to wear special arm bands to distinguish them from hired-out slaves.[55] When black abolitionist David Walker, born in Wilmington to a free black mother and slave father, published a militant antislavery pamphlet in 1829 in Boston, the North Carolina legislature moved swiftly to tighten control over slaves and to restrict the freedom of movement on free Negroes. To the extent that free Negroes gained their liberty at the behest of

---

54. John Hope Franklin, *The Free Negro in North Carolina, 1790–1860* (Chapel Hill: University of North Carolina Press, 1943), chap. 2.
55. Ira Berlin, *Slaves Without Masters: The Free Negro in the Antebellum South* (New York: Pantheon Books, 1974), pp. 92–99.

former owners and could be effectively regulated by statute,
their protection served the interests of the community. That
freedom itself, however, was an elusive, imponderable element
in the social order that defied rational calculation. Berlin quotes
this notice in a Raleigh newspaper: "Ran away from the
subscriber, more than two years ago, a Negro man named
LIBERTY. . . . The fellow may have changed his name." North
Carolina courts, in a series of conflicting decisions in the
early nineteenth century, wrestled with the ramifications of
emancipation. Were the children of manumitted persons free?
Were the offspring of slaves promised manumission entitled to
freedom? Where did the burden of evidence lie in proving that a
black person had been legally manumitted? What legal bearing
did mulatto complexion have on a person's presumption to
freedom? In confronting these issues, North Carolina courts
redefined the freedom that nonwhites might enjoy. Manumission
did not retroactively free the children of a former slave. Whites
could at any time challenge the freedom of a black whom they
believed they owned, and only the strongest evidence of legal
emancipation protected free blacks from reenslavement.[56]

The other major contribution to understanding the social
stresses generated by slavery is Edward W. Phifer's classic article,
"Slavery in Microcosm: Burke County, North Carolina." In this
foothills setting, slavery was not economically crucial as a source
of labor; nevertheless, it was a key element in buttressing the
position of the emergent elite in the county. The 38 percent of
landowners in the county who held slaves were uniformly the
owners of alluvial deltas between the many large streams and
rivers in the region, which was the most fertile land. Slaves and
the agriculture they made possible were the most rewarding
form of speculation. A majority of the largest slave owners were
also merchants, clergymen, doctors, or lawyers. They used their

56. Ibid., p. 14; Franklin, *The Free Negro in North Carolina*, pp. 48–57,
81–101, and Julius Yanuck, "Thomas Ruffin and North Carolina Slave Law,"
Journal of Southern History 21 (1955): 456–75.

slaves in mining, road building, and trade occupations; farming was an activity that marked them as gentlemen, and the profitability from farming the best alluvial land with slave labor supported their economic and social ascendancy. While it is true, Phifer writes, that slaves in a western county received better treatment than those in the plantation east, "there remained the spiritual ignominy of slavery," and his most significant paragraphs based on sensitive use of court records explore the effect of the system on the behavior of slave owners. He finds strong social opprobrium against masters who sold slaves to itinerant slave dealers, but at the same time slave owners were always aware of the market value of slaves in places like Louisiana and Virginia. Owners of small numbers of slaves were most prone to make special provisions in their wills for the distribution of individual slaves to particular heirs; this tendency always fragmented slave families. The supreme importance of inheritance undermined in a critical way the relatively mild regimentation of slaves in the western part of the state. Phifer tells the story of Waightstill Avery, who left a "likely" slave girl to his niece and gave her the option of taking $400 instead. When the estate was settled, the slave girl was in the possession of a relative in Tennessee and apparently had to walk much of the way to her new owner. She injured her foot on the trip and a bitter dispute occurred over the spoiled condition of the property. "Legalism," concludes Phifer, "did not provide for a sense of gratitude or of sympathy for a little ten year old girl who had been abruptly taken from her accustomed surroundings and transferred almost 200 miles over rough mountain trails only to find she was unwanted when she arrived at her destination."[57]

57. Edward W. Phifer, "Slavery in Microcosm: Burke County, North Carolina," *Journal of Southern History* 28 (1962): 137–60. A major gap in the study of social control in North Carolina during this period is white-Indian relations. What little scholarly work exists is still unpublished: Mattie Russell, "William Holland Thomas: White Chief of the North Carolina Cherokees," Ph.D. diss., Duke University, 1956; and Jerry Clyde Cashion, "Cherokee Removal from North

Phifer's article underscores the greatest single need in historical research for this period: intensive local studies based on the enormous county records in the state archives in Raleigh. Detailed studies of property, marriage, family life, inheritance, slavery, local government, and economic change drawn from county records hold the greatest promise of enlarging historical understanding of North Carolina.

This story of cultural dislocation and adjustment in North Carolina during the late eighteenth and early nineteenth centuries therefore sets the agenda of work to be done by this generation of students of the Tar Heel past. There are, in the first place, large and obvious gaps in the biographical and institutional history of the state during this period. We need broadly conceived and psychologically, intellectually, and cul- turally acute biographies of Alston, Steele, Macon, Thomas Ruffin, Gaston, Murphey, and other prominent figures; mono- graphs on taxation, banking, public finance, and the state legislature; and systematic analyses of the legal and constitu- tional thought of Gaston, Ruffin, and other members of the state supreme court and its predecessor, the court of conference. Studies of the impact of migration from the state, modeled on Hugh H. Wooten's article on Iredell County, and of the living patterns of North Carolina emigrant communities in Indiana, Tennessee, and throughout the new southwest will illuminate the social development of the Piedmont and western parts of the state.[58] Lacking the kind of galvanizing events that raise dramatic issues, such as the Revolution, Civil War, Populism, and civil rights movement do for other periods, historians of the late eighteenth and early nineteenth centuries in North Carolina are under a special obligation to examine human life

Carolina" (1966) and "Fort Butler and Cherokee Removal from North Carolina" (1970), typescripts, North Carolina Collection, University of North Carolina at Chapel Hill Library.

58. Hugh H. Wooten, "Westward Migration from Iredell County, 1800– 1850," *NCHR* 30 (1953): 61–71. North Carolina migration to Indiana is the subject of meticulous genealogical research by Dr. John Scott Davenport.

in its most rudimentary settings. No facet of experience was more universal than death; we particularly need extensive work on the prospect and consequences of dying, the role of wills and the machinery of inheritance as conservative instruments of social control, the impact of death on theology and worship, and the relationship of death to other catastrophes in family and community life.[59]

Sensitivity to the frailty of human existence and to the elusive quality of human aspirations holds a key to a deeper understanding of politics and social development. In his provocative and imaginative study of Jefferson's old age, Robert E. Shalhope finds an underlying continuity between early national period faith in the republican experiment and early antebellum racial and social repression. "Pastoral republicanism," in which slavery was an integral element, represented to Jefferson the only values that would enable Americans to "retain their will and individuality in a culture that threatened to become more and more depersonalized."[60] In just this way North Carolinians were caught between a disappearing past and an uncertain future. Their ambivalence and their courage in the midst of that dilemma offer the best hope of understanding— and learning from—the history they made.

59. See David E. Stannard, ed., *Death in America* (Philadelphia: University of Pennsylvania Press, 1975).
60. Shalhope, "Thomas Jefferson's Republicanism," p. 556. In "The South Carolinian as Extremist," *South Atlantic Quarterly* 74 (1975): 86–103, Robert M. Weir attributes antebellum South Carolina's self-destructive defense of its honor and extreme hostility to outsiders to the cultivation of individual integrity and disinterested virtue as the hallmarks of political and social leadership by South Carolinians in the eighteenth century. Lacking such a well defined intellectual inheritance, North Carolinians moved toward passionate affirmation of their virtue and aspiration in a more piecemeal, haphazard fashion. For a case study of this process see Richard N. Current, "That Other Declaration: May 20, 1775–May 20, 1975," *NCHR* 54 (1977): 169–91, especially pp. 170–74.

4

The Historiography of Antebellum North Carolina, 1835–1860

by Harry L. Watson

In 1835 North Carolina revised its constitution for the first time since 1776. In 1860 the election of Abraham Lincoln led the state into civil war and social cataclysm. These two events frame a distinct period in the work of most state historians. At the same time, they constitute the elements of a paradox for state historians and for students of southern history.

The democratic reforms of 1835 are commonly linked to the broad movement known as Jacksonian democracy. In an interpretation that is now standard, the convention's amendments led to more representative government, which led in turn to positive legislation on behalf of economic growth and development. The progress that resulted reversed the stagnation of the Rip Van Winkle period and by 1860 had laid the basis for a healthy, growing, and prosperous society.

In this widely accepted view of state history, the coming of the Civil War was a gratuitous calamity that originated outside the state and imposed itself on the people with sudden and arbitrary fury. It appears in our textbooks as a bitter non sequitur to the happy prosperity of the 1850s. We should not forget, however, that antebellum economic progress was wedded to the institution of slavery. Slavery was undemocratic, both in respect to the slave himself, and in the relations it fostered between white slaveholders and nonslaveholders. The existence of this institution prompted North Carolina's slaveholders to take the state out of the Union and into a war that was contrary to the interests and (until the last feverish moment) the wishes of a majority of the state's population. The power that the state's slaveholders exercised over the minds and ultimately the lives of the state's nonslaveholders shows that we must distinguish between apparently democratic political procedures and genuinely democratic political outcomes. The coming of the Civil War is overwhelming testimony that North Carolina experienced the former variety of democracy without enjoying the latter.

Evidently, the constitutional reforms of 1835 did not make North Carolina very democratic after all. Yet the reality of increased procedural democracy is there for all to see. Reapportionment of the legislature, the rise of political parties, the construction of internal improvements, the beginnings of public education, the success of free suffrage, and the emergence of the ad valorem tax campaign all bespeak an active growth of the principle of equal political and social opportunity for all white men.

Constitutional reform and the Civil War thus suggest a historical paradox. In the age of the common man, a small group continued to dictate public policy. The planters' power derived from slavery, an institution which the rest of the nineteenth-century world condemned as a moral and social anachronism. The planters' heyday, however, was otherwise replete with the signs of vigorous modernization. How could these conditions persist, especially in a place where progress was apparently so valued and slavery apparently so weak?

No North Carolina historian has answered this question entirely, but most of us have dealt with one aspect or another of the problem. Perhaps the most effective way to treat the historiography of the antebellum period is to examine the ways in which the aspects of this paradox have been presented in the years since John W. Moore first composed a history of nineteenth-century North Carolina. Instead of surveying all the literature in strict chronological order, it will be easier to review the comprehensive histories first before taking up the more specialized studies. John W. Moore's *History of North Carolina; From the Earliest Discoveries to the Present Times* appeared in 1880.[1] In spite of numerous flaws and obvious biases, this early book is not without interpretive interest. Moore regarded the Civil War as the central event of recent state history. He believed the war was inevitable and blamed its occurrence on the institution of slavery. Giving scant attention to the convention of 1835, he frankly deplored advances in political democracy like free suffrage and ad valorem taxation. In short, Moore displayed a sharp awareness of the destructive dynamics of the slave-based society he grew up in, but he neglected the historical implications of political democracy.

The work of William K. Boyd stands at an opposite interpretive pole from the conclusions of John W. Moore. Boyd was the second historian to deal comprehensively with the history of antebellum North Carolina. A professional historian with graduate training, Boyd contributed the second volume of a three-volume history of the state that appeared in 1919.[2] Where Moore had attempted to interpret the Civil War for a defeated generation, Boyd sought to explain and legitimize the New South. He expressed this interest by minimizing the growth of sectionalism and taking for his theme the triumph of the common man. "The year 1836 is the first dividing line in the history of the state after the Revolution," he declared.

Prior to that date, political conceptions and ideals of social and economic duty bore the stamp of British heritage; thereafter the spirit of American

1. John W. Moore, *History of North Carolina; From the Earliest Discoveries to the Present Time*, 2 vols. (Raleigh: Alfred Williams & Co., 1880).

2. William K. Boyd, *History of North Carolina: The Federal Period, 1783–1860*, vol. 2 of *History of North Carolina*, by R. D. W. Connor, W. K. Boyd, and J. G. de Roulhac Hamilton, 3 vols. (Chicago and New York: Lewis Publishing Co., 1919).

democracy made rapid progress. The constitutional convention of 1835, the rise of the whig and democratic parties, the establishment of a public school system, the foundation of asylums, the building of railways through state aid, and reform of the law—these matters . . . are evidence of a new order.[3]

Boyd filled his pages with the story of progress and democracy, the themes that Moore either ignored or dismissed. But the Civil War, which was the central and inevitable event of Moore's history, was virtually inexplicable to Boyd. He was critical of slavery, but he did not see it as incompatible with unlimited progress nor productive of an "irrepressible conflict." He neglected the development of sectionalism, ignored the presidential election of 1860, and failed to describe the secession crisis at all. Boyd's history contained in most of its essentials the interpretation of antebellum North Carolina that has been standard for most of this century.

Four other major general histories of North Carolina appeared in the twentieth century. Samuel A'Court Ashe published the second volume of his *History of North Carolina* in 1925; R. D. W. Connor completed *North Carolina: Rebuilding an Ancient Commonwealth* in 1929; and Archibald Henderson's *North Carolina: The Old North State and the New* appeared in 1941. The text that is most familiar today is the joint effort of Hugh Talmage Lefler and Albert Ray Newsome, whose third revised edition of *North Carolina: The History of a Southern State* appeared in 1973. These authors have embellished and corrected the work of Moore and Boyd in matters of fact and detail. Generally speaking, however, the more recent authors have borrowed elements of the two interpretive strands woven by Moore and Boyd without coming any closer to a unified account of antebellum history that,would explain with equal facility the phenomena of democracy, modernization, slavery, and war.

The *History of North Carolina* by Samuel A'Court Ashe resembled the work of John W. Moore by its attention to eminent

3. Ibid., p. v.

individuals and its justification of the Civil War.[4] Unlike Moore, Ashe did not link the Civil War to any inherent characteristic of southern government or society but regarded it as the work of abolitionist busybodies. Like Boyd, Ashe was fascinated with progress. But unlike his predecessor, Ashe had limited enthusiasm for democracy and reserved his highest praise for progressive aristocrats like his father, William S. Ashe. For Ashe the historian the turning point of antebellum history was not the convention of 1835, but the founding of the North Carolina Railroad in 1848. The results of this and other internal improvements were so beneficial in Ashe's eyes that he described the North Carolina of 1860 in lyrical terms.

The decade then drawing to a close might well be called the golden period of [the state's] existence. It was rich in accomplishment and contentment and happiness reigned throughout her borders, while the future promised full reward to industry. . . . In a word, nowhere else was to be found a picture more pleasing to one in sympathy with what is best in human existence. North Carolinians can dwell on it with pride and admiration.[5]

According to Ashe, the Civil War brought this idyl to an arbitrary end. His work reveals the patrician thinking of a Confederate veteran in the twentieth century. For the modern reader who wishes to see a closer connection between political events and social process, Ashe has little to add by way of interpretation.

R. D. W. Connor's general history was similar to the work of William K. Boyd; indeed, Connor cited Boyd frequently in his footnotes.[6] Connor's title, *North Carolina: Rebuilding an Ancient Commonwealth*, suggested the author's interest in progress and the New South. Connor painted a bleak picture of the Rip Van Winkle period and then described how backwardness was reversed by political democracy, public schools, and internal

4. Samuel A'Court Ashe, *History of North Carolina*, 2 vols. (Raleigh: Edwards and Broughton, 1908–1925), vol. 2.
    5. Ibid., 2:529.
    6. R. D. W. Connor, *North Carolina: Rebuilding an Ancient Commonwealth*,

improvements. Connor's treatment of the Civil War was contradictory. He criticized the institution of slavery and argued that it made the war inevitable. But he regretted the fact that North Carolina's social disorganization contributed to Confederate defeat. As a whole, Connor's work was a sound review of contemporary knowledge that made few conceptual advances over its predecessors.

Archibald Henderson made no additional progress in his *North Carolina: The Old North State and the New*.[7] Henderson was chatty, rambling, and negligent of politics. He reported many curious details of social history without providing any framework of social analysis or social theory. A cavalier approach to factual accuracy was the most telling of his shortcomings, and his history had little to offer the demanding reader.

The latest of the general histories of North Carolina is *North Carolina: The History of a Southern State* by Lefler and Newsome.[8] The authors profited from half a century of monographic research and presented to students a text that was for the most part clear and factually accurate. Many of the authors' themes, however, were taken intact from older histories. "The constitutional reforms of 1835," for example, "increased the power of the people and of the West, [and] paved the way for a quarter-century of remarkable development in North Carolina—the first real age of progress in the history of the state."[9] On the subject of slavery, the authors were more ambivalent. They agreed that "the heavy capital investment in land and slaves made capital scarce for the development of manufacturing."[10] They implied that the slave system was thus a

---

1584–1925, 2 vols. (Chicago and New York: American Historical Society, 1929).

7. Archibald Henderson, *North Carolina: The Old North State and the New*, 2 vols. (Chicago: Lewis Publishing Co., 1941).

8. Hugh Talmage Lefler and Albert Ray Newsome, *North Carolina: The History of a Southern State*, 3d rev. ed. (Chapel Hill: University of North Carolina Press, 1973).

9. Ibid., p. 359.

10. Ibid., p. 397.

social obstacle to the progress that originated in political reform. But they also defended the institution of slavery, and presumably the war which was fought to protect it, on the grounds that "idleness, crime, race war, and the collapse of white control and civilization might result if freedom were given to the slaves, most of whom were fresh from savage Africa and were therefore ignorant and lacking in self-control and respect for law."[11] This is hardly a satisfactory conclusion, if only because slavery was either compatible with modernization or it was not.

Lefler and Newsome's difficulties with slavery were consistent with the confusion experienced by earlier writers of comprehensive histories. Like their predecessors, Lefler and Newsome did not explain how political democracy and sectionalism originated in the same society and arose from the same social dynamics. But the authors' interpretative problems reflected more than the flaccidity forced on writers of texts. They also stemmed from the monographs that these two historians were able to consult.

Early historical articles and monographs on antebellum North Carolina concentrated on the expansion of political democracy. The convention of 1835 was therefore a favorite topic. Two early pieces were Henry Groves Connor's "The Convention of 1835" and William K. Boyd's "Antecedents of the North Carolina Convention of 1835."[12] A similar interest inspired John W. Carr's article "The Manhood Suffrage Movement in North Carolina."[13] Fletcher M. Green codified the standard

11. Ibid., p. 429. Most nineteenth-century slaves were born in America. Given the potential consequences that Lefler and Newsome attribute to African origins, the error is a serious inaccuracy.

12. H. G. Connor, "The Convention of 1835," *North Carolina Booklet* (hereafter cited as *NCB*) 11 (April 1912): 201–50; William K. Boyd, "Antecedents of the North Carolina Convention of 1835," *South Atlantic Quarterly* 9 (January–April 1910): 1–29.

13. John W. Carr, "The Manhood Suffrage Movement in North Carolina," *Trinity College Historical Society Papers* 11 (1915): 47–78. See also John Spencer Bassett, "Suffrage in the State of North Carolina, 1776–1861," American Historical Association, *Annual Report* (1894), pp. 269–85.

interpretation of antebellum political reform and extended the concept to the larger region in his *Constitutional Developments in the South Atlantic States, 1776–1860: A Study in the Evolution of Democracy*, which appeared in 1930.[14] Green acknowledged that the planter class dominated southern state governments in the early nineteenth century. He attributed that dominance to formal antidemocratic barriers such as property requirements and religious tests for officeholding and voting. The constitutional abolition of such requirements, Green asserted, was a movement of the plain folk against the planters. The reformers' leaders, men like Edward B. Dudley and John Motley Morehead, were anything but plain folk, and the "reformed" southern governments had no difficulty taking lower-class whites out of the Union and into a war that was hardly consistent with popular interests. Richard P. McCormick, moreover, showed that the passage of free suffrage did not alter the aristocratic character of the North Carolina Senate to any significant extent.[15] *Politicians, Planters, and Plain Folk*, by Ralph A. Wooster, documented the *increased* representation of planters in the North Carolina General Assembly of the 1850s.[16] Such evidence suggests that the formal requirements for voting and officeholding had little to do with whether or not the government was truly democratic. The most recent study of the 1835 convention, Harold J. Counihan's "The North Carolina Constitutional Convention of 1835: A Study in Jacksonian Democracy," does not address this question.[17]

14. Fletcher M. Green, *Constitutional Developments in the South Atlantic States, 1776–1860: A Study in the Evolution of Democracy* (Chapel Hill: University of North Carolina Press, 1930).

15. Richard P. McCormick, "Suffrage Classes and Party Alignments: A Study in Voter Behavior," *Mississippi Valley Historical Review* 46 (December 1959): 397–410.

16. Ralph A. Wooster, *Politicians, Planters, and Plain Folk: Courthouse and Statehouse in the Upper South, 1850–1860* (Knoxville, Tenn.: University of Tennessee Press, 1975), pp. 35, 40.

17. Harold J. Counihan, "The North Carolina Constitutional Convention of 1835: A Study in Jacksonian Democracy," *North Carolina Historical Review* (hereafter cited as *NCHR*) 46 (October 1969): 335–64.

The convention of 1835 is usually linked with the rise of the Whig and Democratic parties. H. M. Wagstaff, the first historian of North Carolina's antebellum parties, concentrated on the parties' positions on constitutional issues.[18] His approach was consistent with an older generation's fascination with the legal background of secession. Writing ten years later, in 1916, J. G. de Roulhac Hamilton established a broader interpretation in *Party Politics in North Carolina, 1835–1860*.[19] Like his associates Boyd and Connor, Hamilton saw the 1835 convention as a triumph of democracy. Its greatest political effect, he believed, was the stimulation of statewide political parties, which he called "the best instruments then devised for expressing the collective will of the people."[20] Hamilton provided a useful introduction to the subject, but he was hampered by the meager availability of manuscript sources. The absence of footnotes handicapped scholarly readers. Hamilton contended that party lines were drawn on the basis of national politics, but he offered no analysis of what sort of persons tended to vote for the Whigs and what sort for the Democrats.

Later historians have improved the scope and depth of Hamilton's research. In the 1930s Clarence Clifford Norton and Herbert Dale Pegg completed monographs on the Democratic and Whig parties respectively.[21] Both of these works were based solidly on published records, party newspapers, and private correspondence. The institutional structure of the parties

18. Henry McGilbert Wagstaff, *States Rights and Political Parties in North Carolina—1776–1861*, Johns Hopkins University Studies in Historical and Political Science, vol. 24, nos. 7–8 (Baltimore: Johns Hopkins Press, 1906).

19. J. G. de Roulhac Hamilton, *Party Politics in North Carolina, 1835–1860*, James Sprunt Historical Publications, vol. 15, nos. 1–2 (Durham: Seeman Printery, 1916).

20. Ibid., p. 15.

21. Clarence Clifford Norton, *The Democratic Party in Ante-Bellum North Carolina, 1835–1861*, James Sprunt Historical Studies, vol. 21, nos. 1–2 (Chapel Hill: University of North Carolina Press, 1930); Herbert Dale Pegg, "The Whig Party in North Carolina," Ph.D. diss., University of North Carolina, 1932, published under the same title by Colonial Press, Chapel Hill, 1968.

received careful attention from both authors, as did the nature of partisan issues and the cycle of election campaigns. Both Norton and Pegg traced the origins of the parties to sectional interests in constitutional reform and internal improvements, but they did not explain why all sections contained many adherents of both parties. They also left vague the connection between national and local party issues. In 1958 William S. Hoffmann offered a detailed account of the political maneuvering behind the appearance of the two parties.[22] Hoffmann's *Andrew Jackson and North Carolina Politics* has been highly praised for its careful explanation of the shifting alignments among political leaders that accompanied the construction of a party system.[23] Hamilton had described political parties as agencies that translated public opinion into public policy. In Hoffmann's analysis, the importance of public opinion diminished, and the movements of politicians became more significant.

Hoffmann's concentration on leadership has left open the question of party membership at the grass-roots level. In 1970 Max R. Williams summarized the existing literature on the Whig party and observed that the traditional accounts failed to recognize the social diversity of its membership.[24] Williams suggested that the old generalization that North Carolina Whigs were the party of reform, of internal improvements, and of the west was subject to so many qualifications and exceptions that its usefulness was limited. Despite his able analysis Williams was no more successful than his predecessors in explaining what drew together this coalition "of westerners and easterners, slaveholders and nonslaveholders, of small farmers, plantation

22. William S. Hoffmann, *Andrew Jackson and North Carolina Politics*, James Sprunt Studies in History and Political Science, vol. 40 (Chapel Hill: University of North Carolina Press, 1958).

23. Richard P. McCormick, *The Second American Party System: Party Formation in the Jacksonian Era* (Chapel Hill: University of North Carolina Press, 1966), p. 368.

24. Max R. Williams, "The Foundations of the Whig Party in North Carolina: A Synthesis and a Modest Proposal," *NCHR* 47 (April 1970): 115–29.

owners, merchants, bankers, professional men, and urban workers."[25] A recent dissertation by Jerry L. Cross also failed to clarify the social origins of the Democratic party.[26]

Like other American voters of the nineteenth century, North Carolinians usually chose a political party early in life or at the time the parties were formed and kept that party identification for the rest of their adult lives. Political scientists have found that voters rarely change party affiliation except in an important political crisis known as a "critical election."[27] The outcome of elections is consequently the result of personal decisions made by the voters long before the elections themselves. The reasons why voters choose their favorite parties is therefore a crucial one for political historians. But the reasons why some North Carolinians became Whigs and others became Democrats still remain unsettled.

A recent sophisticated effort to deal with North Carolina's parties on a statewide basis is Thomas Edward Jeffrey's dissertation, "The Second Party System in North Carolina, 1836–1860."[28] Jeffrey makes a complicated argument, and this is not the place to examine it in detail. Briefly, however, he maintains that North Carolina political parties represented no consistent interest or section. Instead, "each group differed from the other primarily in its belief that it alone should enjoy the perquisites of office."[29] These rival groups of leaders won the loyalty of voters by catering to petty local grievances and prejudices that had nothing to do with national or even state government. Jeffrey thus avoids the paradox of democratic

25. Ibid., p. 129.
26. Jerry L. Cross, "Political Metamorphosis: A Historical Profile of the Democratic Party in North Carolina, 1800–1892," Ph.D. diss., State University of New York at Binghamton, 1975.
27. The term was coined by V. O. Key, Jr. See his "A Theory of Critical Elections," *Journal of Politics* 17 (February 1955): 3–19.
28. Thomas Edward Jeffrey, "The Second Party System in North Carolina, 1836–1860," Ph.D. diss., The Catholic University of America, 1976.
29. Ibid., p. 184.

procedures and undemocratic outcomes by denying that politics consisted of translating rational public opinion into constructive public policy. He suggests that a unified upper class conducted elections to beguile the masses while governing North Carolina to suit itself.

This is an arresting thesis, and there is much evidence to support it. The personal characteristics of Whig and Democratic leaders were indeed strikingly similar. When they were in power, both parties did support comparable measures. Irrational prejudices did sway many voters. But Jeffrey's contention that "few differences of opinion actually separated Democrats and Whigs" strains the evidence unduly.[30] At the time the parties were formed, Democrats and Whigs differed substantially on the values of the positive state and the merits of the Transportation Revolution. Charles Grier Sellers, Jr., sketched out these differences in regional perspective in his 1954 article, "Who Were the Southern Whigs?" In his view, "the Whig party in the South was controlled by urban commercial and banking interests, supported by a majority of the planters, who were economically dependent on banking and commercial facilities."[31] Sellers implies that the Democrats must have drawn their support from farmers and smaller planters who felt victimized by the increased commercialization of society. I have described similar party conflicts of political economy in my own dissertation, " 'Bitter Combinations of the Neighbourhood': The Second American Party System in Cumberland County, North Carolina." Democratic and Whig officeholders may have resembled each other socially and economically, but I am persuaded that their constituents, at least in the crucial formative stages of the party system, did not.[32] The differences may not have been consistent

30. Ibid., p. 230.
31. Charles G. Sellers, Jr., "Who Were the Southern Whigs?" *American Historical Review* (hereafter cited as *AHR*) 59 (January 1954): 346.
32. The economy of Cumberland County was divided between a region of small farms and modest plantations and a commercial center in the town of Fayetteville. The local newspapers reveal intense controversy in the county over

across the state, thus encouraging the idea that both parties were collections of equally diverse types.

The nuances of Whig and Democratic origins are questions that will continue to fascinate the specialist, but they do not exhaust the research topics of North Carolina political history. Perhaps the subspecialty that has attracted the greatest efforts in this field has been biography. Practically every political leader of note in antebellum North Carolina has been the subject of a scholarly biography, whether in the form of a thesis, a dissertation, a series of articles, or a book. This tendency reflects the rise of the Southern Historical Collection and the collections of the Division of Archives and History during the middle years of this century. It also reflects the conviction that senior scholars such as Boyd, Hamilton, Connor, and Green had established the basic framework for understanding the period. The task for their students appeared to be the filling of gaps. For the most part, the biographies that resulted from this situation were sound, creditable pieces that continue to be useful. There is not space here to review the merits of each one. Some of the more notable works in this area are Carolyn Andrews Wallace, "David Lowry Swain, the First Whig Governor of North Carolina"; H. G. Jones, "Bedford Brown: State Rights Unionist"; J. Herman Schauinger, *William Gaston, Carolinian*; Burton Alva Konkle, *John Motley Morehead and the Development of North Carolina*; and Richard L.

---

internal improvements and the needs of business in the 1820s and 1830s. Tax lists and precinct voting returns indicate that the rural- and urban-oriented sides of this debate were generally following the directions of their material interests. Later voting returns and party membership lists demonstrate that the blocs emerging in the twenties over internal improvements became the bases of the second party system. In Cumberland County, the Whigs were the party of modernization and the Democrats were its opponents (Harry Legare Watson, "'Bitter Combinations of the Neighbourhood': The Second American Party System in Cumberland County, North Carolina," Ph.D. diss., Northwestern University, 1976). For the Democrats' ideological hostility to the Transportation Revolution, see Harry L. Watson, "Squire Oldway and His Friends: Opposition to Internal Improvements in Antebellum North Carolina," *NCHR* 54 (April 1977): 106–19.

Zuber, *Jonathan Worth: A Biography of a Southern Unionist*.[33] The now indispensable collection of biographical information is Samuel A'Court Ashe's *Biographical History of North Carolina from Colonial Times to the Present*.[34] The forthcoming *Dictionary of North Carolina Biography*, edited by William S. Powell, should replace Ashe's collection as the standard work of this nature.

Monographs in North Carolina history have followed the more general works in tending to de-emphasize the origins of the Civil War. H. M. Wagstaff was interested in the constitutional theories behind secession, but his early research on state rights has long been outmoded. The only author to study secession in North Carolina extensively has been J. Carlyle Sitterson, whose monograph *The Secession Movement in North Carolina* appeared in 1939.[35] Sitterson prefaced his analysis of the politics of secession with a detailed discussion of economic sections in the state that was also published separately.[36] Sitterson's work suggested that support for secession was basically a party question, with Democrats being mostly in favor and Whigs being mostly opposed. Subsequent research has suggested that party choice was not simply a matter of sectionalism, so it is possible that

33. Caroline Andrews Wallace, "David Lowry Swain, the First Whig Governor of North Carolina," in J. Carlyle Sitterson, ed., *Studies in Southern History in Memory of Albert Ray Newsome*, James Sprunt Studies in History and Political Science, vol. 39 (Chapel Hill: University of North Carolina Press, 1957), pp. 62–81; H. G. Jones, "Bedford Brown: State Rights Unionist," *NCHR* 32 (July and October 1955): 321–45, 483–511; J. Herman Schauinger, *William Gaston, Carolinian* (Milwaukee: Bruce Publishing Co., 1949); Burton Alva Konkle, *John Motley Morehead and the Development of North Carolina, 1796–1866* (Philadelphia: William J. Campbell, 1922); Richard L. Zuber, *Jonathan Worth: A Biography of a Southern Unionist* (Chapel Hill: University of North Carolina Press, 1965).

34. Samuel A'Court Ashe, ed., *Biographical History of North Carolina from Colonial Times to the Present*, 8 vols. (Greensboro: C. L. Van Noppen Co., 1905–17).

35. J. Carlyle Sitterson, *The Secession Movement in North Carolina*, James Sprunt Studies in History and Political Science, vol. 23, no. 2 (Chapel Hill: University of North Carolina Press, 1939).

36. J. Carlyle Sitterson, "Economic Sectionalism in Ante-Bellum North Carolina," *NCHR* 16 (April 1939): 134–46.

secessionism was also more than a party issue. Sitterson wrote a thorough analysis of the leadership of the movement, but this should not discourage further research on the topic. Marc Kruman's recent dissertation includes a new examination of secession in North Carolina; it is hoped that his findings will spark renewed interest in this important subject.[37]

The older writers on antebellum North Carolina politics were convinced that their histories of political change were the story of democracy in action. The most striking aspect of these recent articles and dissertations from a historiographical standpoint is that this conviction seems to have faded. Instead of the people versus the interests, we read of voter manipulation and the indistinguishability of politicians. The ultimate implication of such findings must be that electoral politics, in this period at least, was historically meaningless. If elections were not decided on the basis of the issues and it made no difference who won, we certainly cannot explain the past by studying "Jacksonian democracy." Alternatively, we may conclude that issues and elections were important, but that their significance appeared in terms that were specific to a particular society. In either case, the political historian is drawn to the study of social and cultural history.

Unfortunately, North Carolina social history has not been studied as carefully as the details of antebellum politics. A variety of crops, land tenure patterns, and labor systems existed in antebellum North Carolina. The state is therefore an excellent historical laboratory for a number of important issues in the field. It is time we began to work on these abundant opportunities.

The discussion of North Carolina social history must begin with Guion Griffis Johnson's extraordinary volume, *Ante-Bellum North Carolina: A Social History*.[38] The product of enormous

37. Marc Kruman, "Parties and Politics in North Carolina, 1846–1865," Ph.D. diss., Yale University, 1978.

38. Guion Griffis Johnson, *Ante-Bellum North Carolina: A Social History* (Chapel Hill: University of North Carolina Press, 1937).

research, Johnson's work provided a description of virtually every social institution, religious practice, popular pastime, family practice, and intellectual development in the state from the end of the Revolution to the coming of the Civil War. Johnson treated with careful attention many subjects that only later assumed the status of independent specialities, for example, family history, urban history, and black history. Her research was so inclusive that subsequent students have apparently drawn back from a continued interest in the field. This has been unfortunate, because, like all good authors, Johnson did not answer every question she raised and left many dimensions of social history open for further research. Johnson's greatest virtue was her power of description; the analysis she made of her data was not complex. Like her contemporaries in political history, she saw the antebellum period as a time of admirable improvement that was virtually canceled by the war. There is great opportunity in this field for historians of a less whiggish disposition to reexamine the institutions Johnson described and to explain some problems of fundamental importance to southern history.

The principal area that calls for investigation is the nature of slavery and slave-based society. The history of North Carolina slavery has relied too long on the observation of Frederick Law Olmsted that slavery in the state was more patriarchal, and therefore less harsh, than slavery in Virginia.[39] A reading of the North Carolina slave narratives collected by the WPA can leave the modern student with no such impression.[40] A fascination with the law of slavery and a neglect of the slave's own testimony characterized the work of John Spencer Bassett and Rosser H. Taylor, the earliest students of this subject.[41]

39. Frederick Law Olmsted, *A Journey in the Seaboard Slave States, with Remarks on Their Economy* (New York: Dix & Edwards, 1856), pp. 367–68.
40. George P. Rawick, ed., *The American Slave: A Composite Autobiography*, 19 vols. to date (Westport, Conn.: Greenwood Publishing Co., 1972–), vols. 14–15, *The North Carolina Narratives*.
41. John Spencer Bassett, *Slavery in the State of North Carolina*, Johns

A broader treatment of slavery appears in modern works that cover the entire South, but there are few studies that apply specifically to North Carolina.

The anomalous position of the free Negro is the grand exception to this generalization. There have been at least four monographs written on this subject, the best of which is John Hope Franklin's *The Free Negro in North Carolina, 1790–1860*.[42] Franklin's book is a model of social history for its careful attention to empirical detail and to larger questions of cause and effect. Franklin's research can now be supplemented and seen in comparative perspective by Ira Berlin's recent study of free Negroes throughout the South, *Slaves Without Masters*.[43]

The history of slavery itself in North Carolina, however, has not received much recent attention. Edward W. Phifer's fine article on slavery in Burke County stands out in this area, but one can imagine many other potential articles on aspects of slavery that were peculiar to the upper South. Slave exportation, the problems of the slave community in a small-farm area, and the expansion of slavery into the Piedmont in the wake of transportation improvement are but a few obvious possibilities.[44]

The impact of bondage on white society is the aspect of slavery that is most significant for a comprehensive synthesis on antebellum North Carolina. Hinton Rowan Helper was not the

Hopkins University Studies in Historical and Political Science, vol. 17, nos. 7–8 (Baltimore: Johns Hopkins Press, 1899); Rosser H. Taylor, *Slaveholding in North Carolina: An Economic View*, James Sprunt Historical Publications, vol. 18, nos. 1–2 (Chapel Hill: University of North Carolina Press, 1926).

42. John Hope Franklin, *The Free Negro in North Carolina, 1790–1860* (Chapel Hill: University of North Carolina Press, 1943). See also Rosser H. Taylor, *The Free Negro in North Carolina*, James Sprunt Historical Publications, vol. 17, no. 1 (Chapel Hill: University of North Carolina Press, 1920); James B. Browning, "The Free Negro in Ante-Bellum North Carolina," *NCHR* 15 (January 1938): 23–33; James H. Boykin, *The Negro in North Carolina Prior to 1861: An Historical Monograph* (New York: Pageant Press, 1958).

43. Ira Berlin, *Slaves Without Masters: The Free Negro in the Antebellum South* (New York: Pantheon Books, 1974).

44. Edward W. Phifer, "Slavery in Microcosm: Burke County, North Carolina," *Journal of Southern History* 28 (May 1962): 137–65.

first North Carolinian to say that slavery stifled the economic development of the state and the region, nor was he the last.[45] Traditional accounts are not clear on the question of slavery's general effect; the authors suggest simultaneously that slavery inhibited the economy, that slavery was spreading in the state, and that the economy was getting better and better all the time. Empirical determination of the economic realities of slavery is a perilous undertaking, as Robert W. Fogel and Stanley Engerman have learned by their costly example.[46] The experience of Fogel and Engerman has not invalidated the proper use of quantitative evidence, and the questions they raised remain central to an understanding of the antebellum South. Eugene Genovese has argued that slavery inhibited economic modernization not only by its economic influence but also by the ideology and culture that it encouraged among the master class.[47] Piedmont North Carolina developed minor industries in the antebellum period; Genovese's insight might be amplified by a study of the relation of these workshops to the slave economy.[48]

45. Hinton Rowan Helper, *The Impending Crisis of the South: How to Meet It* (New York: Burdick Brothers, 1857).

46. Robert W. Fogel and Stanley L. Engerman, *Time on the Cross: The Economics of American Negro Slavery*, 2 vols. (Boston: Little, Brown, 1974). Fogel and Engerman's work has been widely attacked by other historians in scholarly reviews, review essays, and book-length treatments. See Herbert G. Gutman, *Slavery and the Numbers Game: A Critique of "Time on the Cross"* (Urbana: University of Illinois Press, 1975); and Paul A. David et al., *Reckoning With Slavery: A Critical Study in the Quantitative History of American Negro Slavery* (New York: Oxford University Press, 1976). But these attacks in turn have had a mixed reception. See the reviews of *Reckoning with Slavery* by Allan G. Bogue in the *AHR* 82 (June 1977): 745–46; and by Harold D. Woodman in the *Journal of American History* 64 (June 1977): 150–51. The controversy over *Time on the Cross* has had the fortunate effect of stimulating econometric research on slavery rather than suppressing it.

47. Eugene D. Genovese, *The Political Economy of Slavery: Studies in the Economy and Society of the Slave South* (New York: Pantheon Books, 1965).

48. A number of articles already exist on North Carolina antebellum industry. Generally speaking, their authors suggest that antebellum industry was heavily dependent on the slave plantation for markets and capital. In the cases of mining and tobacco manufacture, slaves were a source of labor as well. These findings would support the conclusion that the state's "infant industries" were not the germs of an economic departure from slavery before 1860. See Lester

The effect of slavery on agriculture itself is also uncertain. Like the rest of his contemporaries in other fields of state history, C. O. Cathey stressed the improvements being made in agriculture under the slave regime.[49] Genovese has pointed out that these improvements must have depended on slave sales to have been financially feasible, but more empirical evidence on this point is badly needed. We know, moreover, that internal improvements were desired to stabilize the value of lands and to improve the profitability of western agriculture. In other words, railroads were to prop up the plantation system where it existed and to extend it to isolated areas that had previously specialized in subsistence farming. The degree to which these purposes were accomplished remains unexamined. C. K. Brown's *A State Movement in Railroad Development* and the other studies of internal improvements have concentrated on the acts of incorporation, matters of corporate finance, and on the construction process. A recent article by Thomas E. Jeffrey clarifies the role of internal improvements as an issue in party politics, but we still need a study of the social and economic impact of improvement projects that were completed.[50] An

---

Cappon, "Iron-making—A Forgotten Industry of North Carolina," *NCHR* 9 (October 1932): 331–48; Fletcher M. Green, "Gold Mining: A Forgotten Industry of Ante-Bellum North Carolina," *NCHR* 11 (January and April 1937): 1–19, 135–55; Joseph Clarke Robert, "The Tobacco Industry in Ante-Bellum North Carolina," *NCHR* 15 (April 1938): 119–30; Diffie W. Standard and Richard W. Griffin, "The Cotton Textile Industry in Ante-Bellum North Carolina," *NCHR* 34 (January and April 1957): 15–35, 131–64; Adelaide L. Fries, "One Hundred Years of Textiles in Salem," *NCHR* 27 (January 1950): 1–17; and Richard F. Knapp, "Golden Promise in the Piedmont: The Story of John Reed's Mine," *NCHR* 52 (1975): 1–19.

49. Cornelius O. Cathey, *Agricultural Developments in North Carolina, 1783–1860*, James Sprunt Studies in History and Political Science, vol. 38 (Chapel Hill: University of North Carolina Press, 1956). See also Joseph C. Robert, *The Tobacco Kingdom: Plantation, Market, and Factory in Virginia and North Carolina, 1800–1860* (Durham: Duke University Press, 1938); and James M. Clifton, "Golden Grains of White: Rice Planting on the Lower Cape Fear," *NCHR* 50 (October 1973): 365–93.

50. C. K. Brown, *A State Movement in Railroad Development: The Story of North Carolina's First Effort to Establish an East and West Trunk Line Railroad* (Chapel

examination of the Wilmington and Weldon Railroad and the Raleigh and Gaston Railroad, the two lines that primarily served plantation areas, would be especially interesting in this respect.

The social impact of slavery is as important as its economic influences. Helper also maintained that slavery fostered a particularly undemocratic relationship between white slaveholders and nonslaveholders. George M. Fredrickson has suggested that racism lent a special kind of egalitarianism to relations among whites in the antebellum South.[51] The correct answer is crucial to a combined understanding of southern society and politics. The relationship between classes in white society may be sought in the daily details of correspondence and plantation diaries, in minor protest movements of white artisans against slave labor, and in movements of political crisis involving potential class conflict. Secession represents the prototypical crisis, but Sitterson's study of secession does not analyze the event below the level of senior political leadership. Stephen Channing's *Crisis of Fear* deals with the role of racism in uniting all South Carolinians in the secession movement.[52] As the last state to leave the Union, North Carolina's experience in this emergency would be a useful study in contrast.

Social relations within the white community may also be

Hill: University of North Carolina Press, 1928); Charles Clinton Weaver, *Internal Improvements in North Carolina Previous to 1860*, Johns Hopkins University Studies in Historical and Political Science, vol. 21, nos. 3–4 (Baltimore: Johns Hopkins Press, 1903); J. Allen Morgan, "State Aid to Transportation in North Carolina: The Pre-Railroad Era," *NCB* 10 (January 1911): 122–54; Robert B. Starling, "The Plank Road Movement in North Carolina," *NCHR* 16 (January and April 1939): 1–22; 147–73; Reginald Hinshaw, Jr., "North Carolina Canals Before 1860," *NCHR* 25 (January 1948): 1–57; Phillip M. Rice, "The Early Development of the Roanoke Waterway—A Study in Interstate Relations," *NCHR* 21 (January 1954): 50–74; and Thomas E. Jeffrey, "Internal Improvements and Political Parties in Antebellum North Carolina, 1836–1860," *NCHR* 55 (Spring 1978): 111–156.

51. George M. Fredrickson, *The Black Image in the White Mind: The Debate on Afro-American Character and Destiny, 1817–1914* (New York: Harper & Row, 1971), pp. 58–64.

52. Stephen A. Channing, *Crisis of Fear: Secession in South Carolina* (New York: Simon and Schuster, 1970).

studied in topics not normally associated with social history. The history of education in North Carolina has customarily been treated as one more area of progress for patriots to take pride in.[53] Archibald D. Murphey's reports calling for common schools, however, laid great stress on the function of schools as implements of social control.[54] If the implications of his concerns are pursued throughout the antebellum period, we may well discover a strong preoccupation on the part of political leaders with the problem of disciplining the lower classes. This preoccupation did figure prominently in the minds of educational reformers in nineteenth-century Massachusetts; a similar finding for North Carolina would radically revise the standard interpretation of the growth of common schools in the state.[55] Likewise, the history of churches and especially the question of church discipline may reveal far more than the traditional concerns of religious historians. The study of crime and the court system has been sadly neglected in North Carolina historiography, yet no field has greater potential for illuminating questions of social structure and social relations.

The broad purpose of a reexamination of North Carolina social history would be to resolve the paradox alluded to earlier, namely that constitutional reform and secession seemed to emerge from opposing tendencies in state history. Constitutional reform was emblematic of the state's commitment to political and economic modernization. Secession was a desperate attempt to preserve an anachronism. Broadly speaking, the same

53. For the history of common schools, see Edgar Knight, *Public School Education in North Carolina* (Boston: Houghton, Mifflin Co., 1916), and M. C. S. Noble, *A History of the Public Schools of North Carolina* (Chapel Hill: University of North Carolina Press, 1930).

54. Archibald D. Murphey, "Report on Education Made to the General Assembly of North Carolina At Its Session of 1816," in William Henry Hoyt, ed., *The Papers of Archibald D. Murphey*, 2 vols. (Raleigh: North Carolina Historical Commission, 1914), 2:51–61.

55. Michael B. Katz, *The Irony of Early School Reform: Educational Innovation in Mid-Nineteenth Century Massachusetts* (Cambridge, Mass.: Harvard University Press, 1968).

movements existed in every southern state. How two such contradictory movements could exist among the same people is a major challenge of explanation for North Carolina historians and southern historians in general.

For the most part, North Carolina historians have not attempted to find subsuming causes for the modernization movement and the war to save slavery. Other historians of the South are making this effort, however, and the field of North Carolina history is an excellent place to participate in the same pursuit. George M. Fredrickson, for example, has pointed to the overwhelming power of racism in binding all southern white men together. In his eyes, the movement to equalize political privileges among white men and to deny the vote to free blacks were two parts of the same drive to establish *Herrenvolk* democracy as a bulwark against blacks.[56] This analysis suggests a view of the Civil War as a racist effort to protect white supremacy from a Republican president. In another explanation, Eugene D. Genovese has asserted that the modernizing South was undermining the pillars of its own social structure, and that secession was an attempt by the ruling planter class to escape the consequences of this inner contradiction.[57]

Of these authors, Fredrickson emphasizes the role of racist ideology and Genovese the role of class hegemony. My purpose is not to support the ideas of one or the other, but to point out that both have a unified explanation for opposing tendencies in antebellum history. Because North Carolina was an actively modernizing state with a long-established slave economy, it is an excellent place to test these explanations and perhaps to devise better ones. Attention to such problems will build progressively on the state's existing historical literature and will increase our usefulness to the field of southern history as a whole.

56. Fredrickson, *Black Image*, pp. 66–70.
57. Genovese, *Political Economy*, pp. 264–70.

5

The Civil War and Reconstruction, 1861–1876

by Allen W. Trelease

Seventy-five years ago, when J. G. de Roulhac Hamilton began his study of post–Civil War North Carolina, historians of the then-recent Civil War and Reconstruction era had achieved a rare degree of consensus. Not only did they agree with each other on nearly every point of consequence, they had (some of them) the assurance of having scaled the peak of scientific historical objectivity. "The author has sought throughout the work," said Hamilton in the preface to his *Reconstruction in North Carolina*, "to divest himself of any prejudice in his treatment of a period which . . . has been the cause of so much later bitterness, prejudice, and sectional misunderstanding. He has held no thesis, but has sought only to present the truth, and, in the main, to relate rather than interpret."[1]

If there is occasion for surprise at what has happened to the historiography of this period in North Carolina since the turn of the century, it lies less in the revolution that has occurred in Reconstruction historiography since the 1950s than in the lack of significant change concerning the war period that preceded it. To some degree this constancy is the product of neglect. With a few notable exceptions (John G. Barrett's comprehensive military account springs first to mind) North Carolina historians of the last generation have not broadly investigated the war period within the state.

1. J. G. de Roulhac Hamilton, *Reconstruction in North Carolina* (New York: Columbia University Press, 1914), p. v.

The consensus that prevailed in Hamilton's day may be characterized as neo-Confederate. Its leading practitioners were professional historians such as Hamilton, R. D. W. Connor, William K. Boyd, and Archibald Henderson, who belonged generally to the first generation of that species, or highly qualified amateurs like Samuel A. Ashe and Kemp P. Battle. All of these men (except Boyd) were native to the state, and most were as patrician in their backgrounds as the nature of North Carolina society permitted. They were, in short, members of a conservative establishment that dominated the state with hardly a break from the 1870s well into the present century. Several of them either wrote themselves or participated in massive state histories conceived on an appropriate scale in the grand manner of James Ford Rhodes or Edward Channing.[2]

With no need to establish their southern Democratic credentials in their own day, a majority of them seemed retrospectively to vote Whig as they wrote of the Civil War era. All of them identified with the state and felt a need to justify it. Because so many North Carolinians had evidenced attachment to the Union in 1861 and lack of enthusiasm for the Confederacy thereafter, it was possible for these historians to be relatively impartial in treating the secession controversy and the internal divisions of wartime. Nevertheless, most of them leaned toward the Whig-Unionists who acquiesced in separation only after Lincoln's call for troops. They were in the awkward position of wanting to reaffirm their own heritage but not wanting to defend the Negro slavery that led to secession or to support a secession policy itself that had such disastrous consequences. This dilemma helped to produce good history. Samuel A. Ashe came

2. J. G. de Roulhac Hamilton, *History of North Carolina since 1860* (Chicago and New York: Lewis Publishing Co., 1919); Robert Diggs Wimberly Connor, *North Carolina: Rebuilding an Ancient Commonwealth, 1584–1925*, 2 vols. (Chicago and New York: American Historical Society, 1929); Archibald Henderson, *North Carolina: The Old North State and the New*, 2 vols. (Chicago: Lewis Publishing Co., 1941); Samuel A. Ashe, *History of North Carolina*, 2 vols. (Greensboro: C. L. Van Noppen, 1908; Raleigh: Edwards and Broughton, 1925).

closer to favoring the original secessionists in his treatment, but all tried with considerable success to treat both sides fairly.[3]

No one added appreciably to their account of North Carolina's secession until J. Carlyle Sitterson published his monograph on that subject in 1939. And Sitterson's contribution was essentially to amplify and confirm with much greater detail what was by then the traditional account. The center of gravity among Whigs, he found, was much more Unionist than it was among Democrats before Lincoln's call. Geographically he found Unionism strongest along the coast, in the Piedmont, and in some mountain counties, while secession sentiment prevailed chiefly (before the firing on Fort Sumter) in the heavy slaveholding counties of the east and in the southwestern Piedmont.[4] Until later historians think of substantial new questions to ask about the secession movement, Sitterson's careful research and sensible conclusions will surely remain standard.

A similar condition prevails in the military field since the appearance in 1963 of John G. Barrett's *The Civil War in North Carolina*.[5] Until well into the twentieth century, treatments of North Carolina's war record were inclined toward uncritical rapture over the bravery and fighting ability of her troops. Historians of that time were commonly sons of Confederate veterans, like Daniel H. Hill, Jr., if they were not veterans themselves like Samuel Ashe. Though the state itself was never a major battleground during the war, North Carolina's civilian population experienced some of the worst effects of enemy raids, military occupation, and the depredations of rival gangs of

---

3. See Hamilton, *Reconstruction in North Carolina* and *North Carolina since 1860*, and Connor (vol. 2), Henderson (vol. 2), and Ashe (vol. 2) cited in fn. 2. Also see William K. Boyd, "North Carolina on the Eve of Secession," American Historical Association, *Annual Report* (1910), pp. 165–77.

4. J. Carlyle Sitterson, *The Secession Movement in North Carolina* (Chapel Hill: University of North Carolina Press, 1939), pp. 215–20.

5. John G. Barrett, *The Civil War in North Carolina* (Chapel Hill: University of North Carolina Press, 1963).

bushwhackers. Such activity did not lend itself as much to heroic treatment (except for the defense of Fort Fisher) as did the larger scale warfare in Virginia and elsewhere, where most North Carolina men did their fighting and dying. Most treatments of the fighting in North Carolina were relatively straightforward accounts, therefore, with Confederate commanders incurring some condemnation from time to time, especially Braxton Bragg in the Fort Fisher campaign. Indignation reached its greatest proportions in discussing the work of Federal bummers and foragers. Cornelia Phillips Spencer, writing within a year of the war's close, was understandably vigorous in her denunciation of these off-the-field depredations and was unappreciative of General Sherman's method of shortening the war.[6]

No one in recent years has attempted a history of North Carolinians' role in the war outside the state. It may be an unprofitable venture. But John G. Barrett has contributed vitally to our knowledge of the war within the state with two books. Both are informed by the fundamental assumption that we do not have to take sides in refighting the Civil War. *Sherman's March Through the Carolinas*[7] has become the standard treatment of that important episode near the end of the war. Barrett's *Civil War in North Carolina* is an authoritative and comprehensive account of a very miscellaneous subject. Except as it permits or

6. Cornelia Phillips Spencer, *The Last Ninety Days of the War in North Carolina* (New York: Watchman Publishing Co., 1866), pp. 31–32, 55 ff. Despite their understandable bias, at least two military works of the early twentieth century retain great value. D. H. Hill, Jr.'s *North Carolina in the War between the States—Bethel to Sharpsburg*, 2 vols. (Raleigh: Edwards and Broughton, 1926) is a very full account of the first year and a half of the war. Judge Walter Clark edited in five volumes in 1901 a series of North Carolina regimental histories that John Barrett characterizes as indispensable. Walter Clark, ed., *Histories of the Several Regiments and Battalions from North Carolina in the Great War, 1861–1865*, 5 vols. (Raleigh: E. M. Uzzell, 1901). No other southern state, Barrett says, has a publication to compare with it (*Civil War in North Carolina*, pp. 465–66). Clark's work is now being updated and supplemented by Louis H. Manarin and Weymouth T. Jordan, Jr., eds., *North Carolina Troops, 1861–1865: A Roster*, 6 vols. to date (Raleigh: Division of Archives and History, 1966–77).

7. John G. Barrett, *Sherman's March through the Carolinas* (Chapel Hill: University of North Carolina Press, 1956).

even invites more detailed accounts of separate incidents—and there have not been many since his book appeared—it has become the standard account of the war in this state for some time to come.[8]

Political history, broadly construed, has inspired more writing than any other subject. With the disappearance in 1861 of the prewar political parties and the triumph of secession, North Carolina politics quickly settled into a contest over how far and how zealously to support the Confederate government. Public opinion in the state ranged from avid defense of the Confederacy to service in the Union army. In practical political terms the range was from full support of the Richmond government to the advocacy by 1863 of a negotiated peace by separate state action. Emory M. Thomas, in his challenging if overstated book, *The Confederacy as a Revolutionary Experience*, has argued that the Confederate government, driven by the demands of modern total warfare, in effect abandoned state rights and "transformed the South . . . into a centralized, national state. . . . Within the limits of its ability the Davis administration dragged Southerners kicking and screaming into the nineteenth century."[9] Allowing for some exaggeration, this centralizing tendency was strong, and it drove Davis into headlong conflict with Governors Joseph E. Brown of Georgia and Zebulon B. Vance of North Carolina, and with his own vice-president, Alexander H. Stephens. The controversy grew out of the central government's efforts to suspend habeas corpus, conscript men, impress supplies, and tax citizens in kind; there was even resentment over real or fancied discrimination against North Carolina in army promotions and governmental appointments.

Among the traditional school of North Carolina historians,

8. The fullest account of the Stoneman raid is Ina W. Van Noppen, "The Significance of Stoneman's Last Raid," *North Carolina Historical Review* (hereafter cited as *NCHR*) 38 (January–October 1961): 19–44, 149–72, 341–61, 500–526. See also John G. Barrett, "Sherman and Total War in the Carolinas," ibid. 37 (July 1960): 367–81.

9. Emory M. Thomas, *The Confederacy as a Revolutionary Experience* (Englewood Cliffs, N.J.: Prentice-Hall, 1971), pp. 58–59, 78.

Samuel Ashe showed the greatest appreciation of Davis's dilemma and his policies, just as he looked most favorably on secession. In his view, William W. Holden, William A. Graham, and other critics of the central government were unreasonable and irresponsible in their defense of civil liberty and state rights in wartime. "[T]hey inflamed rather than quieted their adherents. . . . [I]nstead of strengthening the Confederate cause, their attitude tended to weaken it." Governor Vance, said Ashe, seemed to have been unduly impressed with these self-seeking politicians. But he was a young man with noble impulses who was in a difficult situation. "If, at times, he became intemperate in expression, it was either to conciliate malcontents or to command attention and secure remedies, rather than merely to harass the Confederate authorities."[10] Those more Whiggish and Unionist (in the 1860–61 sense) than Ashe could rarely find heart to criticize Vance at all. They repeatedly minimized his disruptive role and emphasized (as Ashe did too) his positive contributions in recruiting men, securing supplies, and encouraging the raising of grain crops for food and not for distillation.

This is also the stance taken by Vance's modern biographers, Richard E. Yates and Glenn Tucker. Yates, in two articles and a short book on Vance's governorship appearing between 1937 and 1958, adds detail to the earlier accounts but little new interpretation. He is consistently favorable to his subject.[11] In a highly readable and well researched book that

10. Ashe, *History of North Carolina*, 2: 758–59, 815–17.
11. Richard E. Yates, "Zebulon B. Vance as War Governor of North Carolina, 1862–1865," *Journal of Southern History* 3 (February 1937): 43–75; Yates, "Governor Vance and the End of the War in North Carolina," *NCHR* 18 (October 1941): 315–38; Yates, *The Confederacy and Zeb Vance* [Tuscaloosa, Ala.: University of Alabama Press, 1958); and Glenn Tucker, *Zeb Vance: Champion of Personal Freedom* (Indianapolis: Bobbs-Merrill, 1965). The early biography of Vance by Clement Dowd, *Life of Zebulon B. Vance* (Charlotte: Observer Printing and Publishing House, 1897), is an uncritical panegyric consisting in large measure of excerpts from Vance's correspondence. The book is now outdated and superseded.

supersedes its predecessors, Tucker is aware of and sympathetic to the problems of President Davis and the Richmond government in maintaining Confederate independence amidst growing adversity. But he uniformly takes a Vance's-eye view of matters and emphasizes consistently the governor's positive role.

Albert B. Moore approached his study of *Conscription and Conflict in the Confederacy*, understandably enough, from the point of view of Richmond. To him Vance was a talented demagogue, pandering to "the masses of untutored, provincialistic, and suspicious peasant farmers of North Carolina." As Moore saw it, Vance would support conscription only so far as it accorded with local prejudice. He evolved by the end of the war from "a mild obstructionist to a bold defier."[12] Memory F. Mitchell has more recently taken a comparable view of state rightist obstruction of the conscription laws in North Carolina. In a monograph published in 1965, she concentrates on the state courts rather than the governor. "The fact that the highest court of one state," she says, "could cause dismay, grief, and actual losses to the Confederacy is, in itself, indicative of the character of the central government formed in 1861." The Confederacy's failure to set up an appeals court to review state decisions was, she concludes, one of the defects contributing to the downfall of that government.[13]

It was not only the central government in Richmond that extended its activities and powers in order to win the war. States did likewise, and their actions constitute one of the least publicized aspects of the period. North Carolina was perhaps in the vanguard in this respect, owing to the dynamic personality

12. Albert B. Moore, *Conscription and Conflict in the Confederacy* (New York: Macmillan Co., 1924), pp. 279–83. This view was similar to that of A. Sellew Roberts, "The Peace Movement in North Carolina," *Mississippi Valley Historical Review* 11 (September 1924): 193–95.

13. Memory F. Mitchell, *Legal Aspects of Conscription and Exemption in North Carolina, 1861–1865* (Chapel Hill: University of North Carolina Press, 1965), p. 91.

and the political and administrative skills of Zebulon Vance. All historians have recounted his action in fitting out blockade runners to sell cotton and other local products abroad in return for the supplies that were so badly needed at home and on the front; also his mobilizing men, materiel, and foodstuffs for soldiers and civilians, even to the extent of taking responsibility for clothing North Carolina's troops in the field at state expense. One of the great strengths of Glenn Tucker's biography lies in his account of Vance's achievements in this regard. Yet the subject might still profit from broader investigation than a biography of Vance can well include.

    The peace movement was stronger in North Carolina than in any other southern state. Once the war had begun, North Carolinians divided politically into those who had favored secession from the beginning and sympathized most with the Richmond government, and the Conservatives (chiefly but not entirely Whigs) who had opposed secession before Sumter and Confederate centralization thereafter. The Conservatives were so clearly the majority that they indulged the luxury of dividing among themselves by 1864. Most Conservatives, together with the old secessionists, supported Governor Vance, who wanted peace only on the basis of Confederate independence, but with rather less than more guidance from Richmond. The peace faction favored a negotiated settlement even if it meant doing so by separate state action and restoration to the Union. Its acknowledged leader was William W. Holden, editor of the *Raleigh Standard*, whose erratic career earlier generations of historians delighted to condemn in its every aspect.[14] And discerning threads of continuity provides a continuing challenge for historians today. No one has yet studied the incipient wartime political parties and how they were organized and managed, or what their respective sources of support were. On

    14. A notable exception was the favorable treatment by William K. Boyd in "William W. Holden," Trinity College Historical Society *Papers*, ser. 3 (1899), pp. 38–78, 90–130.

what geographical, economic, or other basis did voters divide in wartime elections? How valid for North Carolina voters is the Alexander and Beringer finding that Confederate congressmen supported the Richmond government in rough correspondence to the proximity of their districts to the war zones?[15]

The traditional historians regarded Holden as an artful demagogue, determined to rule or ruin the state. Connor charged him with fostering army desertions and appealing to nonslaveholders on class grounds. "By the summer of 1864 he had led North Carolina to the very brink of a class war."[16] More recently Holden and his cause fared better in the hands of Horace W. Raper. Agreeing that Holden was heavily influenced by ambition and angry at exclusion from the political and social establishment, he nonetheless gives Holden's arguments a more open hearing than was customary before. A negotiated peace in 1863 or 1864 by separate state action, Holden said, would stave off almost certain destruction at a time when the state still had some bargaining power. It would preserve slavery, he continued, and through it the structure of southern society. (Whatever the validity of this argument, it was hardly a call for class war.) When Holden was badly defeated by Vance in his bid for the governorship in 1864, Raper agreed that Holden had grounds for alleging fraud although Vance would have won anyway.[17]

Closely related to the peace movement, and not always distinguishable from it, was Unionism. This subject has yet to find its historian, both for North Carolina and the South, although most historians of the war have had to mention it. Disaffection to the Confederacy came in many dimensions. It included those Union-loving people whose menfolk took the

15. Thomas B. Alexander and Richard E. Beringer, *The Anatomy of the Confederate Congress: A Study of the Influences of Member Characteristics on Legislative Voting Behavior, 1861–1865* (Nashville: Vanderbilt University Press, 1972).

16. Connor, *North Carolina: Rebuilding an Ancient Commonwealth*, 2:156.

17. Horace W. Raper, "William W. Holden and the Peace Movement in North Carolina," *NCHR* 31 (October 1954): 495, 506, 514.

first opportunity to join the Federal army, and who thus were objects of great sentimental regard in the North. But in substantial measure the term is also applied to those who were simply disaffected from the war as well as draft dodgers, deserters, and bushwhackers (called buffaloes in some parts of the state) who lived by plunder.

Genuine Unionists were treated with some respect by the neo-Confederate historians. They were most noticeable in the far eastern and western ends of the state where Union army occupation or proximity, or the nature of the terrain, made that stance more feasible and more rewarding than elsewhere. The respect may have derived from the fact that these people were only a few steps removed from the reluctant secessionists of 1861. The traditional accounts of Unionism (at the state level) have hardly been added to or improved upon. There have been several broader studies of desertion, disaffection, dissent, and Unionism in the Confederacy that touch upon North Carolina. All are of value, but none exhausts the subject either generally or in this state.[18] Interestingly, at the state level recent attention has centered on eastern North Carolina and efforts by the Federal government to organize a Unionist state government under prewar Congressman Edward Stanly. Both Norman C. Delaney and Norman D. Brown (the latter in a recent biography of Stanly) conclude that there were not enough Unionists in that

18. See Ella Lonn, *Desertion during the Civil War* (New York: Century Co., 1928); Georgia L. Tatum, *Disloyalty in the Confederacy* (Chapel Hill: University of North Carolina Press, 1934); Frank W. Klingberg, *The Southern Claims Commission* (Berkeley and Los Angeles: University of California Press, 1955); Stephen E. Ambrose, "Yeoman Discontent in the Confederacy," *Civil War History* 8 (September 1962): 259–68; Carl N. Degler, *The Other South: Southern Dissenters in the Nineteenth Century* (New York: Harper and Row, 1974), chaps. 5–6. Three useful short studies at the state level are very old and need updating as well as elaboration. See Mary Shannon Smith, *Union Sentiment in North Carolina during the Civil War*, Meredith College *Quarterly Bulletin*, ser. 9, no. 1 (Raleigh, 1915); J. G. de Roulhac Hamilton, "The Heroes of America," *Southern Historical Association Publications* 11 (1907): 10–19; and A. Sellew Roberts, "The Peace Movement in North Carolina."

vicinity to sustain the effort.[19] A statewide account, sorting
out the different kinds of Unionism, where and how they
manifested themselves, and what effect they had on the war is
a great desideratum.

Turning to the politics of Reconstruction, an initial
observation must be made: we have no survey of North Carolina
during Reconstruction that is adequate to the needs of the
present generation. J. G. de Roulhac Hamilton's *Reconstruction
in North Carolina*, published in 1914, is an exasperating mixture
of comprehensiveness, technical proficiency, and breathtaking
prejudice against blacks, Republicans, and the entire Reconstruction experiment. An examination of James W. Garner's earlier
book on Mississippi and William W. Davis's on Florida will
demonstrate the excessiveness of Hamilton's bias even by
the standards of his day.[20] His work has both guided and
misguided later scholars in proportions of which few of us can
yet be fully aware. Its strengths, especially its comprehensiveness, almost foreclosed any further investigation of the period
for the next generation. The ensuing general histories by Ashe,
Connor, Henderson, and of course Hamilton himself, owed
much to his monograph and diverge very little from it.

In the 1950s a modest revisionism set in, reflected in at
least half-a-dozen graduate theses at Chapel Hill, none of which
unfortunately was ever published in full. Two of the best
appeared in 1951. Horace W. Raper wrote a very competent
political biography of Governor William W. Holden, who had
finally been elected to that office as a Republican in 1868. Raper

19. Norman C. Delaney, "Charles Henry Foster and the Unionists of
Eastern North Carolina," *NCHR* 37 (July 1960): 348–66; Norman D. Brown, "A
Union Election in Civil War North Carolina," ibid. 43 (Autumn 1966): 381–400;
Brown, *Edward Stanly: Whiggery's Tarheel "Conqueror"* (University, Ala.: University
of Alabama Press, 1974). For a competent unpublished account of mountain
Unionism, see William D. Cotton, "Appalachian North Carolina: A Political
Study, 1860–1889," Ph.D. diss., University of North Carolina at Chapel Hill, 1954.
20. James W. Garner, *Reconstruction in Mississippi* (New York: Macmillan

daringly defended the subject on some occasions while accepting much of the traditional world view handed down by Hamilton. The work is today in need of revision, but it is a necessary starting point for whoever undertakes a badly needed biography of this influential man.[21] Jack B. Scroggs's more original and pathbreaking dissertation was on carpetbagger influence in the reconstruction of the South Atlantic states. A section of it, pointing out the constructive and lasting achievements of these men in constitutional reform, was published as an article and has become a staple of the Reconstruction literature.[22] Less advanced than Scroggs but clearly edging into the revisionist era was Jonathan Daniels's sprightly *Prince of Carpetbaggers*, a biography that captures beautifully General Milton S. Littlefield's ingratiating personality and sharp acquisitive instincts, if not entirely the ideology of radical Republicanism which he espoused.[23]

Less gingerly than Daniels in accepting the ideals, policies, and actions of the Radicals were Otto H. Olsen and W. McKee Evans, both of whom made major contributions in the 1960s. This was in keeping with national trends and corresponded with the implications of the civil rights movement —the Second Reconstruction—then under way. Olsen's article

---

Co., 1901); William W. Davis, *The Civil War and Reconstruction in Florida* (New York: Columbia University Press, 1913).

21. Horace W. Raper, "William Woods Holden: A Political Biography," Ph.D. diss., University of North Carolina at Chapel Hill, 1951. See also Raper, "William W. Holden and the Peace Movement."

22. Jack B. Scroggs, "Carpetbagger Influence in the Political Reconstruction of the South Atlantic States, 1865–1876," Ph.D. diss., University of North Carolina at Chapel Hill, 1951; Scroggs, "Carpetbagger Constitutional Reform in the South Atlantic States, 1867–1868," *Journal of Southern History* 27 (November 1961): 475–93. See also Cotton, "Appalachian North Carolina"; Austin M. Drumm, "The Union League in the Carolinas," Ph.D. diss., University of North Carolina at Chapel Hill, 1956; and Richard L. Hoffman, "The Republican Party in North Carolina, 1867–1871," M.A. thesis, University of North Carolina at Chapel Hill, 1960.

23. Jonathan Daniels, *Prince of Carpetbaggers* (Philadelphia: J. B. Lippincott Co., 1958).

on the Ku Klux Klan in North Carolina politics and his biography of carpetbagger Albion W. Tourgée exhibited a constructive side of Republicanism and a vicious aspect of the Democratic opposition that was almost totally missing from the pages of Hamilton.[24] Allen Trelease also called attention to the Democratic propensity to violence in his study of the Ku Klux Klan, published in 1971, several chapters of which related partly or wholly to North Carolina.[25] Evans's work, *Ballots and Fence Rails: Reconstruction on the Lower Cape Fear*, is one of the major pieces of Reconstruction literature, regardless of locale. Essentially a study of Reconstruction in Wilmington, it presents the economic, political, and racial dynamics of that period as they affected both parties and both races within the Republican party in terms that, apart from detail, are applicable throughout the South.[26]

Evans also avoids the temptation (to which revisionists are susceptible) to exalt Radical motivations and achievements too highly. Republican ambivalence on the race question during and after Reconstruction was the theme of Gordon McKinney's article on southern mountain Republicans.[27] The limitations as well as the achievements of Republican reform were also touched upon in Allen Trelease's recent roll-call analysis of the North Carolina House during its single term under Republican control.[28] An even more recent article by Suzanne Lebsock indicates that Republican governments across the South compiled a very modest record of achievement in facing one of the

24. Otto H. Olsen, "The Ku Klux Klan: A Study in Reconstruction Politics and Propaganda," *NCHR* 39 (Summer 1962): 340–62; Olsen, *Carpetbagger's Crusade: The Life of Albion Winegar Tourgée* (Baltimore: Johns Hopkins University Press, 1965). See also Olsen, "Reconsidering the Scalawags," *Civil War History* 12 (December 1966): 304–20, which relates primarily to North Carolina.

25. Allen W. Trelease, *White Terror: The Ku Klux Klan Conspiracy and Southern Reconstruction, 1866–1872* (New York: Harper and Row, 1971).

26. W. McKee Evans, *Ballots and Fence Rails: Reconstruction on the Lower Cape Fear* (Chapel Hill: University of North Carolina Press, 1966).

27. Gordon B. McKinney, "Southern Mountain Republicans and the Negro, 1865–1900," *Journal of Southern History* 41 (November 1975): 493–516.

28. Allen W. Trelease, "Republican Reconstruction in North Carolina: A

most basic demands of nineteenth-century women: control over their own property.[29] The whole question of Republican policy and accomplishment needs closer scrutiny than it has received in this and other states in order to substantiate or modify the party's recent reformist reputation. Education historians, beginning early in the century, have perhaps pushed this inquiry furthest. Similarly, there is room for systematic investigation of both political parties, who belonged to them and why, and how they were organized and run. Quantitative studies should be made of voting behavior as well as legislative activity.

Economic subjects are more neglected. The older historians treated economic topics, and sometimes well, but this was seldom their major concern, and economic theory and method have come far since they wrote. The traditional view was that the Civil War had a staggering effect on the southern economy, setting back agricultural production in particular by many years.[30] But this view is now questioned. The acknowledged setback is attributable, in recent views, not so much to the war itself as to a slower postwar increase in the world demand for cotton, and to emancipation that gave blacks the freedom (within limits) to work less than they had been forced to do as slaves. Black women in particular chose to work less in the fields.[31] There has been a good deal of recent study concerning the economic impact of the war, but almost none of it is primarily

Roll-Call Analysis of the State House of Representatives, 1868–1870," ibid. 42 (August 1976): 319–44.

29. Suzanne D. Lebsock, "Radical Reconstruction and the Property Rights of Southern Women," ibid. 43 (May 1977): 195–216.

30. See James L. Sellers, "The Economic Incidence of the Civil War in the South," *Mississippi Valley Historical Review* 14 (September 1927): 179–91; Eugene M. Lerner, "Southern Output and Agricultural Income, 1860–1880," *Agricultural History* 33 (July 1959): 117–25; and Paul W. Gates, *Agriculture and the Civil War* (New York: Alfred A. Knopf, 1965), pp. 371–73.

31. See Peter Temin, "The Post-Bellum Recovery of the South and the Cost of the Civil War," *Journal of Economic History* 36 (December 1976): 898–907, and Roger Ransom and Richard Sutch, "The Impact of the Civil War and of Emancipation on Southern Agriculture," *Explorations in Economic History* 12 (January 1975): 1–28.

based on or related to North Carolina. Standing virtually alone is a 1957 essay by C. O. Cathey that treats wartime agriculture in the state, including the transition from cotton and tobacco to food crops and the thwarting of a prewar trend toward better farming methods.[32]

In business and industrial history, most attention has been devoted, appropriately enough, to railroads. The traditional historians had comparatively little to say on this subject except as they investigated and excoriated Republican railroad frauds.[33] In the past generation there has been a great expansion of railroad studies at the national and regional levels. They include institutional histories of the industry as a whole and of particular roads, sociological studies of railroad managers, and accounts of governmental railway policy at every level.[34] These studies deal only lightly with North Carolina, and many of their generalizations could profitably be tested at the state level. Similarly, James F. Doster, after asking "Were Southern Railroads Destroyed by the Civil War?" and answering, "generally, no," gave little attention to this state.[35] Charles L. Price, who has concentrated on North Carolina railroads in this era, found that the Federal army did very little to maintain the state's railway system during and immediately after the war.[36]

32. Cornelius O. Cathey, "The Impact of the Civil War on Agriculture in North Carolina," in J. Carlyle Sitterson, ed., *Studies in Southern History in Memory of Albert Ray Newsome* (Chapel Hill: University of North Carolina Press, 1957), pp. 97–110.

33. See especially Hamilton, *Reconstruction in North Carolina*, chap. 11.

34. See particularly Robert C. Black III, *The Railroads of the Confederacy* (Chapel Hill: University of North Carolina Press, 1952); John F. Stover, *The Railroads of the South, 1865–1900* (Chapel Hill: University of North Carolina Press, 1955); Carter Goodrich, "Public Aid to Railroads in the Reconstruction South," *Political Science Quarterly* 71 (September 1956): 407–42; Maury Klein and Kozo Yamamura, "The Growth Strategies of Southern Railroads, 1865–1893," *Business History Review* 41 (Winter 1967): 358–77; Maury Klein, "Southern Railroad Leaders, 1865–1893: Identities and Ideologies," ibid. 42 (Autumn 1968): 288–310.

35. James F. Doster, "Were Southern Railroads Destroyed by the Civil War?" *Civil War History* 7 (September 1961): 310–20.

36. Charles L. Price, "The United States Military Railroads in North Carolina, 1862–1865," *NCHR* 53 (July 1976): 243–64.

Price's studies are concerned both with railway operations and the legislative or policy aspects of the subject between 1861 and 1871, but his dissertation on the Reconstruction period has not been published.[37]

Less has been done on other aspects of business in the period, despite the availability of manuscript and other primary source materials. Two valuable articles, by J. Carlyle Sitterson and Richard W. Griffin, establish that a large proportion of the state's postwar business leaders, especially those in textiles and tobacco, were born into families who had developed those industries before the war.[38] The recent splendid study by Robert F. Durden of the Duke family accentuates the dearth of such studies in other fields of endeavor during this period.[39]

In the area of social history, earlier historians often referred to the suffering incurred by the civilian population of the state during the Civil War, and the efforts made by Governor Vance and others to alleviate it. Although the subject has attracted historians at the regional level in recent times,[40] it has not drawn much systematic attention at the state level. More might be said, for example, of the food riots that occurred in Salisbury, High Point, and elsewhere, and the conditions that evoked them. How long after the war, moreover, did war-induced deprivation last?

37. Price, "North Carolina Railroads during the Civil War," *Civil War History* 7 (September 1961): 298–309; Price, "The Railroads of North Carolina during the Civil War," M.A. thesis, University of North Carolina at Chapel Hill, 1951; Price, "Railroads and Reconstruction in North Carolina, 1865–1871," Ph.D. diss., University of North Carolina at Chapel Hill, 1959.

38. J. Carlyle Sitterson, "Business Leaders in Post-Civil War North Carolina, 1865–1900," in Sitterson, ed., *Studies in Southern History*, pp. 111–21; Richard W. Griffin, "Reconstruction of the North Carolina Textile Industry, 1865–1885," *NCHR* 41 (Winter 1964): 34–53.

39. Robert F. Durden, *The Dukes of Durham, 1865–1929* (Durham: Duke University Press, 1975).

40. See Charles W. Ramsdell, *Behind the Lines in the Southern Confederacy* (Baton Rouge: Louisiana State University Press, 1944); Mary E. Massey, *Ersatz in the Confederacy* (Columbia, S.C.: University of South Carolina Press, 1952); and Massey, *Refugee Life in the Confederacy* (Baton Rouge: Louisiana State University Press, 1964).

In 1970 John Hope Franklin wrote a short suggestive article, "Public Welfare in the South during the Reconstruction Era, 1865–1880."[41] He traced the efforts and accomplishments made in such areas as education, land distribution, poor relief, child welfare, public health, care of the insane, and the physically handicapped. Except for education, most of these topics were virtually unexplored in North Carolina when he wrote and remain so now. Roy M. Brown produced in 1928 a useful but now dated survey, *Public Poor Relief in North Carolina*, covering the period from colonial times to the twentieth century,[42] and Kenneth St. Clair wrote a valuable article in 1941 titled "Debtor Relief in North Carolina during Reconstruction."[43] But these works by no means exhaust the subjects raised by Franklin.

Education has been more fully dealt with, thanks to several individuals writing since the turn of the century who specialized in that field. J. G. de Roulhac Hamilton's partisan handling of this subject in his Reconstruction history exhibits him at his worst.[44] But his contemporary, Edgar Wallace Knight, produced several books and articles on education in the South and especially in this state that (no matter how reluctantly) credited the Reconstructionists with important achievements in this field. Knight insisted correctly that the Republicans did not create the first public school systems in the South; in North Carolina that distinction belongs primarily to Calvin H. Wiley before the war. But they did introduce prescribed school terms, Negro education, and school support by a uniform system of taxation.[45] The Republicans won somewhat greater and less

41. John Hope Franklin, "Public Welfare in the South during the Reconstruction Era, 1865–1880," *Social Service Review* 44 (December 1970): 379–92.

42. Roy M. Brown, *Public Poor Relief in North Carolina* (Chapel Hill: University of North Carolina Press, 1928).

43. Kenneth St. Clair, "Debtor Relief in North Carolina during Reconstruction," *NCHR* 18 (July 1941): 215–35.

44. Hamilton, *Reconstruction in North Carolina*, chap. 16.

45. Edgar W. Knight, "Some Fallacies Concerning the History of Education in the South," *South Atlantic Quarterly* 13 (October 1914): 371–81. See

grudging support a generation later from Daniel Jay Whitener
and David H. Prince, who were correspondingly critical of
Democratic parsimony.[46] All of these are legislative and
institutional histories. No one has gotten far into the philosophy
and sociology of education for this period: What are the schools
supposed to teach, and for what purpose?

Historical sociology is the province of two recent students
of the period who have attempted to blaze new trails. Edward
Magdol, believing that we need "to reconceptualize Reconstruction historiography from the point of view of the Southern
lower classes," has chosen as a case study the black and Lumbee
Indian community of Robeson County. He characterizes it as a
mestizo or maroon culture comparable to those in the Everglades
and Latin America where escaped slaves, sometimes with Indian
allies, were able to establish their own societies. Even if Henry
Berry Lowry and his band suggest a parallel of this nature,
however, Robeson County with its triracial society seems to be a
hazardous place from which to launch generalizations applicable
to the South as a whole.[47] By contrast, Gail O'Brien examines

especially Knight's *The Influence of Reconstruction on Education in the South* (New
York: Columbia University Press, 1913), which deals almost entirely with the
Carolinas, and *Public School Education in North Carolina* (Boston: Houghton Mifflin
Co., 1916). Similar views appear in Charles L. Coon, "School Support and Our
North Carolina Courts, 1868–1926," *NCHR* 3 (July 1926): 399–438; and M. C. S.
Noble, *A History of the Public Schools of North Carolina* (Chapel Hill: University of
North Carolina Press, 1930).

46. Daniel J. Whitener, "Public Education in North Carolina during
Reconstruction, 1865–1876," in Fletcher M. Green, ed., *Essays in Southern History
Presented to Joseph Gregoire de Roulhac Hamilton* (Chapel Hill: University of North
Carolina Press, 1949), pp. 67–90; and Whitener, "The Republican Party and Public
Education in North Carolina, 1867–1900," *NCHR* 37 (July 1960): 382–96; David H.
Prince, "A History of the State Department of Public Instruction in North
Carolina, 1852–1956," Ph.D. diss., University of North Carolina at Chapel Hill,
1959.

47. Edward Magdol, "Against the Gentry: An Inquiry into a Southern
Lower-Class Community and Culture, 1865–1870," *Journal of Social History* 6
(Spring 1973): 259–83. See the perceptive account of the Lowry band and its
background in W. McKee Evans, *To Die Game: The Story of the Lowry Band, Indian*

the elite of Guilford and Mecklenburg counties from roughly 1850 to 1880. She finds in both cases that there was great continuity and little social change throughout the period. So far as Republicans achieved political offices during Reconstruction, however—and that was more common in Guilford than Mecklenburg—it brought to power men who had not been leaders before.[48] The implications of this work bear investigation on a broader stage.

O'Brien's work also falls into the timely realm of urban history. North Carolina was overwhelmingly rural, but enough has been done already on her cities during this period to justify pushing the inquiry forward. W. McKee Evans's study of postwar Wilmington has already been mentioned. Howard N. Rabinowitz has recently published several seminal articles on urban race relations in the South between 1865 and 1890, using Raleigh as one of the cities studied. These works will be noted more fully below. Both Frank E. Vandiver and Emory M. Thomas have noted the impact of war conditions on southern towns after 1860. They grew so much in size and influence that Thomas refers to an "urban revolution" in the Confederacy. Wilmington, Charlotte, and other towns in this state must have experienced some of the conditions that Thomas found in his study of Richmond.[49] Later, as political parties vied with each other for power and patronage, they used their control of state legislatures to manipulate local governments for their own advantage. It

---

Guerillas of Reconstruction (Baton Rouge: Louisiana State University Press, 1971).

48. Roberta Gail O'Brien, "War and Social Change: An Analysis of Community Power Structure, Guilford County, North Carolina, 1848–1882," Ph.D. diss., University of North Carolina at Chapel Hill, 1975; Gail W. O'Brien, "Power and Influence in Mecklenburg County, 1850–1880," *NCHR* 54 (April 1977): 120–44.

49. See Frank E. Vandiver, "Some Problems Involved in Writing Confederate History," *Journal of Southern History* 36 (August 1970): 404–5; Emory M. Thomas, *The Confederacy as a Revolutionary Experience*, pp. 85–86, 94–98; Thomas, *The Confederate State of Richmond: A Biography of the Capital* (Austin: University of Texas Press, 1971).

would be instructive to see in some detail how this worked and with what consequences for the cities (and counties too) and their inhabitants.[50]

Virtually nothing has been written about women's history in North Carolina during this period, except incidentally as part of regional or national or more general state studies.[51] The state historians of the early twentieth century paid their compliments to the patriotism and stamina of North Carolina women in wartime. They occasionally noted too the desperation with which some women were driven to take part in bread riots or to plead with soldier husbands to come home and save the farm and family.[52] But the larger modern view of what women's history should include, as reflected in Ann Firor Scott's *The Southern Lady*, has not yet appeared.[53]

The first observation to be made concerning black history is that North Carolina lacks a study of blacks either in the Civil War or during Reconstruction. Valuable studies of both kinds have appeared in recent years for other states. There has, however, been some specialized investigation in North Carolina, paralleling work done in other states and the South generally. In the country as a whole, white historians had little to say on

50. For a summary account of southern urban developments in this period and suggested areas of further research, see Blaine A. Brownell and David R. Goldfield, eds., *The City in Southern History: The Growth of Urban Civilization in the South* (Port Washington, N.Y.: Kennikat Press, 1977), pp. 8–16, 20–22, 92–122.

51. For traditional treatments, see Matthew Page Andrews, *The Women of the South in War Times* (Baltimore: Norman, Remington Co., 1920); Francis Butler Simkins and James W. Patton, *The Women of the Confederacy* (Richmond: Garrett and Massie, Inc., 1936); Mary Elizabeth Massey, *Bonnet Brigades* (New York: Alfred A. Knopf, 1966); Bell I. Wiley, *Confederate Women* (Westport, Conn.: Greenwood Press, 1975).

52. The only book concentrating on North Carolina is a collection of short celebratory sketches. Lucy London Anderson, *North Carolina Women of the Confederacy* (Fayetteville, N.C.: Cumberland Printing Co., 1926).

53. Ann Firor Scott, *The Southern Lady: From Pedestal to Politics, 1830–1930* (Chicago: University of Chicago Press, 1970). See also Lebsock, "Radical Reconstruction and Property Rights of Southern Women."

this subject before the 1950s, the major exception being Bell I. Wiley's *Southern Negroes, 1861–1865*, published in 1938.[54] Nor did black scholars have much to say about North Carolina during the Civil War and Reconstruction as contrasted with Alrutheus Ambush Taylor's works on Virginia, Tennessee, and South Carolina, for instance.[55]

This situation began to change in the late 1940s with the appearance of specialized articles in the *North Carolina Historical Review* on Federal use of Negro labor during the war, on wartime legislation affecting blacks in North Carolina, and on the work of black delegates to the 1868 constitutional convention.[56] Two major books of regional scope appeared in the 1950s, Benjamin Quarles's *The Negro in the Civil War*[57] and George R. Bentley's *A History of the Freedmen's Bureau*,[58] but they failed to stimulate any corresponding state studies.

As the civil rights movement heightened in the 1960s, the volume of work in black history burgeoned. It shows no sign of abating. Some of the general or regional studies of this period relate to North Carolina, for example Robert F. Durden's account

54. Bell I. Wiley, *Southern Negroes, 1861–1865* (New Haven: Yale University Press, 1938). William A. Mabry surveyed the Reconstruction period in *The Negro in North Carolina Politics since Reconstruction* (Durham: Duke University Press, 1940).

55. Alrutheus Ambush Taylor, *The Negro in the Reconstruction of Virginia* (Washington, D.C.: Association for the Study of Negro Life and History, 1926); Taylor, *The Negro in Tennessee, 1865–1880* (Washington, D.C.: Associated Publishers, 1941); Taylor, *The Negro in South Carolina during the Reconstruction* (Washington, D.C.: Association for the Study of Negro Life and History, 1924).

56. Tinsley Lee Spraggins, "Mobilization of Negro Labor for the Department of Virginia and North Carolina, 1861–1865," *NCHR* 24 (April 1947): 160–97; B. H. Nelson, "Some Aspects of Negro Life in North Carolina during the Civil War," ibid. 25 (April 1948): 143–66; Leonard Bernstein, "The Participation of Negro Delegates in the Constitutional Convention of 1868 in North Carolina," *Journal of Negro History* 34 (October 1949): 391–409.

57. Benjamin Quarles, *The Negro in the Civil War* (Boston: Little, Brown, 1953).

58. George R. Bentley, *A History of the Freedmen's Bureau* (Philadelphia: University of Pennsylvania Press, 1955).

of the debate over emancipation in the Confederacy[59] and
William Preston Vaughn's *Schools for All*, dealing with black
education and especially the issue of school segregation in the
Reconstruction South.[60] Howard N. Rabinowitz has recently
published four articles of major importance relating to southern
blacks, especially urban blacks, in the period from 1865 to 1890.
Based on several cities, including Raleigh, they deal respectively
with health and welfare services, the shift from white to black
teachers in Negro schools, the treatment blacks received from
local governments under Republican and Democratic control,
and racial segregation patterns. He finds that blacks benefited
from Republican control, where and as long as it existed, in a
variety of ways, including greater employment opportunities
(public and private) and access to social and health services.
Moreover, Republicans accorded separate but equal accom-
modations to blacks in public facilities, replacing a policy of
general exclusion in previous times. When Redeemers took over,
they retained the separate facilities but allowed those for blacks
to deteriorate.[61]

　　The growth of black history is hardly reflected in North
Carolina state studies for this period, however, with only four
notable articles appearing since 1960. Two dealt with the actions
of church denominations (the Presbyterians and Baptists) toward
blacks during Reconstruction, one with Negro legislators, and
the most recent with Negro education in the state during the

　　59. Robert F. Durden, *The Gray and the Black: The Confederate Debate on
Emancipation* (Baton Rouge: Louisiana State University Press, 1972).
　　60. William Preston Vaughn, *Schools for All: The Blacks and Public Education
in the South, 1865–1877* (Lexington: University Press of Kentucky, 1974).
　　61. Howard N. Rabinowitz, "From Exclusion to Segregation: Health and
Welfare Services for Southern Blacks, 1865–1890," *Social Service Review* 48 (September 1974): 327–54; Rabinowitz, "From Exclusion to Segregation: Southern
Race Relations, 1865–1890," *Journal of American History* 63 (September 1976):
325–50; Rabinowitz, "From Reconstruction to Redemption in the Urban South,"
Journal of Urban History 2 (February 1976): 169–94; and Rabinowitz, "Half a Loaf:
The Shift from White to Black Teachers in the Negro Schools of the Urban South,
1865–1890," *Journal of Southern History* 40 (November 1974): 565–94. Also see his

early Reconstruction period.[62] Virtually every aspect of the black experience in North Carolina from wartime slavery to postwar freedom and political power needs further investigation. So does the changing relationship between the races and the impact of blacks on the society as a whole.

Most future research, whether relating to black history or other aspects of this period, will necessarily depend chiefly on source materials that are already known.[63] But new questions, new assumptions, and new research methods, often borrowed from other disciplines, will continue to produce fresh insights from traditional sources. And many of the sources are under-utilized from any standpoint. These include the county court records to 1868, the voter registration books of 1867–68, and pension applications in the state archives; manuscript letters illustrating conditions of military life and social conditions during and after the war; and papers related to economic and business history in both the Duke University Library's Manuscript Department and the Southern Historical Collection in Chapel Hill. The Civil War and Reconstruction era within North Carolina is emphatically not an overworked field.

---

book, *Race Relations in the Urban South, 1865–1890* (New York: Oxford University Press, 1978).

62. John L. Bell, Jr., "The Presbyterian Church and the Negro in North Carolina during Reconstruction," *NCHR* 40 (Winter 1963): 15–36; Bell, "Baptists and the Negro in North Carolina during Reconstruction," ibid. 42 (Autumn 1965): 391–409; Elizabeth Balanoff, "Negro Legislators in the North Carolina General Assembly, July 1868–February 1872," ibid. 49 (January 1972): 22–55; Roberta Sue Alexander, "Hostility and Hope: Black Education in North Carolina during Presidential Reconstruction, 1865–1867," ibid. 53 (Spring 1976): 113–32.

63. Among the documentaries published by the North Carolina Division of Archives and History that contain materials pertinent to the period are Noble J. Tolbert, *The Papers of John Willis Ellis*, 2 vols. (Raleigh, 1964); J. G. de Roulhac Hamilton and Max R. Williams, eds., *The Papers of William Alexander Graham*, 6 vols. to date (Raleigh, 1957–76); Henry T. Shanks, ed., *The Papers of Willie Person Mangum*, 5 vols. (Raleigh, 1950–56); Frontis W. Johnston, ed., *The Papers of Zebulon Baird Vance*, 1 vol. to date (Raleigh, 1963); and Wilfred Buck Yearns, ed., *The Papers of Thomas Jordan Jarvis*, 1 vol. to date (Raleigh, 1969).

6

The Reconstruction That Took: North Carolina in the New South, 1877–1912

by Robert F. Durden

That Radical Reconstruction after the Civil War failed to achieve its purposes in the South is a universally recognized fact. Not only were the newly gained rights of the freedmen placed in jeopardy by 1877, to be gradually whittled away in succeeding years by the dominant whites, but the national Republican party did not even succeed in establishing the strong southern wing that architects of Congressional Reconstruction had envisioned. The political remodeling of the South in the image of the North and under the tutelage of Republicans proved to be an unattainable goal.

Despite these facts, there was, to use historian Carl Degler's telling phrase, a "Reconstruction that took." That was the acceptance of industrialization by a majority of the southern people as the great hope for the future. "By the time the First World War broke out in Europe," Degler maintains, "the American South had been 'northernized' to a degree only hoped for by the most ambitious of Reconstructionists. Moreover, this was permanent change, for the northern industrial way had been voluntarily accepted by the South." Quite aware that only a beginning of industrialization had been made by 1914 and that the greater part of the southern people still remained tied to the land, Degler nevertheless insists that the "decisive break with the agrarian tradition had been made" and that the South was at least launched on the path leading toward its ultimate return to the main currents of the nation's life.[1]

For North Carolina the last quarter of the nineteenth century, when the factories began to multiply in number, was the period when the hope for industrialization became dominant. Yet only isolated fragments of the fundamentally important story have thus far been told. Ironically, historians of modern Europe in North Carolina's universities probably know more about the workers and their conditions, tools, and labor patterns in various factories in small French towns in the nineteenth century than we know about what went on in the textile, tobacco, and furniture establishments of North Carolina. Moreover, industrialization and the special kind of limited urbanization that has accompanied it in this state have surely affected family patterns, social and religious norms, and attitudes toward such fundamental things as class and race. Yet we remain woefully ignorant concerning these matters.

The first historians of North Carolina's industrialization were obviously naïve in their assessments of their subject's importance. Some of them were overly sanguine about the economic and social benefits of industrialization. Holland Thompson, a native Tar Heel and pioneer economic historian of the South, published his study of North Carolina's cotton textile industry in 1906. Admitting that North Carolina was still an overwhelmingly rural state with fewer than 18 percent of its people living in incorporated towns in 1900, Thompson nevertheless insisted that "a great economic change" was clearly under way. North Carolina had built almost two hundred cotton mills in two decades, and he estimated that from 150,000 to 200,000 people had already moved from the country to take

1. Carl Degler, *Out of Our Past: The Forces that Shaped Modern America* (New York: Harper & Row, 1970), p. 256. The impact of industrialization is emphasized less in the classic study of the South in this period, C. Vann Woodward, *The Origins of the New South, 1877–1913*, vol. 9 in Wendell H. Stephenson and E. Merton Coulter, eds., *A History of the South* (Baton Rouge: Louisiana State University Press, 1951).

factory jobs. "The whole attitude of mind," he suggested, "has changed more during the last fifteen years than in the fifty preceding." Anticipating Degler, Thompson concluded that "commercialism is doing what bayonets could not do."[2] Now glaringly outdated in many respects, Thompson's book, sad to state, has never been replaced in the seventy years since it appeared. While studies of various aspects of the cotton textile industry in North Carolina have been written, no historian has attempted, as Thompson did, to take a comprehensive, chronological view of the subject.

Similarly, much remains to be done in the field of labor history, but Melton A. McLaurin has written a helpful study of southern cotton mill workers in the last quarter of the nineteenth century, while Elizabeth H. Davidson has examined the subject of child labor in southern textile mills.[3]

If recent historians have failed to grapple with the cotton textile industry as a whole, such is happily not the case with another industry that still looms large in North Carolina— tobacco. Nannie May Tilley's classic study of the bright-leaf tobacco industry appeared in 1948. Covering the agricultural as well as the manufacturing aspects of the industry, Tilley's careful and exhaustive work has well stood the test of time.[4] Unfortunately for all who are interested in the history of North Carolina, the same author's manuscript history of the R. J. Reynolds Tobacco Company in Winston-Salem has never been released for publication by Reynolds Industries. What the Reynolds family was to Winston-Salem, Washington Duke and his sons were to Durham, and Robert F. Durden has published a

2. Holland Thompson, *From the Cotton Field to the Cotton Mill: A Study of the Industrial Transition in North Carolina* (New York: Macmillan, 1906), pp. 1–9.

3. Melton A. McLaurin, *Paternalism and Protest: Southern Cotton Mill Workers and Organized Labor, 1876–1905* (Westport, Conn.: Greenwood Press, 1971); Elizabeth H. Davidson, *Child Labor Legislation in the Southern Textile States* (Chapel Hill: University of North Carolina Press, 1939).

4. Nannie Mae Tilley, *The Bright-Tobacco Industry* (Chapel Hill: University of North Carolina Press, 1948).

history of them and of their role in building an important part
of the tobacco as well as the textile and electric power industries
in North Carolina. No adequate published work is available on
Daniel A. Tompkins, one of the central figures in Piedmont
North Carolina's early industrial development, but there is a
dissertation on him by Howard B. Clay.[5]

More neglected than textiles and tobacco, the furniture
industry began to become important in this state toward the end
of the last century. It has grown to play a national and even an
international role today; yet no historian has tried to tell the
story. There is not much more than a short article in the *North
Carolina Historical Review* and a few articles in trade journals
that have been published on the history of one of the state's
major industries.[6]

To be sure, historians have included North Carolina
developments in treating various aspects of the South's
economic history. John F. Stover, for example, has carefully
studied southern railroads from the end of the Civil War to 1900,
and Anthony Tang has analyzed economic development in the
southern Piedmont with special attention to the impact on
agriculture.[7] The fact remains, however, that in southern history
as a whole, just as in North Carolina history, economic
developments have been deplorably neglected.

Perhaps the ultimate illustration of this neglect is to be
found in the area of agriculture. In the late nineteenth and early

5. Robert F. Durden, *The Dukes of Durham, 1865–1929* (Durham: Duke
University Press, 1975); Howard B. Clay, "Daniel Augustus Tompkins: An
American Bourbon," Ph.D. diss., University of North Carolina at Chapel Hill,
1951.

6. Charles H. V. Ebert, "Furniture Making in High Point [since 1889],"
North Carolina Historical Review (hereafter cited as *NCHR*) 36 (July 1959): 330–39;
David N. Thomas, "Getting Started in High Point," *Forest History* 11 (1967):
22–32.

7. John F. Stover, *The Railroads of the South, 1865–1900* (Chapel Hill:
University of North Carolina Press, 1955); Anthony Tang, *Economic Development in
the Southern Piedmont, 1860–1950: Its Impact on Agriculture* (Chapel Hill: University
of North Carolina Press, 1958).

twentieth centuries industrialization, after all, was but the wave of the future. It represented "the Reconstruction that took," but the process of its taking required quite a few decades. And the fact was that the majority of Tar Heels, white and black, continued to make their livelihoods from the land. Of the agrarian revolt of the 1890s, to be discussed shortly, our knowledge is largely political, while the economic and social realities of agrarian life around the turn of the century remain virtually unknown.

Although North Carolina's industrialization has not resulted in as extensive an urbanization as has been the case in so much of the world, Tar Heel cities have grown significantly in the past century, and adequate histories of them are, on the whole, lacking. William K. Boyd's history of Durham, for example, is fifty years old and sorely in need of updating. One type of study that is needed may be found in Samuel M. Kipp's dissertation on urban growth and social change in Greensboro between 1870 and 1920. Articles by Kay H. Huggins on city planning in North Carolina in the first three decades of this century and by Sarah M. Lemmon on Raleigh as a "New South" city are among the few examples of urban history that can be found.[8] Urban history has been neglected, but what might be called regional history has fared better. Western North Carolina, so distinctive in many ways, has been well covered for the period since the Civil War in a study by Ina W. and John J. Van Noppen.[9]

Historians may have shunned much of North Carolina's

8. William K. Boyd, *The Story of Durham: City of the New South* (Durham: Duke University Press, 1927); Samuel M. Kipp III, "Urban Growth and Social Change in the South, 1870–1920: Greensboro, North Carolina, as a Case Study," Ph.D. diss., Princeton University, 1974; Kay H. Huggins, "City Planning in North Carolina, 1900–1929," *NCHR* 46 (Autumn 1969); and Sarah M. Lemmon, "Raleigh: An Example of the 'New South'?" ibid. 43 (Autumn 1966). Kipp's findings are succinctly stated in "Old Notables and Newcomers: The Economic and Political Elite of Greensboro, North Carolina, 1880–1920," *Journal of Southern History* 43 (August 1977).

9. Ina W. Van Noppen and John J. Van Noppen, *Western North Carolina since the Civil War* (Boone, N.C.: Appalachian Consortium, 1973).

economic and urban past, but they have not been guilty of ignoring her political history. Here the picture brightens, or perhaps one should say, the bibliography thickens. A regrettable fact is, however, that the most comprehensive single study of Tar Heel political history in this period has never been published. Despite that, numerous historians have utilized Joseph F. Steelman's dissertation, "The Progressive Era in North Carolina, 1884–1917," in their own researches; and Steelman has published a series of eight articles in the *North Carolina Historical Review* that are related in part to his dissertation.[10] Steelman and others have added a great deal of information to the older, standard published work on the period by J. G. de Roulhac Hamilton.[11] More importantly, these later historians tell a more complex story than did Hamilton, who tended to look much more kindly upon white Democrats than he did upon Republicans and blacks.

Several political biographies illumine and enliven the period although they are not as comprehensive as Steelman's dissertation. The Bourbon Democrats of the late nineteenth century have not been covered as fully as the leaders of the

10. Joseph F. Steelman, "The Progressive Era in North Carolina, 1884–1917," Ph.D. diss., University of North Carolina at Chapel Hill, 1955. The articles, in order of their appearance and all in the *NCHR*, are "Jonathan Elwood Cox and North Carolina's Gubernatorial Campaign of 1908," 41, no. 4 (1964): 436–47; "Republicans in North Carolina: John Motley Morehead's Campaign to Revive a Moribund Party, 1908–1910," 42 (April 1965): 153–68; "The Trials of a Republican State Chairman: John Motley Morehead and North Carolina Politics, 1910–1912," 43, no. 1 (1966): 31–42; "Richmond Pearson, Roosevelt Republican, and the Campaign of 1912 in North Carolina," 43 (April 1966): 122–39; "Vicissitudes of Republican Party Politics: The Campaign of 1892 in North Carolina," 43 (October 1966): 430–42; "The Progressive Democratic Convention of 1914 in North Carolina," 46 (April 1969): 83–104; "Republican Party Strategists and the Issue of Fusion with Populists in North Carolina, 1893–1894," 47 (July 1970): 244–69; and "Edward J. Justice: Profile of a Progressive Legislator, 1899–1913," 48 (April 1971): 148–61. See also Steelman's "Progressivism and Agitation for Legal Reform in North Carolina, 1897–1917," in *Essays in American History* (Greenville: Department of History, East Carolina University, 1964), 1:77–93.

11. J. G. de Roulhac Hamilton, *North Carolina since 1860*, vol. 3 of *History of North Carolina*, by R. D. W. Connor et al., 3 vols. (Chicago: Lewis Publishing Company, 1919).

subsequent period. There is still a need, for example, of a scholarly and critical examination of the postwar political career of Zebulon B. Vance; but W. Buck Yearns has edited the first volume of the Thomas J. Jarvis papers, and Lala Carr Steelman is at work on a study of Elias Carr.[12] Perhaps the best of the political biographies to have appeared so far is a life of Charles Brantley Aycock by Oliver H. Orr, Jr. Managing the difficult task of writing a book that is scholarly and sprightly at the same time, Orr is basically sympathetic toward the Democratic leader who, championing both "white supremacy" and universal education, won the governorship in 1900. More than most southern leaders of his time, Aycock possessed the sensitivity and intelligence to realize that he operated under ironclad constraints of a parochial sectionalism and racism; he knew that truly national, broad-gauged paths of service were virtually closed to his generation of southerners.[13]

A powerful figure in Democratic politics and journalism during Aycock's lifetime, Josephus Daniels long outlived the popular governor. Daniels's own memoir of his early career, *Editor in Politics*, should be read together with Joseph L. Morrison's study of Daniels during the years before he joined the cabinet of President Woodrow Wilson. In those later years under Wilson and then President Franklin D. Roosevelt, Daniels, according to some observers, "got religion" and markedly toned down both himself and his *Raleigh News and Observer* from the flamboyance that was so characteristic in the 1890s and the early twentieth century. Blatantly racist when that paid off for Tar Heel Democrats, Daniels also advocated a whole series of reforms ranging from free silver to prohibition and railway regulation.

12. W. Buck Yearns, ed., *The Papers of Thomas Jordan Jarvis*, vol. 1 (Raleigh: Department of Archives and History, 1969).

13. Oliver H. Orr, Jr., *Charles Brantley Aycock* (Chapel Hill: University of North Carolina Press, 1961). An older study is Robert D. W. Connor and Clarence Poe, *The Life and Speeches of Charles Brantley Aycock* (New York: Doubleday, Page and Company, 1912).

Despite all the paradoxes and ironies that are involved, he and his newspaper remain central to any study of the Populist and Progressive eras in North Carolina.[14]

Moving into national prominence earlier than Daniels, Walter Hines Page was another journalist and publisher who looms large in North Carolina's intellectual history during this period. An older study of him by Burton J. Hendrick will now need to be supplemented by the more critical, new biography of Page by John M. Cooper, Jr. Page, John Spencer Bassett, A. J. McKelway, and other Tar Heels are also interestingly treated in a study by Bruce Clayton of southern intellectuals around the turn of the century.[15]

Furnifold M. Simmons was another Democrat who rose to prominence in the 1890s and remained powerful, as a United States senator and state political leader, until 1930. More than three decades ago, the late J. Fred Rippy published a volume of Simmons's memoirs and addresses. Richard L. Watson, Jr., at work on a longer study of Simmons, has written a useful article on him in the *North Carolina Historical Review*.[16]

Walter Clark, as chief justice of the North Carolina Supreme Court, never loomed as large in the public arena as did Aycock, Daniels, or Simmons; yet he was an influential and controversial figure whose full story has never been told. Aubrey L. Brooks published an overly sympathetic account of Clark's life, and Brooks also collaborated with Hugh T. Lefler in

14. Josephus Daniels, *Editor in Politics* (Chapel Hill: University of North Carolina Press, 1941); Joseph L. Morrison, *Josephus Daniels Says . . . : An Editor's Political Odyssey from Bryan to Wilson and F.D.R., 1894–1913* (Chapel Hill: University of North Carolina Press, 1962).

15. Burton J. Hendrick, *The Life and Letters of Walter H. Page*, 3 vols. (New York: Doubleday, Page and Co., 1922–25); and *The Training of an American* (Boston and New York: Houghton Mifflin Company, 1928); John M. Cooper, Jr., *Walter Hines Page: The Southerner as American, 1855–1918* (Chapel Hill: University of North Carolina Press, 1977); Bruce Clayton, *The Savage Ideal: Intolerance and Intellectual Leadership in the South, 1890–1914* (Baltimore: Johns Hopkins University Press, 1972).

16. J. Fred Rippy, ed., *Furnifold Simmons, Statesman of the New South:*

editing a useful collection of Clark's papers. As adept at operating offstage as he was on, Clark remains an enigmatic but important figure in North Carolina's Populist and Progressive periods.[17]

Like Josephus Daniels and unlike Aycock and Clark, Josiah W. Bailey lived to achieve prominence in the New Deal era of Franklin D. Roosevelt. Bailey first gained influence and power as a Baptist editor around the turn of the century, and John R. Moore has written a careful biography of him that treats the early period as well as his later senatorial career.[18]

North Carolina Republicans, without a continuing daily newspaper, were underrepresented, and often misrepresented too, in the printed media of the 1890s and early twentieth century. Historians, probably influenced in part by the paucity of Republican newspaper sources, have been more attracted to subjects chosen from the majority Democrats than from the minority Republicans. Jeffrey J. Crow and Robert F. Durden, however, have written a political biography of the most prominent—and most controversial—Republican of his day, Daniel L. Russell. Elected to the governorship by Republican and some Populist voters in 1896, Russell espoused various reforms before his administration was checked by the Democrats in the famous white-supremacy legislative campaign of 1898. Still seeking revenge against the Democrats after their across-the-board victory of 1900, Russell made one final, spectacular foray against those whom he regarded as "the enemy," that is, Tar Heel Democrats. He engineered a once-famous interstate lawsuit wherein South Dakota successfully sued North Carolina in the

---

Memoirs and Addresses (Durham: Duke University Press, 1936); Richard L. Watson, Jr., "Furnifold M. Simmons: 'Jehovah of the Tar Heels'?," NCHR 44 (1967).

17. Aubrey L. Brooks, Walter Clark: Fighting Judge (Chapel Hill: University of North Carolina Press, 1944); Aubrey L. Brooks and Hugh T. Lefler, eds., The Papers of Walter Clark, 1857–1924, 2 vols. (Chapel Hill: University of North Carolina Press, 1948–50).

18. John R. Moore, Josiah William Bailey of North Carolina: A Political Biography (Durham: Duke University Press, 1968).

United States Supreme Court for payment on certain bonds of
the Reconstruction era. As the so-called Redeemer Democrats
of the 1870s never allowed a whole generation of Tar Heels
to forget the alleged horrors of "Holden and Radical rule," the
white-supremacist Democratic Redeemers of 1898 and 1900 long
played on the themes of "Russellism" and "Negro domination"
as they consolidated their power in the early decades of this
century.[19] The struggle of Tar Heel Republicans to rebuild their
party after the disfranchisement of the blacks is the subject of
David C. Roller's unpublished study of North Carolina's
Republican party in the Progressive era.[20]

Tar Heel blacks, like the Republicans, have not received
as much attention from historians as they deserve. Voting in
large numbers under the fairer election laws enacted by the
Populist-Republican fusionists in the 1890s, blacks nevertheless
held very few offices except on the local level in a few cities in
the eastern counties. Yet that limited, local participation in the
process of self-government furnished Tar Heel Democrats with
their justification for the white-supremacy campaigns of 1898
and 1900. For the South as a whole, a recent study by J. Morgan
Kousser employs a new methodology to study suffrage restriction and the establishment of the Democratic party's hegemony
in the South during the three decades between 1880 and 1910.
Kousser pays a significant amount of attention to North
Carolina, and his book should be consulted by any student of
Tar Heel political history in that period.[21]

Concentrating on North Carolina blacks, Helen G.

19. Jeffrey J. Crow and Robert F. Durden, *Maverick Republican in the Old
North State: A Political Biography of Daniel L. Russell* (Baton Rouge: Louisiana State
University Press, 1977); Robert F. Durden, *Reconstruction Bonds and Twentieth-
Century Politics: South Dakota v. North Carolina (1904)* (Durham: Duke University
Press, 1962).

20. David C. Roller, "The Republican Party of North Carolina, 1900–
1916," Ph.D. diss., Duke University, 1965.

21. J. Morgan Kousser, *The Shaping of Southern Politics: Suffrage Restriction
and the Establishment of the One-Party South* (New Haven: Yale University Press,
1974).

Edmonds in *The Negro and Fusion Politics in North Carolina, 1894–1901* provided a helpful study that has largely replaced an older work by William A. Mabry.[22] While Edmonds's book is largely political history, Frenise A. Logan treats a broader array of subjects in a study of North Carolina blacks from the end of Reconstruction to 1894, and John E. Fleming has written a dissertation on the adjustment to freedom of Burke County's blacks after the Civil War.[23]

Areas of Afro-American history in North Carolina that have yet to be explored fully are education and religion. Historians need to tell us more about the black public schools and churches and what happened in them in the decades before the Supreme Court ruled against segregated schools in 1954. Louis R. Harlan has provided for all the South Atlantic states a useful overview of some of these educational matters in a book that is aptly titled *Separate and Unequal*, and Richard B. Westin wrote a dissertation on public education for Tar Heel Negroes in the late nineteenth and early twentieth centuries.[24] In the area of public colleges for blacks, Wade Boggs has written a dissertation on state-supported higher education for Tar Heel blacks between 1877 and 1945.[25]

Around the turn of the century, black businessmen in Durham launched an insurance company that has grown into

22. Helen G. Edmonds, *The Negro and Fusion Politics in North Carolina, 1894–1901* (Chapel Hill: University of North Carolina Press, 1951); William A. Mabry, *The Negro in North Carolina Politics since Reconstruction*, Trinity College Historical Society Papers, vol. 23 (1940).

23. Frenise A. Logan, *The Negro in North Carolina, 1876–1894* (Chapel Hill: University of North Carolina Press, 1964); John E. Fleming, "Out of Bondage: The Adjustment of Burke County Negroes after the Civil War, 1865–1890," Ph.D. diss., Howard University, 1974.

24. Louis R. Harlan, *Separate and Unequal: Public School Campaigns and Racism in the Southern Seaboard States, 1901–1915* (Chapel Hill: University of North Carolina Press, 1958); Richard Barry Westin, "The State and Segregated Schools: Negro Public Education in North Carolina, 1863–1923," Ph.D. diss., Duke University, 1966.

25. Wade H. Boggs III, "State-Supported Higher Education for Blacks in North Carolina, 1877–1945," Ph.D. diss., Duke University, 1972.

one of the largest black-owned businesses in the nation, and
Walter B. Weare has skillfully told its story in a recent volume.[26]
An unusual mixture of black history and economic history may
be found in Edward Burgess's unpublished study of a black
business and civic leader, Warren Coleman, and his effort to
launch a textile mill utilizing black laborers in Concord around
the turn of the century.[27] Other interesting chapters of Tar Heel
black history are treated in Willard B. Gatewood's account of
North Carolina's black regiment in the Spanish-American War
and Dorothy Gay's essay on Raleigh's Negro community in
the 1890s.[28]

Although the definitive work on the turbulent and
critically important 1890s has yet to be done, Helen Edmonds's
study *The Negro and Fusion Politics in North Carolina* is useful
for Afro-American history as well as for any student of North
Carolina Populism. Unfortunately, no comprehensive study of
Tar Heel Populism has yet been published. Simeon Delap penned
a sketchy monograph on the subject in 1922, and Philip R. Muller
wrote a dissertation on North Carolina Populism in 1971.[29]

National historians of Populism from John Hicks in 1931 to
Lawrence Goodwyn in 1976 have, of course, dealt with the
People's party in North Carolina. One might add that interpreta-
tions of this state's Populists have varied widely. Hicks portrayed
them sympathetically and placed them in the mainline of
Populist development. On the other hand, Goodwyn, writing

---

26. Walter B. Weare, *Black Business in the New South: A Social History of the
North Carolina Mutual Life Insurance Company* (Urbana: University of Illinois Press,
1973).

27. Edward Burgess, "Tar Heel Blacks and the New South Dream: The
Coleman Manufacturing Company, 1896–1906," Ph.D. diss., Duke University,
1977.

28. Willard B. Gatewood, "North Carolina's Negro Regiment in the
Spanish-American War," *NCHR* 58 (1971); Dorothy A. Gay, "Crisis of Identity:
The Negro Community in Raleigh, 1890–1900," *NCHR* 50 (April 1973).

29. Simeon A. Delap, *The Populist Party in North Carolina*, Trinity College
Historical Society Papers, vol. 14 (1922); Philip R. Muller, "New South Populism:

from an ideological perspective derived from the "midroad" Populists of the deep South and especially Texas, views the Tar Heel Populists as largely misled and seduced into what he terms a "shadow movement" that sought free silver rather than the full range of Populist demands.[30] A recent study by Robert C. McMath, Jr., of the Farmers' Alliance, the important agrarian organization that preceded the Populist party, also contains extensive material on North Carolina, and McMath published an article in the *North Carolina Historical Review* on three of the local or suballiances in North Carolina.[31]

Perhaps the most important volume concerning the agrarian revolt that focuses attention extensively on North Carolina is the classic biography of Leonidas LaFayette Polk by the late Stuart Noblin. Founder of the *Progressive Farmer* and national president of the Farmers' Alliance at the time of his death in 1892, Polk is depicted by Noblin in a careful but sympathetic fashion that countless historians have found highly useful for almost three decades.[32]

Marion Butler succeeded Polk as the foremost agrarian leader in North Carolina. Butler also achieved national prominence as a Populist spokesman and United States senator, but he has found no biographer comparable to Noblin. He is dealt with

------

North Carolina, 1884–1900," Ph.D. diss., University of North Carolina at Chapel Hill, 1971. A much older dissertation is Florence E. Smith, "The Populist Movement and Its Influence in North Carolina, 1892–1896," University of Chicago, 1929.

30. John D. Hicks, *The Populist Revolt: A History of the Farmers' Alliance and the People's Party* (Minneapolis: University of Minnesota Press, 1931); Lawrence Goodwyn, *Democratic Promise: The Populist Moment in America* (New York: Oxford University Press, 1976).

31. Robert C. McMath, Jr., *Populist Vanguard: A History of the Southern Farmers' Alliance* (Chapel Hill: University of North Carolina Press, 1975); and "Agrarian Protest at the Forks of the Creek: Three Subordinate Farmers' Alliances in North Carolina," *NCHR* 51 (Winter 1974): 41–63.

32. Stuart Noblin, *Leonidas LaFayette Polk: Agrarian Crusader* (Chapel Hill: University of North Carolina Press, 1949).

at some length, however, in Robert F. Durden's study of the
Populist role in the presidential campaign of 1896.[33]

Sharing in the political hopes and fears of Tar Heel
men, be they Democrats, Republicans, or Populists, were, no
doubt, countless women, both black and white. Some of these
women aspired to participate directly in the processes of self-
government; others sought fulfillment in nonpolitical directions.
The history of their part in North Carolina's Populist-Progressive
era is not yet available, and that is clearly one of the more
obvious and embarrassing gaps in the historiography of the
period. Anne F. Scott has included significant material on North
Carolina women in her seminal study, *The Southern Lady: From
Pedestal to Politics*; and Noreen D. Tatum also includes Tar Heel
examples in her book on women's work in the southern branch
of the Methodist church in the years from Reconstruction to
1940.[34]

Tar Heel women may or may not have had reservations
about the New South dream of industrialization and economic
development that became dominant in the late nineteenth
century, but it is clear that most of the articulate religious
spokesmen in North Carolina shared and helped promulgate the
dream. Baptist and Methodist leaders, speaking for the largest
denominations in the state, are the subjects of Frederick A.
Bode's new study of how the churchmen helped establish the
dominance of New South ideology in North Carolina.[35] John
Carlisle Kilgo, controversial Methodist preacher and president of
Trinity College before he became a bishop, is one of the key

33. Robert F. Durden, *The Climax of Populism: The Presidential Election of
1896* (Lexington: University of Kentucky Press, 1965).

34. Anne F. Scott, *The Southern Lady: From Pedestal to Politics, 1830–1930*
(Chicago: University of Chicago Press, 1970); Noreen D. Tatum, *Crown of Service*
(Nashville: Parthenon Press, 1960).

35. Frederick A. Bode, *Protestantism and the New South: North Carolina
Baptists and Methodists in Political Crisis, 1894–1903* (Charlottesville: University
Press of Virginia, 1975).

figures in Bode's book. Kilgo was also the subject of an earlier biographical study by Paul N. Garber. But the best analysis of Kilgo's college presidency, as well as of Trinity College between its move to Durham in 1892 and the organization of Duke University around Trinity College in 1924, is Earl Porter's *Trinity and Duke*.[36]

The University of North Carolina, so frequently the indirect target of attacks from denominational leaders like Kilgo and Josiah Bailey, began to come into its own as an outstanding, modern university in the early decades of this century. Those changes at Chapel Hill are the subjects of Louis R. Wilson's volume on the making of a modern university between 1900 and 1930. Probably no other single institution in North Carolina played a more crucial role in bringing about the final burial in this century of the state's former Rip Van Winkle image than did the awakened and expanded University of North Carolina at Chapel Hill.[37] The state's public school system also grew and improved in the early decades of this century, and one of the leaders in that development, Charles Lee Coon, is the subject of George-Anne Willard's dissertation. Another educational leader, Charles D. McIver, is the subject of a careful biography by Rose H. Holder.[38]

A popular writer of the 1920s recalled that as late as the turn of the century North Carolina had reminded him of "a desolated maiden who quits washing her neck and ears" and that, with one or two exceptions, North Carolina "was by [all]

36. Paul N. Garber, *John Carlisle Kilgo: President of Trinity College, 1894–1910* (Durham: Duke University Press, 1937); Earl W. Porter, *Trinity and Duke, 1892–1924: Foundations of Duke University* (Durham: Duke University Press, 1964).

37. Louis Round Wilson, *The University of North Carolina, 1900–1930: The Making of a Modern University* (Chapel Hill: University of North Carolina Press, 1957).

38. George-Anne Willard, "Charles Lee Coon (1868–1927): North Carolina Crusader for Educational Reform," Ph.D. diss., University of North Carolina at Chapel Hill, 1974; Rose H. Holder, *McIver of North Carolina* (Chapel Hill: University of North Carolina Press, 1957).

odds the slouchiest and the shabbiest and the most slothful of the States lying below the Mason-Dixon Line." Yet in two decades' time, he declared, the state had drastically changed. When North Carolina "came forth from the trance," he continued, "she came a 'rearin' and a 'bustin.' An awakening of civic pride, of communal cooperation, followed close along the path where private enterprise had shown the way. The State arose from the dust heap, swapped off her tattered sackcloth for tailormade raiment and set her shining face to the future. . . . She just naturally took hold of the wings of the morning."[39]

Sober historians must acknowledge that the popular writer not only enjoyed poetic license but just plain exaggerated. No miracles happened in North Carolina between 1900 and 1923, or, for that matter, between 1877 and 1913. No dramatic, total transformations occurred. And yet changes, in the mental or spiritual no less than the material realms, were clearly under way and having a profound impact on the lives of most Tar Heels. The poet may wish to say that North Carolina "took hold of the wings of the morning." The historian had best settle for the less impassioned conclusions that industrialization, "the Reconstruction that took," was exerting its quiet but inexorable influence on the Old North State and that about it we actually know remarkably little.

39. Irvin S. Cobb, "North Carolina," *Hearst's International* (November 1923), pp. 140, 142.

7

North Carolina in the Twentieth Century, 1913–1945

by Sarah McCulloh Lemmon

Although writings on the period of North Carolina history from 1913 to 1945 are sparse, there is a vast quantity of research materials available; many monographs therefore need to be written before the period can be properly interpreted by the generalist.

Two general histories, one of the state and one of the region, must be read by the person who wishes to understand North Carolina history during the generation of two wars and a depression. These two works are *North Carolina: The History of a Southern State* by Hugh T. Lefler and A. Ray Newsome, and *Emergence of the New South* by George B. Tindall.[1] In the third edition of *North Carolina*, Lefler and Newsome devote some fifty pages to politics, economic growth, and education and include a brief section on cultural history from 1912 to 1948. Presented administration by administration, the chapters demonstrate the authors' belief in the theory of progress with quantities of statistics but with little evaluation, interpretation, or comment. Agricultural changes and the "second" industrial revolution are treated as an entity from 1930 to 1961 and are likewise heavily illustrated with statistics and charts. Tindall's work, on the other hand, is confined to the time period under

1. Hugh Talmage Lefler and Albert Ray Newsome, *North Carolina: The History of a Southern State*, 3d ed. (Chapel Hill: University of North Carolina Press, 1973); George Brown Tindall, *The Emergence of the New South, 1913–1945*, vol. 10 of *A History of the South*, ed. Wendell Holmes Stephenson and E. Merton Coulter (Baton Rouge: Louisiana State University Press, 1967).

consideration but includes the entire South. It is a masterful
blend of sociology, economics, history, political science, and
literary criticism, with the disciplines listed in descending order
of content. North Carolina provides much of the illustrative
material and many of the statistics used by Tindall, as when he
interprets the defeat of Furnifold Simmons for the United States
Senate in 1930 as the basis for the New Deal coalition. North
Carolina is also the heroine in the dramatic struggle for liberal
change in the South. The volume, however, except for a few
chapters, is one to use as a reference but not as general reading.
This may also be said of Lefler and Newsome's study.

The second category of works on the period from 1913 to
1945 consists of the edited volumes of the papers of the various
governors, each prefaced with a biographical introduction
usually written by a close associate of the governor during his
term of office and published by the Department of Archives and
History under one of its titles. The governors during this
period were Locke Craig, Thomas Bickett, Cameron Morrison,
Angus McLean, O. Max Gardner, J. C. B. Ehringhaus, Clyde
Hoey, J. Melville Broughton, and R. Gregg Cherry.[2] Although
brief, the biographies are fairly complete in relating public

2. *Public Letters and Papers of Locke Craig, Governor of North Carolina,
1913–1917*, comp. and ed. May F. Jones (Raleigh: Edwards & Broughton, 1916);
*Public Letters and Papers of Thomas Walter Bickett, Governor of North Carolina,
1917–1921*, comp. Santford Martin, ed. Robert B. House (Raleigh: Edwards &
Broughton, 1923); *Public Papers and Letters of Cameron Morrison, Governor of North
Carolina, 1921–1925*, comp. William H. Richardson, ed. David Leroy Corbitt
(Raleigh: Edwards & Broughton, 1927); *Public Papers and Letters of Angus Wilton
McLean, Governor of North Carolina, 1925–1929*, ed. David Leroy Corbitt (Raleigh:
Council of State, 1931); *Public Papers and Letters of Oliver Max Gardner, Governor of
North Carolina, 1929–1933*, comp. Edwin Gill, ed. David Leroy Corbitt (Raleigh:
Council of State, 1937); *Addresses, Letters, and Papers of John Christoph Blucher
Ehringhaus, Governor of North Carolina, 1933–1937*, ed. David Leroy Corbitt
(Raleigh: Council of State, 1950); *Addresses, Letters, and Papers of Clyde Roark Hoey,
Governor of North Carolina, 1937–1941*, ed. David Leroy Corbitt (Raleigh: Council
of State, 1944); *Public Addresses, Letters, and Papers of Joseph Melville Broughton,
Governor of North Carolina, 1941–1945*, ed. David Leroy Corbitt (Raleigh: Council
of State, 1950); *Public Addresses and Papers of Robert Gregg Cherry, Governor of North
Carolina, 1945–1949*, ed. David Leroy Corbitt (Raleigh: Council of State, 1951).

careers and are sometimes even sparked with humor and personal anecdotes. The published papers are too frequently routine, consisting of prepared speeches, messages to the General Assembly, proclamations of National Dairy Week, and the like. These nine volumes of papers, though essential for the historian of the period, are but bare bones indeed. One must note in all fairness that much of the material does not lend itself to interpretation.

A third category of writings is that of biographies. Only one governor, O. Max Gardner, has been honored by a published work in a book by Joseph L. Morrison, former professor of journalism at the University of North Carolina at Chapel Hill.[3] This work was commissioned by the Gardner family. There was obviously a tremendous amount of research done for this book and a tone of impartiality has been maintained. Nevertheless the image of Governor Gardner emerges as that of a hero, almost a superman, whose death before he could serve as ambassador to Great Britain was viewed as a singular loss to the country. There is no mention of the powerful Gardner machine that succeeded Furnifold Simmons's nor of other perhaps less favorable interpretations of his career as governor and chief political leader of the state after 1933, thus leaving room for future evaluations of this colorful leader. One additional governor, Cameron Morrison, has been the subject of an unpublished doctoral dissertation.[4] Morrison was a "business progressive" who opposed raising taxes but favored bonded indebtedness for road and harbor improvements. The author credits him with success in building highways and in reducing lynching. However, the study is not a biography but an evaluation of his four years of public service, not touching at all

3. Joseph L. Morrison, *Governor O. Max Gardner: A Power in North Carolina and New Deal Washington* (Chapel Hill: University of North Carolina Press, 1971).
4. Nathaniel Fuqua Magruder, "The Administration of Governor Cameron Morrison of North Carolina, 1921–1925," Ph.D. diss., University of North Carolina at Chapel Hill, 1968.

on his senatorial career and his final defeat by "Our Bob"
Reynolds.

Josephus Daniels has inspired more biographical attempts
than any other North Carolinian of the period. Morrison,
author of the Gardner study, has published two works on
Daniels: *Josephus Daniels Says . . .* , dealing with his life from
Bryan to Wilson, and *Josephus Daniels, the Small-d Democrat*.[5]
With an easy-to-read style, the author depicts his subject as an
old-fashioned editor who never ceased growing, "who had a
conscious political philosophy and acted upon it."[6] However,
he greatly admires the famous editor, is negative toward his
opponents, and underplays his errors and mistaken judgments.
There is also a published doctoral dissertation on Josephus
Daniels as ambassador to Mexico.[7] These three studies plus
Daniels's own memoirs lead to the call for a definitive biography,
perhaps in two volumes.

One North Carolina businessman has been memorialized
by LeGette Blythe, who glowingly describes the life of William
Henry Belk.[8] A collection of reminiscences, newspaper reports,
and papers and scrapbooks of the Belk family, the Belk biography
is somewhat disjointed and succumbs to adulation. Belk
deserves a better work, one that will place him properly in the
framework of southern economic development and that will
compare him with other southern businessmen during the
decades of the bull market and Great Depression.

Suzanne Cameron Linder's approach in her life of William

5. Joseph L. Morrison, *Josephus Daniels Says . . . : An Editor's Political
Odyssey from Bryan to Wilson and F.D.R., 1894–1913* (Chapel Hill: University of
North Carolina Press, 1962); Joseph L. Morrison, *Josephus Daniels, the Small-d
Democrat* (Chapel Hill: University of North Carolina Press, 1966).
6. I. B. Holley, Jr., review in *North Carolina Historical Review* (hereafter
cited as *NCHR*) 44 (1967): 215.
7. E. D. Cronon, *Josephus Daniels in Mexico* (Madison: University of
Wisconsin Press, 1963).
8. LeGette Blythe, *William Henry Belk: Merchant of the South*, enlarged
edition (Chapel Hill: University of North Carolina Press, 1958).

Louis Poteat probably falls between that of Morrison and Blythe.[9] Although well researched and seen by one reviewer as "perceptive and moving,"[10] the book is thoroughly admiring of and sympathetic with its subject. The narration and description of the life of this famous Baptist educator, who spoke so firmly for academic freedom, make for fascinating reading, but Mrs. Linder has not estimated Poteat's lasting place in the state's history except in a sentimental way.

The career of Josiah Bailey, the Baptist editor turned politician, has been described by John Robert Moore in a book devoted chiefly to his senatorial career.[11] Bailey, at first liberal, stayed with the Democratic party in 1928 as did O. Max Gardner, thereby laying the foundation for Bailey's defeat of bolter Furnifold Simmons in the 1930 race for the United States Senate. Although he gradually became more conservative as the New Deal developed, Bailey was an international interventionist and supported Franklin D. Roosevelt's policies with regard to World War II. The book is not a definitive biography, however, because it deals chiefly with one phase of a many-faceted career. Indeed, Moore spends more time on the national scene than on the North Carolina one. A full study of Bailey set in a broad perspective is still needed.

The best of the biographies dealing with persons in the generation from 1913 to 1945 is that of Eugene Clyde Brooks by Willard B. Gatewood.[12] In a "substantial and . . . eloquent" book,[13] the author sees Brooks's greatest achievement as occurring during his tenure as state superintendent of public

9. Suzanne Cameron Linder, *William Louis Poteat: Prophet of Progress* (Chapel Hill: University of North Carolina Press, 1966).

10. Joseph F. Steelman, review in *NCHR* 44 (1967): 93.

11. John Robert Moore, *Senator Josiah William Bailey of North Carolina: A Political Biography* (Durham: Duke University Press, 1968).

12. Willard Badgette Gatewood, *Eugene Clyde Brooks: Educator and Public Servant* (Durham: Duke University Press, 1960). Lanier Branson, *Eugene Cunningham Branson, Humanitarian* (Charlotte: privately printed, 1967) contains excellent notes and numerous letters for a future biography of another noted educator.

13. Daniel J. Whitener, review in *NCHR* 38 (1961): 412.

instruction when, from 1919 to 1923, he held back the forces
of retrenchment and reaction that followed World War I. This
is certainly one of the best biographies of North Carolina
educational leaders yet written.

If the reader must be cautious in perusing a biography lest
it be biased, he must be additionally so in reading memoirs.
Yet, would that there were more of these personal testimonials
to life during the years under consideration. Josephus Daniels
and Clarence Poe, thus far, appear to be the only persons to have
published their recollections. Daniels's two volumes on the
Wilson years are more pertinent to the national than to the state
scene; yet they are essential reading for anyone wishing to
study North Carolina up to 1923.[14] Clarence Poe's recollections of
eighty years are just that, not chosen for their significance and
not always in logical sequence, yet reflecting events of his career
involving Herbert Hoover and Harry S. Truman; his crusade
for improved health, education, and farming; and his editorship
of the famous weekly, *The Progressive Farmer*.[15] These memoirs
will prove useful to future historians.

The next category of writings to be considered is that of
works on special topics. The period between 1913 and 1945
is rich in events of social, cultural, political, and economic
significance. One thinks of World War I, the Jazz Age, the Great
Depression, the New Deal, the rise of totalitarianism, and
World War II, to select the obvious. Of these events, only the
First World War has inspired any appreciable number of
publications. Perhaps because this war was the terminal point
of individual heroism and the first implementation of the mass
destruction hinted at in the American Civil War, it produced
literature glorifying the knight in shining armor but also
remembering blackly and bitterly the hell-holes in the front lines

14. Josephus Daniels, *The Wilson Era: Years of Peace, 1910–1917* (Chapel
Hill: University of North Carolina Press, 1944); *The Wilson Era: Years of War and
After, 1917–1923* (Chapel Hill: University of North Carolina Press, 1946).

15. Clarence Hamilton Poe, *My First 80 Years* (Chapel Hill: University of
North Carolina Press, 1963).

of Flanders. The world's first military aviators felt themselves to be feudal champions in single combat, as expressed by James R. McConnell in *Flying for France*, and in the *War Letters of Kiffin Rockwell*; the infantryman slogging in the mud was described in *Tarheel Tommy Atkins* and in *Sergeant Hallyburton*; the technical work of the modern engineer was revealed by Colonel Joseph Hyde Pratt in his diary.[16] The famous "Old Hickory" (Thirtieth) Infantry Division has its own history in the war, written by Elmer A. Murphy and Robert S. Thomas.[17] None of these books is a history per se; all reflect only one viewpoint; they are the material from which history is written; and they were drawn upon by Sarah M. Lemmon in *North Carolina's Role in the First World War*.[18] This pamphlet, like so much other twentieth-century history, is chiefly descriptive with little interpretation. The author's hope was that eventually the account of each state's service and experience in the First World War might be written, thus making it possible for a national historian to write a definitive work about the war at the grass-roots level. One work of larger stature has been published on North Carolina during the war: Alex M. Arnett's book *Claude Kitchin and the Wilson War Policies*, which is well researched and impartial.[19] Kitchin, North Carolina's most outstanding congressman of the war years, opposed America's entrance into the war, but following the declaration of war against Germany he worked

16. James R. McConnell, *Flying for France: With the American Escadrille at Verdun* (Garden City: Doubleday, Page, 1917); *War Letters of Kiffin Yates Rockwell*, with memoirs and notes by Paul Ayres Rockwell (Garden City: Country Life Press, 1925); Benjamin Muse, *Tarheel Tommy Atkins* (New York: Vantage Press, 1963); Charles W. Hyams, *Sergeant Hallyburton: The First American Soldier Captured in the World War* (Moravian Falls, N.C.: Dixie Publishing Co., 1923); "Diary of Col. Joseph Hyde Pratt, Commanding 105th Engineers, A. E. F.," *NCHR* 1 (1924): 35–70; ibid. 2 (1925): 117–44, 269–99.

17. Elmer A. Murphy and Robert S. Thomas, *The Thirtieth Division in the World War* (Lepanto, Ark.: Old Hickory Publishing Co., 1936).

18. Sarah McCulloh Lemmon, *North Carolina's Role in the First World War* (Raleigh: Department of Archives and History, 1966).

19. Alex Mathews Arnett, *Claude Kitchin and the Wilson War Policies* (Boston: Little, Brown & Co., 1937).

long and hard to support the drive for victory. It is obvious that Arnett admires a man who holds to his convictions in the face of adverse public opinion; yet he does not make Kitchin larger than life size. Two other scholarly publications on World War I have appeared: articles entitled "North Carolina Council of Defense" and "Southern Women in the War," both by William J. Breen and both published in the *North Carolina Historical Review*.[20]

The twenty years between the two world wars have not been dealt with to any great extent by scholars. Although a number of dramatic political events occurred in the state during this time, only one book other than a biography has been published that treats politics. Elmer Puryear's research on Democratic party dissension from 1928 to 1936 was the subject of his doctoral dissertation that was published in 1962, and Richard L. Watson, Jr., has analyzed Senator Furnifold Simmons's bolt from Democratic regularity in 1928 and his consequent defeat in 1930.[21] Other suggestive articles have appeared, including Ronald Marcello, "The Selection of North Carolina's WPA Chief, 1935: A Dispute over Political Patronage"; David Porter, "Representative Warren, the Water Bloc, and the Transportation Act of 1940"; and Joseph Steelman, "The Progressive Democratic Convention of 1914 in North Carolina"; all of which are in the *North Carolina Historical Review*.[22]

20. William J. Breen, "The North Carolina Council of Defense during World War I, 1917–1918," *NCHR* 50 (1973): 1–13; and "Southern Women in the War: The North Carolina Woman's Committee, 1917–1919," ibid. 55 (1978): 251–83.

21. Elmer Lee Puryear, *Democratic Party Dissension in North Carolina, 1928–1936*, James Sprunt Studies in History and Political Science, vol. 44 (Chapel Hill: University of North Carolina Press, 1962); Richard L. Watson, Jr., "A Political Leader Bolts—F. M. Simmons in the Presidential Election of 1928," *NCHR* 37 (1960): 516–43; and Watson, "A Southern Democratic Primary: Simmons vs. Bailey in 1930," ibid. 42 (1965): 21–46.

22. Ronald Ely Marcello, "The Selection of North Carolina's WPA Chief, 1935: A Dispute Over Political Patronage," *NCHR* 52 (1975): 59–76; David Porter, "Representative Lindsay Warren, the Water Bloc, and the Transportation Act of 1940," *NCHR* 50 (1973): 273–88; Joseph F. Steelman, "The Progressive Democratic Convention of 1914 in North Carolina," *NCHR* 46 (1969): 83–104.

Marcello's article was drawn from his unpublished dissertation, "The North Carolina Works Progress Administration and the Politics of Relief," in which he demonstrates that the creation of administrative jobs and the distribution of funds for projects profoundly influenced municipal and county elections.[23]

Although the number of publications on politics is scanty indeed, even less has been written on taxation and finance. North Carolina is a state whose careful fiscal policies have produced exceptionally favorable comment from fiscal experts, yet only a thesis by Josephine L. Doughton on the passage of the sales tax law in 1931–33, and an article on the history of the North Carolina Department of Revenue touch on the state's financial history.[24]

Education fares somewhat better. There are, of course, a number of familiar histories (and some not so familiar) of institutions of higher learning that include the years we are considering in one or more chapters, such as Mary Lynch Johnson, *A History of Meredith College*; Jacob C. Leonard, *History of Catawba College*; a dissertation by Elizabeth Ann Bowles on the University of North Carolina at Greensboro from 1892 to consolidation in 1931; and others, some in preparation, including the history of Saint Mary's School and College in Raleigh.[25] Public education has fared less well, however, in the utilization of sources available and in scholarly attention. Three unpublished theses constitute the total: one on public education during the depression, one on public library service in North Carolina

23. Ronald Ely Marcello, "The North Carolina Works Progress Administration and the Politics of Relief," Ph.D. diss., Duke University, 1969.

24. Josephine Lane Doughton, "Passage of the Sales Tax Law in North Carolina, 1931–1933," M.A. thesis, University of North Carolina at Chapel Hill, 1949; Allen J. Maxwell and William O. Suiter, "The North Carolina Department of Revenue," *NCHR* 21 (1944): 265–93.

25. Mary Lynch Johnson, *A History of Meredith College*, 2d ed. (Raleigh: Edwards & Broughton Co., 1972); Jacob C. Leonard, *History of Catawba College* (Columbia, Mo., n.p., 1927); Elizabeth Ann Bowles, "The University of North Carolina at Greensboro, 1892–1931," Ph.D. diss., University of North Carolina at Chapel Hill, 1965.

and its relation to the WPA, and one survey of the history of the department of public instruction from 1850 to 1956.[26] There is also a dissertation by Charles Monroe Hyder on the North Carolina Education Association from 1884 to 1967 that points out the influence wielded by that organization on teacher training, salaries, school curriculum, and length of term, especially following its change of name in 1922.[27]

Coverage of the fields of agriculture, industry, and transportation is miniscule. For a state noted in all three fields, it is indeed astounding that only two publications could be located on these topics. Stuart Noblin has published a short history of the Grange in North Carolina, and Capus Waynick has written a history of the state highway system to 1952.[28] Noblin's book, commissioned by the Grange, is carefully done but contains no citations. It is factual, rather dull, a good collection of data for future writers of North Carolina history, but not a booklet for reading unless one is a member of the organization. Waynick's glossy production sketches the history of roads from the colonial period, dwelling with admiration on the Good Roads movement of the late teens and twenties; highway

26. Thomas Raikes Slinkard, "Public Education in North Carolina during the Depression, 1929–1933," M.A. thesis, University of North Carolina at Chapel Hill, 1948; Elaine Von Oesen, "Public Library Service in North Carolina and the W.P.A.," M.A. thesis, University of North Carolina at Chapel Hill, 1951; David Hyde Prince, "A History of the State Department of Public Instruction in North Carolina, 1852–1956," M.A. thesis, University of North Carolina at Chapel Hill, 1959.

27. Charles Monroe Hyder, "Development of the North Carolina Education Association, 1884–1967," Ph.D. diss., Duke University, 1968.

28. Stuart Noblin, *The Grange in North Carolina, 1929–1954: A Story of Agricultural Progress* (Greensboro: North Carolina State Grange, 1954); Capus Waynick, *North Carolina Roads and Their Builders* (Raleigh: Superior Stone Co., 1952). Waynick drew upon C. K. Brown, *The State Highway System of North Carolina* (Chapel Hill: University of North Carolina Press, 1931) for the decade of the twenties. The historical account was brought up to 1966 in John Harden, *North Carolina Roads and Their Builders*, vol. 2 (Raleigh: Superior Stone Co., 1966). For a sketch of North Carolina's Mother of Good Roads, see Jeffrey J. Crow, "People in Public Works: Harriet M. Berry," *American Public Works Association (APWA) Reporter* 44 (November 1977): 4–5.

commissioners; and contractors. Its illustrations, which are chiefly photographs, are excellent and nostalgic. One business has received attention, the North Carolina Mutual Life Insurance Company of Durham.[29] The author has written as much a social and intellectual history as a business one. Walter Weare concludes that the company was a product of Afro-American institutions, especially the church and the mutual benefit society; that it was aligned with the philosophy of Booker T. Washington rather than that of W. E. B. Dubois; and that it combined black needs with the American business ethos.

One book deals with the social history of the twenties. Willard B. Gatewood's *Preachers, Pedagogues, and Politicians* examines the climate affecting religion and education in the state at the time of the controversy over evolution.[30] In fact, this controversy was the only social event of the decade to be studied by more than one author. Gatewood has thoroughly researched his subject, has written well, shows a sense of humor, and includes some psychological analysis. He concludes that continuing antiintellectualism and irrationality were accentuated by the alienation and anomie that followed World War I. If the reader combines this book with Linder's biography of Poteat and with a recent distinguished lecture by Thomas C. Parramore on Dr. R. T. Vann's role in the debate over evolution, he will have an informed view of a major event of social history in the state.

A fascinating social history of rural North Carolina may be found in the pages of Jane S. McKimmon's book, *When We're Green We Grow*. Here may be rediscovered the old ways of life as they came in contact with world wars, depression, the boll weevil, and were consciously modified by the work of home

29. Walter Burdette Weare, *Black Business in the New South: A Social History of the North Carolina Mutual Life Insurance Company* (Urbana: University of Illinois Press, 1973).

30. Willard Badgette Gatewood, *Preachers, Pedagogues, and Politicians: The Evolution Controversy in North Carolina, 1920–1927* (Chapel Hill: University of North Carolina Press, 1965).

demonstration agents from 1911 to 1945, as seen by the state's
pioneer woman agent.[31]

Another aspect of social history is touched on by a book
on the North Carolina chain gang, published in 1927, which
provides the scholar with detailed materials for a yet unwritten
history of penology.[32] There is also a short narrative about the
North Carolina Cancer Society, containing a few pages on its
formative period of the 1930s. The existence of a few articles
and master's theses on the history of various phases of public
health in the state might be noted here for those who are
interested in medical history. The remaining publications on
social history are chiefly articles in the *North Carolina Historical
Review* that have been developed largely from theses and
doctoral dissertations. A. Elizabeth Taylor has written the
definitive articles on woman suffrage in North Carolina and
should publish a book.[33] Two articles deal with the social
aspects of the depression and the New Deal: Robert V. Parker
has written on the Bonus March of 1932, and Thomas S. Morgan
has examined the enactment of unemployment legislation.[34]
Morgan's article was drawn from his dissertation, "A Step
Toward Altruism: Relief and Welfare in North Carolina, 1930–
1938," in which the battle between New Dealers and the old
North Carolina Department of Charities and Public Welfare
over control of new social legislation is viewed as resulting in
victory for the state's public welfare structure rather than that
of the New Deal.[35] Religion in the twenties is the subject of

31. Jane Simpson McKimmon, *When We're Green We Grow* (Chapel Hill:
University of North Carolina Press, 1945).

32. Jesse F. Steiner and Roy M. Brown, *The North Carolina Chain Gang*
(Chapel Hill: University of North Carolina Press, 1927).

33. A. Elizabeth Taylor, "The Woman Suffrage Movement in North
Carolina," *NCHR* 38 (1961): 46–62, 173–89.

34. Robert V. Parker, "The Bonus March of 1932: A Unique Experience in
North Carolina Political and Social Life," *NCHR* 51 (1974): 64–89; Thomas Sellers
Morgan, Jr., "The Movement to Enact Unemployment Insurance Legislation in
North Carolina, 1935–1936," *NCHR* 52 (1975): 283–302.

35. Thomas Sellers Morgan, Jr., "A Step Toward Altruism: Relief and

research by Edward W. Phifer, who describes a typical revival in
Burke County and its aftereffects.[36] This is a subject that can
easily be explored for other preachers and other towns in the
state to provide an extensive coverage of a major religious
phenomenon of the decade. Kay H. Huggins has written on
city planning in North Carolina, blazing a trail for the study of
other significant movements in urban history.[37] Her topic
suggests many related ones that have not yet been investigated,
including land booms in North Carolina, the rise of suburbs
in each city, a history of city government, a history of city-
county-state relations, and more. Pearsall has made a unique
contribution to the cultural history of the state by writing
on the North Carolina Symphony Orchestra from 1932 to 1962,
describing its origin, its support by the WPA, and its revival and
expansion into a professional touring orchestra under the
leadership of Dr. and Mrs. Benjamin Swalin. Pearsall was
especially impressed by the symphony's program for children.[38]
The North Carolina Art Society needs a similar scholarly study.

The decade of the thirties closed with war. World War II
did not produce the spate of writing that World War I did. Only
one scholarly book has appeared, Spencer B. King's dissertation
on the selective service in North Carolina, a thorough analysis
that is partly sociological and extremely statistical.[39] King has
constructed a composite picture of the state's entire male
population of military age and has thus encapsulated a historical

Welfare in North Carolina, 1930–1938," Ph.D. diss., University of North Carolina
at Chapel Hill, 1969.

36. Edward W. Phifer, Jr., "Religion in the Raw: Cyclone Mack in Burke
County, August-September, 1920," NCHR 48 (1971): 225–44. See, for example,
James T. Baker, "The Battle of Elizabeth City: Christ and Antichrist in North
Carolina," ibid. 54 (1977): 393–408.

37. Kay Haire Huggins, "City Planning in North Carolina, 1900–1929,"
NCHR 46 (1969): 377–97.

38. Howard Turner Pearsall, "The North Carolina Symphony Orchestra
from 1932 to 1962," Ph.D. diss., Indiana University, 1969.

39. Spencer B. King, Selective Service in North Carolina in World War II
(Chapel Hill: University of North Carolina Press, 1949).

image in a moment of time. Gertrude Carraway wrote a booklet on Camp Lejeune, but there appears to be nothing on the history of Fort Bragg.[40] LeGette Blythe prepared an admiring account of the Thirty-eighth Hospital Evacuation Unit, which was composed chiefly of personnel from Mecklenburg County.[41] There are also a number of other unit histories, rather like college yearbooks, that are doubtless of great interest to those who served in them. Many of these are in the North Carolina Collection at Chapel Hill. Finally, Sarah M. Lemmon's booklet on the state's role in World War II is a good summary, descriptive rather than analytical, of activities on both the home front and the battlefields.[42] In its pages are many hints of topics that are available for scholarly research.

We have now reviewed all the publications, dissertations, and theses that have been written on the history of the state of North Carolina from 1913 to 1945. The list is short, with the most noteworthy items being the two books by Gatewood, Arnett's book on Claude Kitchin, two volumes of Josephus Daniels's memoirs, two biographies by Morrison, and one by Moore. Daniels, Kitchin, Gardner, Bailey, Poteat, and Brooks are the only persons who have been the subjects of scholarly biographies, which is far too limited a number. The evolution controversy has attracted attention, as has the WPA of the New Deal and selective service in World War II, but little else. It is indeed time that researchers turned their efforts toward the period from 1913 to 1945, because it contains some of the most significant and seminal events of our century.

The paucity of historical writings may be due to many causes, not the least of which is the complexity of the time period. Two world wars, a crash, and the New Deal tend to

40. Gertrude Sprague Carraway, *Camp Lejeune Leathernecks* (New Bern: Owen G. Dunn, 1946).

41. LeGette Blythe, *38th Evac* (Charlotte: Heritage Printers, 1966).

42. Sarah McCulloh Lemmon, *North Carolina's Role in World War II* (Raleigh: Department of Archives and History, 1964).

emphasize global and national events to the extent that the state
and local historian hesitates to delve into what must seem a
relatively unimportant historical layer. To allow such neglect
to become permanent would be, however, a grave mistake.
Until the depths are explored, the superstructure is unsound,
like a house built on sand. Interpretations are superficial
unless substantiated at the grass roots. It is essential, therefore, that numerous monographs on North Carolina history be
researched and published in order to allow valid syntheses and
interpretations to be developed.

Nor should monographs be limited to topics in support of
political events and business cycles. The social and intellectual
scenes provide a kaleidoscope of changing colors, with the speed
of change itself so rapid that the historian can indeed research,
chronicle, and interpret such changes in one lifetime. While
one of the greatest challenges to the twentieth-century historian
is the sheer quantity of records available, this fact is also one
of the greatest advantages, in that it makes it possible to weave a
full tapestry of civilization instead of a mere limning of a few
outstanding happenings and persons.

Potential topics for further research and writing in the
period from 1913 to 1945 abound. The number of books already
published on the evolution controversy of the 1920s suggests the
possibility of a study of the relationships of church to state,
to higher education, to international isolationism, to the Great
Depression, and to World War II. A scholar familiar with
quantitative analysis might correlate roll-call votes in the General
Assembly with religious and/or educational affiliation, perhaps
with some interesting results.

A few research articles on aspects of the New Deal have
been mentioned. Monographs using historical methodology
are needed on the Agricultural Adjustment Administration in
North Carolina, the Civilian Conservation Corps, the banking
crisis, and the National Labor Relations Act, to name a few.
Most of the research on the New Deal era has been either

sociological or economic in nature; there is need for a historical assessment now that we are a generation away from those events. One of the greatest beneficiaries of the New Deal was organized labor; yet in labor history only the Gastonia and Marion textile strikes have ever been scrutinized by the historical eye.[43] Admittedly it is difficult to gain access to the state AFL-CIO files, but hopefully some persistent soul will soon break the barrier. Certainly in a state still heavily agricultural, it seems criminal that tobacco alone has achieved its own history. The cotton crisis of 1913–14, the boll weevil onslaught of the 1920s, the attack on cotton by synthetics, price supports under the New Deal, and the impact of World War II on cotton farming all create an outline of a history that begs to be written. Apply the same outline to peanuts, soy beans, truck farming, and the pickle industry, and the list of feasible topics grows ever longer. Histories of cattle raising, chicken and egg farming, the farmers' cooperative movement, the Rural Electrification Authority, soil and water conservation, and the outdoor recreation industry can also be written. Sources might include not only the government documents and newspapers of the day but also the papers of Dudley Warren Bagley of Currituck County, first chairman of North Carolina's REA, deposited at the Southern Historical Collection at Chapel Hill. A biography of Jane Simpson McKimmon, founder of North Carolina's extension homemaker service, would cover much of the history of rural North Carolina. Her papers are at the Division of Archives and History in Raleigh, and her record is part of the history of North Carolina State University as well.

Industrial history, except for the furniture industry, is also lacking, although every factory or plant should be the object of research. The sum of many local accounts will eventually

43. Liston Pope, *Millhands and Preachers* (New Haven: Yale University Press, 1942) contains some historical background and a statement of the events of the Gastonia strike, but it is essentially an example of *Wissensociologie* rather than history.

equal the needed synthesis with its generalizations, interpretations, and evaluations. Some possible accounts to be based on known collections of papers are: railroads and highways from the Alexander Boyd Andrews Collection; the Ivanhoe Manufacturing Company of Smithfield; the Chatham Manufacturing Company of Surry County; the Durham Cotton Manufacturing Company; Durham's industrial growth from the papers of Julian S. Carr and James Southgate; and a publishing company in Greensboro from the papers of Charles L. Van Noppen. Adding newspapers as an industrial category, one can write a history of the *Raleigh Times* to 1938 using the papers of John A. Park; and of the *Charlotte Observer* to 1935 using the papers of Wade Hampton Harris. In addition, the Clarence W. Griffin Collection contains material on the North Carolina Press Association. Furthermore, what of the shipping industry, the rise of motor carriers, the early airlines and air terminals? What of the fabulous motion-picture industry in its North Carolina aspects, from theater construction to the Great Depression's triple feature to the drive-in? What of touring drama companies, the Little Theater movement, the advent of the radio? These are all legitimate topics of social history.

The educational event most often alluded to between 1913 and 1945 is the 1931 consolidation of the University at Chapel Hill, Woman's College, and State College into one university. Many other events of importance occurred, however. A history of each institution, private as well as public, has not yet been written; from such monographs will eventually come a history of junior colleges, of independent colleges, of academies, and an assessment of their respective roles in the cultural life of North Carolinians. How were they affected by the depression? By World War II? What role has been played by the American Association of University Women in women's colleges, and by churches in black colleges? What has been the history of teacher training since Charles D. McIver and J. Y. Joyner? Of the curriculum in the public schools? A number of collections related

to education are available: that of Aaron Burtis Hunter of Saint
Augustine's; of Lillian Dodd, a Raleigh teacher; of Daphne
Carroway, teacher and famous "story-teller"; of William Henry
Jones, cofounder of Biltmore Junior College in Asheville; of
John Jay Blair, state director of schoolhouse planning; and of
Charles M. Hunter, founder of Berry O'Kelly Teacher Training
and Industrial School at Method.

There are still biographies waiting to be written. Blacks
and women and their roles in the state's history have been
almost ignored. Charles M. Hunter, black educator, and Jane S.
McKimmon, both already mentioned, deserve full-scale biographies. So do Nell Battle Lewis, Raleigh free-lance writer and
personality; and Gertrude Weil, Goldsboro feminist and religious
leader. Elizabeth Henderson Cotten left many papers relative
to women's affairs before 1947, and Gabrielle deRosset Waddell
kept eighteen diaries and notebooks covering her life to 1936.
The need for publication of Taylor's research on woman suffrage
in North Carolina has been pointed out, but it should be
followed by a study of the League of Women Voters and perhaps
a quantitative study of women in public office. A history of civil
rights for blacks and women in North Carolina has not yet been
written. Until this is done, the perspective on the later drives
for such rights after 1950 is lacking.

There is need for a complete history of North Carolina's
roles in World War I and World War II, building on Lemmon's
beginning. An enormous quantity of unused material is
deposited in Raleigh at the state archives, and some is in the
Southern Historical Collection at Chapel Hill. Not only are there
several hundred boxes of papers arranged by counties and
by wartime commissions, but also the private collections of
James A. Higgs, Kiffin Rockwell, Fred A. Olds, Daniel Harvey
Hill, James Hinton Pou, R. Gregg Cherry, Mrs. Elle Goode
Hardeman, and Robert Watson Winston. The roles of women
and of blacks on the home front can be extracted readily from
such resources as these. Newspaper editorials and cartoons are

sources for studies of attitudes toward the 1917 Bolshevik Revolution, the occupation of the Rhineland in 1936, the bombing of Hiroshima, and many other public events that stirred controversy.

To conclude this discussion of possible topics, let me submit a miscellaneous yet intriguing list: the North Carolina National Guard with General Pershing in the pursuit of Pancho Villa; a history of hurricanes; the fishing industry; histories of the state mental hospitals, many of which have been besieged by controversial administrators and policies; histories of the Episcopal and Roman Catholic dioceses in North Carolina. Are there any histories yet of Greek Orthodox and Jewish congregations in North Carolina? If not, they are long overdue.

There is no dearth of historical materials, as is readily apparent. To all sources that have been mentioned above, one should add the city and county newspapers, various weekly and monthly journals, court records from local to supreme court levels, journals of the General Assembly, statutes, municipal and county records, reports of state officials and commissions, and more. The sheer quantity of available materials can discourage the scholar who is accustomed to finding only an occasional nugget of information. For this very reason, the general synthesis and interpretation must be deferred until many small studies have been completed. Much of the history of North Carolina since 1920 has been preempted by the sociologists. Because their methodology is different, their studies cannot substitute for those of the historian. Let the graduate student now begin to mine this golden vein. Let definitive works gradually appear. And finally, one day, let a complete interpretation of these significant years, solidly grounded on earlier research and splendidly written, be honored by receiving the Mayflower Cup for nonfiction. Then shall we be satisfied that justice has been done to North Carolina history from 1913 to 1945.

8

North Carolina, 1946–1976: Where Historians Fear to Tread

by H. G. Jones

If history is the record of the past, the three decades since World War II are no less eligible for historical treatment than earlier periods. Certainly there is no paucity of source materials. Indeed, except for documentation shielded by governmental or private restrictions, sources of recent history are more voluminous and more readily available than those for any other period. To be sure, the era has been characterized by a paperwork explosion in which the quality of documentation appears to have deteriorated at least in proportion to the increasing quantity. Furthermore, the substitution of nonpaper recording mediums confronts potential researchers with new and sometimes perplexing challenges in the interpretation of data.

Still, the grist for the historian's mill is source material. But as the grist has piled up in the postwar period, the historian's mill has almost ceased to operate. In fact, because so little has been published by historians about the last three decades, this chapter, except for its inclusion in the table of contents, need not have been prepared. Why have so few historians written about North Carolina's last thirty years? The reasons may be more obvious than justified.

The very nature of the craft makes the historian reluctant to tamper with evidence until it has been lodged in the archives and allowed to mellow with age, for the historian's credibility depends largely upon his objectivity, and although the detachment of time is no assurance of increased objectivity, it does—or should—temper the passion of one's own personal views of events and issues. Robert Moats Miller described the problem in his review of Numan V. Bartley's book on race and politics in the 1950s: "The writing of recent history may or may not be more difficult than exploration of the distant past, but surely the reviewing of a volume dealing with the 1950s is a contingent enterprise, for the reviewer cannot segregate . . . the events 'objectively' described from his own subjective memories of them."[1]

Another explanation for the scarcity of historical studies for postwar North Carolina lies in the significance of the year 1945: It is a clear and easily remembered date that ended a war unparalleled in history. Although the United States has been engaged in two other wars in the last three decades, the adjective "postwar" means, in common parlance, since 1945.

But 1945 was the beginning of another era too, an era that has witnessed such rapid and enormous changes that the date may be considered more as a waterfall than as a watershed. These changes, providing delight to the political scientist, are often too recent, too close, and sometimes too intimate to permit the historian to feel at ease in analyzing them. Neither personal observation nor statistical sampling is a substitute for the historical method, and though social scientists may rush in, historians may prefer to wait until the causes, results, and implications become clearer.

Still another factor in the paucity of historical studies of recent years is the virtual absence of teachers of North Carolina history who are specialists in the twentieth century. Graduate students tend to conduct their investigations into subjects that are of interest to their professors. Is it any surprise, therefore, that doctoral candidates have generally steered clear of postwar North Carolina as a subject for dissertations?

1. Robert Moats Miller, review of Numan V. Bartley, *The Rise of Massive Resistance: Race and Politics in the South During the 1950s*, in *North Carolina Historical Review* (hereafter cited as *NCHR*) 47 (July 1970): 329.

Thirty-four years after the close of World War II, there exists no published work interpreting the postwar era in North Carolina. Except for a few chapters tacked onto general histories and for a few more specialized studies, historians have left the field to social scientists.

Of the general histories, the appearance in 1954 of Hugh T. Lefler and Albert Ray Newsome's *North Carolina: The History of a Southern State* was a major event, for it made available the first one-volume, college-level textbook in North Carolina history.[2] The Second World War had been over only a few years, so it is not surprising that this landmark publication offered no separate treatment of the postwar years. It is surprising, however, that fewer than 70 of the book's 592 pages of text were devoted to the twentieth century, and this portion is more a summary than a careful story development characteristic of the authors' coverage of the earlier centuries. Except for a few statistics and a tracing of political campaigns, the book gave scant coverage to the postwar years.

Lefler's third edition of the same title, published in 1973, is more attractively printed, and it more adequately covers the twentieth century with expanded and rewritten chapters.[3] Still, while the political review flows rather freely, the chapters on agricultural and industrial changes tend to pile statistic upon statistic with little accompanying interpretation. The result is that the portion devoted to the twentieth century remains the weakest part of the volume. Characteristic of textbooks, the Lefler-Newsome volume is straightforward history with few

2. Hugh T. Lefler and Albert Ray Newsome, *North Carolina: The History of a Southern State* (Chapel Hill: University of North Carolina Press, 1954). Lefler's *History of North Carolina*, 2 vols. of text, 2 vols. of biographies (New York: Lewis Historical Publishing Company, 1956), provides somewhat similar treatment for the modern period.

3. Newsome died in 1951, but the book continued to carry his name as coauthor. Other writers of North Carolina history who died in the postwar period included H. M. Wagstaff, 1945; Adelaide Fries, 1949; R. D. W. Connor, 1950; Douglas L. Rights, 1956; J. G. de R. Hamilton, 1961; Archibald Henderson, 1963; D. J. Whitener, 1964; D. L. Corbitt, 1967; and Christopher Crittenden, 1969.

anecdotes and fewer injections of the authors' viewpoints. Only occasionally a provocative qualifier springs forth to challenge the reader, as, for instance, when the purpose of the consolidation of three institutions into the University of North Carolina in 1931 is described as "ostensibly to save money."[4]

Books about the regions of the state have done no better for recent history. Aside from a brief discussion of tourism and a few statistics to demonstrate economic progress, *Western North Carolina since the Civil War*, by Ina Woestemeyer Van Noppen and John J. Van Noppen, gives little notice of the postwar period. Nor is much recent history found in David Stick's *The Outer Banks of North Carolina, 1584–1958*, Wilma Dykeman's *The French Broad*, or Malcolm Ross's *The Cape Fear*, each of which makes a substantial contribution to the history of earlier periods.[5]

County histories, too, have generally ignored the postwar era. The very latest, *Burke: The History of a North Carolina County, 1777–1920*, by Edward W. Phifer, Jr., excuses its omission by its title; but William S. Powell's *When the Past Refused to Die: A History of Caswell County, 1777–1977*, lives up to its title only by means of a few references to recent incidents, such as the celebrated Mack Ingram case. Other good local histories, such as James W. Wall's history of Davie County and Ethel Stephens Arnett's history of Greensboro devote little space to the postwar period.[6]

4. Lefler and Newsome, *North Carolina* (1954 ed.), p. 555.

5. Ina Woestemeyer Van Noppen and John J. Van Noppen, *Western North Carolina since the Civil War* (Boone: Appalachian Consortium Press, 1973); David Stick, *The Outer Banks of North Carolina, 1584–1958* (Chapel Hill: University of North Carolina Press, 1958); Wilma Dykeman, *The French Broad* (New York: Rinehart, 1955); Malcolm Ross, *The Cape Fear* (New York: Holt, Rinehart and Winston, 1965).

6. Edward W. Phifer, Jr., *Burke: The History of a North Carolina County, 1777–1920* (Morganton: Author, 1977); William S. Powell, *When the Past Refused to Die: A History of Caswell County, 1777–1977* (Durham: Moore Publishing Company, 1977); James W. Wall, *History of Davie County in the Forks of the Yadkin* (Mocksville:

If the recent past has been pretty well ignored in state, regional, and county histories, it has fared only a little better in more specialized works, including institutional histories. Medical history is recorded in an imposing series of essays written by competent authorities and published in *Medicine in North Carolina*, edited by Dorothy Long. Several chapters, such as V. K. Hart's "The History of Blue Cross and Blue Shield in North Carolina," cover postwar developments. *The Tar Heel Press*, an entertaining book by Thad Stem, ends with a few pages relating to recent newspaper history; and Capus M. Waynick and John Harden, in *North Carolina Roads and Their Builders*, graphically trace the construction and management of the state's vast road system through the Kerr Scott road-building era.[7]

Louis Round Wilson's account of the University of North Carolina under consolidation brings a judicious if not altogether disinterested eye to the subject and leaves questions for future researchers to answer, while William S. Powell gives a nostalgic view of the Chapel Hill branch in his pictorial history of the first state university. Robert Rieke describes the emergence of a major university, the University of North Carolina at Charlotte, with a style and tone that lift the story above the pedestrian narratives so characteristic of many institutional histories. J. Winston Pearce's history of Campbell College is primarily concerned with the early years of the institution but takes the admiring story down to the postwar period. Much more satisfactory for recent decades is the second edition of Mary Lynch Johnson's *History of Meredith College*, half of which is

Davie County Historical Publishing Association, 1969); Ethel Stephens Arnett, *Greensboro, North Carolina: The County Seat of Guilford* (Chapel Hill: University of North Carolina Press, 1955).

7. Dorothy Long, ed., *Medicine in North Carolina: Essays in the History of Medical Science and Medical Service, 1524–1960*, 2 vols. (Raleigh: North Carolina Medical Society, 1972); Thad Stem, *The Tar Heel Press* ([Southport]: North Carolina Press Association, 1973); Capus M. Waynick and John Harden, *North Carolina Roads and Their Builders*, 2 vols. (Raleigh: Superior Stone Company, 1952–1966).

devoted to the postwar era. An interesting as well as contro-versial institutional history is Martin Duberman's *Black Mountain: An Exploration in Community*, which opens to public view the goings-on at the innovative college that closed in 1956. Shed of its psychoanalytic shroud, *Black Mountain* may be the best history ever written about a North Carolina institution.[8]

A superlative may also be used to describe *The North Carolina State Ports Authority* by Charles Edward Landon.[9] This well-documented study of a postwar agency can serve as a model for other departmental histories that ought to be written.

Among studies of the state's educational policies and services in the postwar period are Rebecca Murray's history of public school kindergartens and *School and Taxes in North Carolina* by Betsy Levin, Thomas Muller, and William Scanlon. The mention of only these works is a reminder of the dearth of historical studies on the public school system in the postwar era.[10]

Postwar publications on penology in North Carolina include the Osborne Association's survey of the Tar Heel prison system and the Institute of Government's study of local jails. The North Carolina Advisory Committee on Civil Rights has also published *Prisons in North Carolina*. All of these works offer little history and much opinion, but they and similar studies

8. Louis Round Wilson, *The University of North Carolina under Consolida-tion, 1931–1963: History and Appraisal* (Chapel Hill: Author, 1964); William S. Powell, *The First State University: A Pictorial History of the University of North Carolina* (Chapel Hill: University of North Carolina Press, 1972); Robert Rieke, *A Retrospective Vision: The University of North Carolina at Charlotte, 1965–1975* (Char-lotte: University of North Carolina at Charlotte, 1977); J. Winston Pearce, *Campbell College: Big Miracle at Little Buies Creek (1887–1974)* (Nashville: Boardman Press, 1976); Mary Lynch Johnson, *History of Meredith College* (Raleigh: Meredith College, 1972); Martin Duberman, *Black Mountain: An Exploration in Community* (New York: E. P. Dutton & Company, 1972).

9. Charles Edward Landon, *The North Carolina State Ports Authority* (Durham: Duke University Press, 1963).

10. Rebecca Murray, *History of the Public School Kindergarten in North Carolina* (New York: MSS Information Corporation, 1974); Betsy Levin, Thomas Muller, and William Scanlon, *Schools and Taxes in North Carolina* (Washington, D.C.: Urban Institute, 1973).

deserve the attention of a state with the nation's highest prison population per capita.[11]

Moya Woodside's *Sterilization in North Carolina* is a pioneer study that reveals, among other facts not customarily confronted by historians, that women may continue to achieve orgasm after sterilization. No mention is made of its effect upon men.[12]

Organizational histories tend to be traced to the date of writing, sometimes to include references to officers who sponsored their publication. Among the postwar productions are Stuart Noblin's study of the Grange in North Carolina; Thad Stem's survey of the PTA; and Brian Haislip's history of the Z. Smith Reynolds Foundation. The indefatigable Albert Coates has recently embraced women's organizations in two new books.[13]

Corporate histories, like organizational histories, are often written for self-serving purposes. Yet, they too have a role in recording the history of recent times. Walter B. Weare, in *Black Business in the New South*, and Jack Riley, in *Carolina Power and Light Company*, deal primarily with the earlier history of these corporations; but William J. Kennedy, Jr., devotes more than half of the *North Carolina Mutual Story* to the postwar period.[14]

11. Osborne Association, *Survey Report on North Carolina Prison System* (Raleigh: North Carolina State Highway and Public Works Commission, 1950); *Lock-Up: North Carolina Looks at Its Local Jails* (Chapel Hill: Institute of Government, 1969); North Carolina Advisory Committee on Civil Rights, *Prisons in North Carolina* (Raleigh: United States Commission on Civil Rights, 1976).

12. Moya Woodside, *Sterilization in North Carolina* (Chapel Hill: University of North Carolina Press, 1950).

13. Stuart Noblin, *The Grange in North Carolina, 1929–1954* (Greensboro: North Carolina State Grange, 1954); Thad Stem, *PTA Impact: 50 Years in North Carolina, 1919–1969* (Raleigh: North Carolina Congress of Parents and Teachers, 1969); Brian Haislip, *A History of the Z. Smith Reynolds Foundation* (Winston-Salem: John F. Blair, 1967); Albert Coates, *Citizens in Action: Women's Clubs, Civic Clubs, Community Chests: Flying Buttresses to Governmental Units* (Chapel Hill: Author, 1976); and Coates, *By Her Own Bootstraps: A Saga of Women in North Carolina* (Chapel Hill: Author, 1975).

14. Walter B. Weare, *Black Business in the New South: A Social History of the North Carolina Mutual Life Insurance Company* (Urbana: University of Illinois Press,

198   Writing North Carolina History

There are no general works on the labor movement in North Carolina in the postwar era, though at least two books give labor's side of controversies. Boyd E. Payton, an official of the Textile Workers Union of America who served a prison term for conspiracy in a dynamiting plot connected with the strike at the Harriet-Henderson Cotton Mills at Henderson in 1959, argues his innocence and the rightness of his cause in *Scapegoat: Prejudice, Politics, Prison*. Crystal Lee Jordan's story of the lengthy strike at the J. P. Stevens Company in Roanoke Rapids is told by Henry P. Leifermann in his book on her.[15]

The cultural history of North Carolina in the twentieth century, and particularly in recent decades, remains inadequately treated. However, despite its title, Ola Maie Foushee's *Art in North Carolina* is devoted mainly to the spirited movement in the 1950s that led to the creation of the North Carolina Museum of Art. Here is the story of North Carolina's emergence as the "state of the arts," including the internecine squabbles within the North Carolina Art Society. Charles W. Stanford has traced his role in the establishment of the innovative Mary Duke Biddle Gallery for the Blind at the Museum of Art.[16]

The Penland School of Handicrafts has been the subject of several books, including *Gift from the Hills* by Lucy Morgan and LeGette Blythe. Two beautiful books edited by John Coyne have brought Penland's pottery and jewelry to national attention.[17]

1973); Jack Riley, *Carolina Power and Light Company, 1908–1958* (Raleigh: Carolina Power and Light Company, 1958); William J. Kennedy, Jr., *The North Carolina Mutual Story: A Symbol of Progress, 1898–1970* (Durham: North Carolina Mutual Life Insurance Company, 1970).

15. Boyd E. Payton, *Scapegoat: Prejudice, Politics, Prison* (Philadelphia: Whitmore Publishing Company, [1970]); Henry P. Leifermann, *Crystal Lee: A Woman of Inheritance* (New York: Macmillan, 1975).

16. Ola Maie Foushee, *Art in North Carolina: Episodes and Developments, 1585–1970* (Chapel Hill: Author, 1972); Charles W. Stanford, *Art for Humanity's Sake: The Story of the Mary Duke Biddle Gallery for the Blind* (Raleigh: North Carolina Museum of Art, 1970).

17. Lucy Morgan and LeGette Blythe, *Gift from the Hills* (Indianapolis: Bobbs-Merrill, 1958; enl. ed., Chapel Hill: University of North Carolina Press,

Richard Walser's favorite pastime is tilling literary gardens, and in his *Literary North Carolina* he mentions hundreds of writers, including a few contemporary historians. Himself a former English professor, Walser has contributed much to the history of North Carolina literature through his own research and writing.[18]

The harvest of biographies and autobiographies of North Carolinians in the postwar period is also disappointing. Not one is likely to become a classic.

William Franklin Graham, a native North Carolinian who maintains his home at Montreat but spends most of his time outside the state, ranks as the best known Tar Heel of the era. Billy Graham's meteoric rise to the status of spiritual hero of millions and the friend of presidents has attracted biographers, not all of whom are admirers. He is represented in the North Carolina Collection by ninety-seven catalog cards, ranging from citations to Charles T. Cook's *The Billy Graham Story: "One Thing I Do"* and Lewis Gillenson, *Billy Graham: The Man and His Message*, both published in 1954, to more than a dozen books that carry Graham's own name as author.[19] While existing biographies deal mainly with Graham the evangelist, the definitive book on Graham the man is yet to be written.

Probably the runner-up to Graham as the state's most famous postwar resident is Samuel J. Ervin, Jr., who gained national notice for his stand against Senator Joseph R. McCarthy in the 1950s and whose face and stories became familiar to

1971); John Coyne, ed., *The Penland School of Crafts Book of Pottery* (Indianapolis: Bobbs-Merrill, 1975); and Coyne, ed., *The Penland School of Crafts Book of Jewelry Making* (Indianapolis: Bobbs-Merrill, 1975).

18. Richard Walser, *Literary North Carolina* (Raleigh: North Carolina Department of Archives and History, 1970).

19. Charles T. Cook, *The Billy Graham Story: "One Thing I Do"* (Wheaton, Illinois: Van Kampen Press, 1954); Lewis Gillenson, *Billy Graham: The Man and His Message* (Greenwich, Connecticut: Fawcett Publications, 1954). Among the early articles about the rising star of evangelism is "Evangelical Faith and Billy Graham" by James L. McAllister, then a Duke University ministerial student, in *Social Action* 19 (March 1953): 3–36.

many more millions during the Watergate hearings two decades later. Thus far he has become the subject of two biographies. Paul R. Clancy's biography is a newspaperman's account, interestingly written without citations and portraying the subject as many Americans came to feel about him. It is a highly favorable depiction. Dick Dabney asserts in his biography that "Sam Ervin is a good man: a truth-teller, even when he is wrong." Dabney's book is more critical than Clancy's, but it is also factually less dependable, and it reflects unnecessarily the author's own views of contemporary issues. Senator Ervin found so many errors in Dabney's account that he placed an itemized list of them with his papers in the Southern Historical Collection. Ervin is also a key figure in Samuel Dash's careful reconstruction of the story of the Watergate hearings.[20]

Luther H. Hodges, secretary of commerce under President Kennedy and President Johnson, also attained national attention, but thus far only one biography has appeared. Pete Ivey's *Luther H. Hodges: Practical Idealist* is an uncritical review of the subject's Horatio Alger story.[21] His long tenure as governor, his cabinet service in Washington, and his role in the creation of the Research Triangle combine to make Hodges an attractive subject for a more substantial biography.

Maurice F. Tauber wrote *Louis Round Wilson: Librarian and Administrator* back in 1967 when his subject was ninety-one years old.[22] He could have waited for the Wilson centennial, celebrated in 1976, because the famed librarian is still alive and mentally active. The book, by an admiring colleague, is

20. Paul R. Clancy, *Just a Country Lawyer: A Biography of Senator Sam Ervin* (Bloomington: Indiana University Press, 1974); Dick Dabney, *A Good Man: The Life of Sam J. Ervin* (Boston: Houghton Mifflin, 1976); Samuel Dash, *Chief Counsel: Inside the Ervin Committee—The Untold Story of Watergate* (New York: Random House, 1976).

21. Pete Ivey, *Luther H. Hodges: Practical Idealist* (Minneapolis: Denison, 1968).

22. Maurice F. Tauber, *Louis Round Wilson: Librarian and Administrator* (New York: Columbia University Press, 1967).

more than a biography. It is virtually a history of librarianship during much of the twentieth century, for Wilson became librarian of the University of North Carolina back in 1901.

Moses Rountree's book on Henry Belk offers an uncritical biography of the remarkable blind editor whose influence grew as his handicap worsened. James H. Blackmore's biography of W. R. Cullom gives the warm story of the Wake Forest minister. William Stevens has written a friendly account of J. E. Broyhill and the development of Broyhill Industries. The book also concerns the author, who is Broyhill's son-in-law and the unsuccessful Republican candidate for the United States Senate in 1974.[23]

Sports figures, too, continue to attract biographers. Among the crop in recent years are two books by Bill Libby. The first deals with Perquimans County's Jim "Catfish" Hunter, the baseball pitcher; the second with Tar Heel racer Richard Petty of Randolph County.[24]

Among other biographies published in recent years but whose contents pertain mainly to the prewar era are Wilma Dykeman and James Stokely, *Seeds of Southern Change: The Life of Will Alexander*, about a major contributor to improved race relations; Ruby Lanier, *Blanford Barnard Dougherty: Mountain Educator*, about the perspicacious founder of Appalachian State University; LeGette Blythe, *Robert Lee Stowe: Pioneer in Textiles*, about a successful Belmont industrialist; and LeGette Blythe, *William Henry Belk*, about the founder of the Belk department store chain.[25]

23. Moses Rountree, *Henry Belk: Son of Sweet Union* (Durham: Moore Publishing Company, 1975); James H. Blackmore, *The Cullom Lantern: A Biography of W. R. Cullom* (Raleigh: Edwards & Broughton, 1963); William Stevens, *Anvil of Adversity: Biography of a Furniture Pioneer* (New York: Popular Library, 1968).

24. Bill Libby, *Catfish: The Million Dollar Pitcher* (New York: Coward, McCann & Geoghegan, 1976); Libby, *"King Richard": The Richard Petty Story* (Garden City: Doubleday, 1977).

25. Wilma Dykeman and James Stokely, *Seeds of Southern Change: The Life of Will Alexander* (Chicago: University of Chicago Press, 1962); Ruby Lanier,

Autobiographies, too, have concentrated on pre–World War II years, but some, such as Aubrey Lee Brooks, *A Southern Lawyer*, and David Ovens, *If This Be Treason*, manage to drop in a few postwar references. Ovens at the age of eighty-four still had his sense of humor, for in the preface he advises friends who find errors in the book, "Don't phone me about them. It is too late now."[26]

Collected biographies often record the lives of persons who will never rate more than a brief sketch, and few historians are fully appreciative of the contributions of the compilers. For instance, Ruby K. Marsh, in a poorly written and mimeographed book titled *Keepers of Memories*, publishes sketches of about a hundred surviving widows of Confederate soldiers.[27] These rare individuals were mostly overlooked by historians during the centennial of the Civil War.

William S. Powell's *North Carolina Lives* is the best collection of contemporary biographical sketches. There are thousands of them. Each carries the inherent weakness and strength of having been initially drafted by its subject, but there remains merit in publications like *North Carolina Lives* and the two volumes of biographies accompanying Hugh Lefler's *History of North Carolina*.[28] Future researchers, especially quantifiers, will be more comfortable using these collections as edited by

---

Blanford Barnard Dougherty: Mountain Educator (Durham: Duke University Press, 1974); LeGette Blythe, *Robert Lee Stowe: Pioneer in Textiles* (Belmont: N.p., 1965); and Blythe, *William Henry Belk* (Chapel Hill: University of North Carolina Press, 1950).

26. Aubrey Lee Brooks, *A Southern Lawyer* (Chapel Hill: University of North Carolina Press, 1950); David Ovens, *If This Be Treason* (Charlotte: Heritage House, 1957).

27. Ruby K. Marsh, *Keepers of Memories: Biographical Sketches of Confederate Widows Living in North Carolina Today—1961–1965* (Asheboro: N.p., 1965).

28. William S. Powell, *North Carolina Lives: The Tar Heel Who's Who* (Hopkinsville, Kentucky: Historical Record Association, 1962); Hugh T. Lefler, *History of North Carolina*, 2 vols. of text, 2 vols. of biographies (New York: Lewis Historical Publishing Company, 1956). Powell is now at work on a monumental *Dictionary of North Carolina Biography*, the first volume of which is appearing in 1979.

historians than in using the commercial who's whos that have sprung up in recent years in the state and region.[29]

As noted earlier, Pete Ivey's brief treatment of Luther Hodges is the only biography of a postwar North Carolina governor, and it does not measure up to professional standards. Perhaps the availability in print of a substantial amount of documentation on the governors has inhibited writings about them. Following a tradition established over a half century ago, the state has continued to publish a selection of the public addresses and releases of each governor, and these volumes, distributed free to libraries and to friends of the chief executives, provide useful source materials for researchers. However, despite the fact that the volumes are edited by professional historians, they undeniably put forward the best side of each leader. Public addresses and press releases of a chief executive, for instance, reflect a governor's point of view—or that of his staff—and seldom allude to contrary opinions. Furthermore, the biographical prefaces are written by friends selected by the governor or by his family, and the sketches therefore tend to be panegyrics. The inherent characteristic of subjectivity notwithstanding, the volumes constitute an important service to scholarship.[30]

29. There has been a small plague of commercial ventures into biographical book publishing in recent years. One, *Who's Who in North Carolina* (Atlanta: United States Public Relations Service, Inc., 1973), starts off with a full-page photograph of and an introduction by Senator Ervin, who points out that the book records biographical sketches of 7,000 contemporary North Carolinians, "each of whom has given in his own way to the development of community, state, and nation." Sam Ervin's sketch is not among them. Terry Sanford, the only governor or former governor included, was accorded three lines; I was given five lines; and Cornelis Johannes Hogervorst of Wilmington was allotted thirty lines. Biographical sketches of several dozen black and Indian leaders are carried in *Paths Toward Freedom: Biographical History of Blacks and Indians in North Carolina by Blacks and Indians* (Raleigh: North Carolina State University, Center for Urban Affairs, 1976).

30. The volumes for Cherry, Kerr Scott, and Umstead were edited by David Leroy Corbitt and published by the Council of State; the three volumes for Hodges were edited by James W. Patton and published by the Council of State; and Memory F. Mitchell edited the volumes for Sanford, Moore, and Robert

To make sure that his administration was given credit for its accomplishments, Governor W. Kerr Scott upon leaving office issued a small booklet titled *A Report to the People*. Terry Sanford's friends published a more extensive review of his administration under the title *New Day*. And associates of Robert Scott brought out *The Long View*. All three reports, of course, contain undisguised praise for the respective gubernatorial administrations.[31]

Luther H. Hodges went a step further; he wrote his own extensive review. *Businessman in the Statehouse* is of more than routine importance because it publicizes the energetic and sometimes unorthodox approaches to government by a governor who was by then the secretary of commerce in the Kennedy administration.[32]

After he left office, Terry Sanford wrote two books, but neither is intended to be a full review of his administration. The first is *But What About the People?* and calls for greater responsiveness of government to public needs, particularly in the field of education; the second, *Storm Over the States*, continues to argue for a more activistic state government and for restructuring to give more power to the chief executive.[33] He thus gives a

Scott, the first published by the Council of State, the latter two by the Division of Archives and History. These volumes, of course, are highly selective and contain only a teasing fraction of the vast amount of documentation in the records of the governor's office which are preserved in the state archives. For a discussion of North Carolina's handling of the records of the chief executive, see Robert W. Scott, "Governor's Records: Public Records," *American Archivist* 33 (January 1970): 5–10.

31. *A Report to the People: The Administration of Governor W. Kerr Scott, 1949–53* (Raleigh: Governor's Office?, 1952); Sam Ragan, ed., *The New Day* (Zebulon: Record Publishing Company, [1965]); Russell Clay, David Murray, Sam Ragan, and Roy Wilder, Jr., eds., *The Long View: The Administration of Governor Robert W. Scott, 1969–1973* (Raleigh: Governor's Office?, 1973).

32. *Luther H. Hodges, Businessman in the Statehouse: Six Years as Governor of North Carolina* (Chapel Hill: University of North Carolina Press, [1962]). In 1963 Prentice-Hall published a book of essays by Hodges under the title *The Business Conscience*, one of the few works by North Carolinians translated into Japanese.

33. Terry Sanford, *But What About the People?* (New York: Harper and Row, 1966), and *Storm Over the States* (New York: McGraw-Hill, 1967).

verbal justification for the reorganization of state government that was undertaken by the Robert Scott and James Holshouser administrations.

The Governor, by Bruce and Nancy Roberts, is a unique record of the inner workings of the governor's office.[34] Under an arrangement with Governor Robert Scott, the husband-and-wife journalistic team was given access to conferences and interviews that are normally held in great confidence. In fact, the authors were permitted to follow the governor over a period of several months. Though profusely illustrated, The Governor is more than a picture book; it is an account of the daily life and problems of a governor. For historians, it records vividly some of the heated negotiations surrounding the consolidation of the state university system; for the public, it provides vicariously the experience of sitting in on discussions from which evolved far-reaching governmental decisions and policies.

Where historians have been reluctant to tread, social scientists and journalists have shown less inhibition, and although their books vary in quality and usefulness, some of them are of first importance in the study of history.

The most ambitious publication in the field of state government appeared in 1955. Robert S. Rankin, a Duke University political scientist, provided an adequate but unexciting textbook on the organization and functioning of state government.[35] Unfortunately, Rankin's subsequent membership on the United States Civil Rights Commission prevented him

34. Nancy and Bruce Roberts, The Governor (Charlotte: McNally and Loftin, 1972).
35. Robert S. Rankin, The Government and Administration of North Carolina (New York: Crowell, 1955). Earlier, Paul W. Wager had written The State and Its Government (New York: Oxford Book Company, 1947) and County Government across the Nation (Chapel Hill: University of North Carolina Press, 1950), but these also were not updated. Two Institute of Government publications designed primarily for local officials but that are useful for a wider audience are Henry W. Lewis's short An Introduction to Local Government (Chapel Hill: Institute of Government, 1963) and Joseph S. Ferrell's more substantial County Government in North Carolina (Chapel Hill: Institute of Government, rev. ed., 1975).

from updating the volume, and no other has been published to take its place. Moreover, the reorganization of state government in the 1970s and the casualness with which the General Assembly now alters the functions of state agencies present obstacles to any publication proposing to describe the organization and functions of government, for such a textbook would be out of date within a few years.

Certainly the outstanding compendium of North Carolina data published since 1945 is *North Carolina Atlas: Portrait of a Changing Southern State*, edited by James W. Clay, Douglas M. Orr, Jr., and Alfred W. Stuart, all of the Department of Geography and Earth Sciences at the University of North Carolina at Charlotte. Their splendid study, which largely supersedes Richard E. Lonsdale's *Atlas of North Carolina*, published eight years earlier, is a result of the collaboration of more than two dozen specialists (including historian William Powell), whose profusely illustrated essays coalesce into a veritable sourcebook, supplementing the approach of the historian with the skills of social scientists. Scores of maps and charts provide graphic images of the radical changes taking place in postwar North Carolina.[36] Under broad topics of human settlement and profile, physical resources and environmental quality, the economy, and services and amenities, this volume challenges some of the assumptions of historians. For instance, in questioning the validity of the traditional division of the state into eastern, Piedmont, and mountain regions, the editors say, "a difficulty arises when, over time, the similarities between counties within a grouping changes [*sic*] and certain counties really become more like those in a different region. If this occurs without an appropriate adjustment in the definition of regions,

36. James W. Clay, Douglas M. Orr, Jr., and Albert W. Stuart, eds., *North Carolina Atlas: Portrait of a Changing Southern State* (Chapel Hill: University of North Carolina Press, 1975); Richard E. Lonsdale, *Atlas of North Carolina* (Chapel Hill: University of North Carolina Press, 1967). The Lonsdale atlas was in itself a superior achievement and except for the energy of the Charlotte professors would still be the best work of its type. It remains a valuable supplement to the Clay-Orr-Stuart volume.

then those who persist in using traditional definitions are in danger of having weak or false perceptions of contemporary realities." An accompanying map in color graphically shows that "county types" challenge the traditional classification of the state by regions.[37]

The Institute for Research in Social Sciences (IRSS) at the University of North Carolina continued to produce useful studies, but the most influential publications of its founder, Howard W. Odum, and his colleague, Rupert B. Vance, belong to the prewar period. Among their later works were Odum's *Way of the South* and Vance's *Urban South*, both written too early to capture the essence of the revolution just beginning, though the latter did observe that the growth of urbanism was creating new problems as others were being superseded. Vance urged greater interplay among the various social sciences in the study of urbanism and regionalism.[38] The *Washington Post* commented: "Certainly there was no one—unless it was Franklin Roosevelt— whose influence was greater than Odum's on the development of the region below the Potomac."[39] Dewey W. Grantham, Jr., has noted more recently, however, that sociologists of the South are turning away from regionalism. An excellent evaluation of Odum's work comprises a chapter in Morton Philip Sosna's dissertation on white southern racial liberalism, 1920 to 1950.[40] Guy and Guion Johnson are currently preparing for publication a fifty-year history of the IRSS.

The Duke University economists Calvin B. Hoover and

37. Clay, Orr, and Stuart, *North Carolina Atlas*, p. 317.

38. Howard W. Odum, *The Way of the South* (New York: Macmillan, 1947); Rupert B. Vance, *The Urban South* (Chapel Hill: University of North Carolina Press, 1954).

39. Quoted in George B. Tindall, "The Significance of Howard W. Odum to Southern History: A Preliminary Estimate," *Journal of Southern History* 24 (1958): 285.

40. Dewey W. Grantham, Jr., "The Regional Imagination: Social Scientists and the American South," ibid. 34 (1968); Morton Philip Sosna, "In Search of the Silent South: White Southern Racial Liberalism, 1920–1950," Ph.D. diss., University of Wisconsin, 1972. See also Sosna's *In Search of the Silent South: Southern Liberals and the Race Issue* (New York: Columbia University Press, 1977).

B. U. Ratchford also did most of their influential work prior
to the war, but in their postwar book, *Economic Resources and
Policies of the South*, they noted that research laboratories were
replacing the "wailing wall."[41] Similarly, S. Huntington Hobbs,
Jr., professor of rural-social economics at Chapel Hill, remained
active after the war. His economic and social profile of North
Carolina, published in 1958, contained brief chapters on a
variety of subjects ranging from industry and agriculture to
governmental services. Sadly, however, the data was poorly
organized and often without lucid interpretation.[42]

　　A sociologist, a statistician, and a theologian have recently
collaborated on a controversial study of a North Carolina city.
Starting with Liston Pope's classic *Millhands and Preachers*,
John R. Earle, Dean D. Knudsen, and Donald W. Shriver, Jr.,
compare modern-day conditions in Gastonia with those of 1940
in their perceptive analysis titled *Spindles and Spires*.[43] In many
ways, what they found is encouraging. For instance, they
conclude that race relations and labor-management relations

41. Calvin B. Hoover and B. U. Ratchford, *Economic Resources and Policies
of the South* (New York: Macmillan, 1951).
42. S. Huntington Hobbs, Jr., *North Carolina: An Economic and Social Profile*
(Chapel Hill: University of North Carolina Press, 1958).
43. Liston Pope, *Millhands and Preachers* (New Haven: Yale University
Press, 1942); John R. Earle, Dean D. Knudsen, and Donald W. Shriver, Jr., *Spindles
and Spires: A Re-Study of Religion and Social Change in Gastonia* (Atlanta: John Knox
Press, 1976). Earle, Knudsen, and Shriver made considerable use of oral interviews. Oral history projects offer considerable potential for research in modern
history. In addition to other less concentrated programs, the projects at Duke
University and the University of North Carolina at Chapel Hill have recorded and
often transcribed interviews with scores of North Carolinians. In the Southern
Oral History Program at Chapel Hill, for instance, citizens such as Terry Sanford,
Wilbur Hobby, Frank Rouse, Jesse Helms, Floyd McKissick, and Robert Morgan
have been interviewed; and transcripts and tapes are available for use in the
Southern Historical Collection. Included in the Southern Historical Collection
also are more than 200 transcripts and tapes used by Jack Bass and Walter DeVries
in the preparation of their book, *The Transformation of Southern Politics: Social
Change and Political Consequence since 1945* (New York: Basic Books, 1976). Reed M.
Wolcott, a northern journalist, used oral interviews in her disturbing book, *Rose
Hill* (New York: G. P. Putnam's Sons, 1976).

have improved significantly. And, describing progress as "economic crisis and renewal," the editors confirm considerable progress. Even a sixfold increase in per-member contributions to church budgets reflects economic advancement, if not deeper pietism.

In its 1954 ruling in the case of *Brown* v. *Board of Education of Topeka*, the United States Supreme Court sparked a controversy that still engages the pens of social scientists and some historians alike. If the ruling seemed to be a bad dream for some whites and a dream come true for blacks, there were a few citizens who foresaw the enormity of the problems that the state must resolve in the subsequent adjustment of traditional relations between the races.

One of these was Albert Coates, director of the Institute of Government, whose report to Governor William B. Umstead, furnished only a few weeks after the landmark decision, revealed a clarity of evaluation not common during this traumatic period.[44] Fortunately for North Carolina, Governor Umstead, and, following his death, Governor Hodges, chose to follow the middle road, which accepted the inevitability of compliance while using delaying tactics to prepare the citizens for the change. Consequently, the minimum integration of the schools during the next six years enabled North Carolina to avoid the degree of resistance and violence characteristic of most of the other southern states.

The extent of adjustment required among rank-and-file Tar Heels before compliance could be achieved was indicated in an analysis of the attitudes of 287 white males in Guilford County less than four years after the court's ruling. In *Desegregation and Readiness*, Melvin M. Tumin revealed the intensity of white feelings against Negroes in general and

44. Albert Coates, *A Report to the Governor of North Carolina on the Decision of the Supreme Court of the United States* (Chapel Hill: Institute of Government, 1954), reprinted in *Law and Government, a Series: The School Segregation Decision* (Chapel Hill: Institute of Government, 1954).

integration in particular. Not unexpectedly, the study indicated that negative attitudes were more prevalent among those of the lowest income, education, and social levels.[45]

In 1957 three North Carolina cities, including Greensboro, admitted a few blacks to previously all-white schools. The experiences of Greensboro, North Carolina, and Greenville, South Carolina, are studied by William Bagwell in his book on school desegregation in the Carolinas.[46] Bagwell traces the successful efforts of local leaders who worked quietly to smooth the way for the new experience of interracial education. The story is not always pretty, but it illustrates the debt owed to persons of good will who sought to insure peaceful change in a climate of opinion already described by Tumin.

Although the movement to desegregate business services was well under way in the South, a group of students from North Carolina Agricultural and Technical College introduced a new weapon in the battle in February 1960. Miles Wolff painstakingly traces the origin of the new technique in *Lunch at the Five and Ten: The Greensboro Sit-Ins, a Contemporary History*.[47] By midsummer Woolworth's and other stores with lunch counters yielded, and the sit-in became a persuasive tactic in other cities and states. Wolff's book is a noteworthy contribution to history.

John Ehle is best known for his fiction, but despite verbal challenges to some facets of his reporting of the Chapel Hill demonstrations of 1964, his *Free Men* constitutes a personal narrative of importance.[48] The reader vicariously accompanies Ehle into campus and town meetings and private conversations, stands in the crowd as an onlooker, and even finds himself

45. Melvin M. Tumin, *Desegregation and Readiness* (Princeton: Princeton University Press, 1958).
46. William Bagwell, *School Desegregation in the Carolinas: Two Case Studies* (Columbia: University of South Carolina Press, 1972).
47. Miles Wolff, *Lunch at the Five and Ten: The Greensboro Sit-Ins, a Contemporary History* (New York: Stein and Day, 1970).
48. John Ehle, *The Free Men* (New York: Harper and Row, 1965).

with arms linked across Franklin Street. The book does not
pretend to be objective history, but it is a compelling account of
social change.

The struggle of blacks for their civil rights was accompanied by a struggle for leadership among blacks. In *Negro
Political Leadership in a Southern City*, Margaret Elaine Burgess
gives an unusually intimate peek into the divisions within the
Negro community in Durham, thinly disguised in the book as
"Crescent City." There, as in many other southern towns, the
long-respected black business leaders, willing to cooperate with
their white counterparts for long-range gains, are challenged
by militant blacks intent upon forcing immediate concessions.
An article by Frederic N. Cleaveland and Bradbury Seasholes
compares the patterns of black activity in Durham and Winston-
Salem.[49]

Ten years after the *Brown* decision, a book described by
one reviewer as likely to become "a source for future historians
of the Negro revolution" was published under the auspices of
the Sanford administration. In his role as a peacemaker,
Governor Sanford had established the North Carolina Mayors'
Co-operating Committee, headed by the former diplomat, Capus
Waynick. In *North Carolina and the Negro*, Waynick and his
assistants briefly review racial progress since 1954 in fifty-five
municipalities in which the committee, or its local counterparts, had negotiated for the extension of civil rights for blacks.
The report, though perhaps unrealistically optimistic, nevertheless documents a record that few Tar Heels a decade earlier
would have predicted.[50]

49. Margaret Elaine Burgess, *Negro Political Leadership in a Southern City*
(Chapel Hill: University of North Carolina Press, 1962); Frederic N. Cleaveland
and Bradbury Seasholes, "Negro Political Participation in Two Piedmont Cities,"
in F. Stuart Chapin, Jr., and Shirley Weiss, eds., *Urban Growth Dynamics* (Chapel
Hill: University of North Carolina Press, 1962).

50. Capus M. Waynick, John C. Brooks, and Elsie W. Pitts, eds., *North
Carolina and the Negro* (Raleigh: North Carolina Mayors' Co-operating Committee,
1964).

While North Carolinians—at least most white North Carolinians—tend to look back with pride upon the past twenty-five years and applaud their adjustment to changing times, writers reporting progress in the entire South seldom give North Carolina high marks. Historian Charles P. Roland in his book on the South since World War II expresses considerable disappointment because the southern state with the best race relations prior to the *Brown* decision failed to lead the region in the integration of blacks into society after 1954. In a recent study of southern governors and the Second Reconstruction, Earl Black implies a similar disappointment, but he observes that North Carolina escaped much of the demagoguery characteristic of several neighboring states because Tar Heel governors sought to keep the peace and encouraged local solutions to racial problems. On a discordant note, however, Neil R. McMillan classifies the Patriots of North Carolina as a "sedate version" of the Citizens Council and attributes to the Patriots and their successors, the North Carolina Defenders of States' Rights, the names of some of the "most respected men of North Carolina." He could have added, however, that neither organization exercised much political leverage in the state.[51]

Politics has always been a favorite form of recreation in North Carolina, and it continues to provide a popular topic

51. Charles P. Roland, *The Improbable Era: The South since World War II* (Lexington: University Press of Kentucky, 1975); Earl Black, *Southern Governors and Civil Rights: Racial Segregation as a Campaign Issue in the Second Reconstruction* (Cambridge: Harvard University Press, 1976); Neil R. McMillan, *The Citizens Council: Organized Resistance to the Second Reconstruction, 1954–1964* (Urbana: University of Illinois Press, 1965). Among other books on the South that pay less notice to North Carolina are Numan V. Bartley, *The Rise of Massive Resistance: Race and Politics in the South During the 1950s* (Baton Rouge: Louisiana State University Press, 1969); Reed Sarratt, *The Ordeal of Desegregation: The First Decade* (New York: Harper and Row, 1966); and Benjamin Muse, *Ten Years of Prelude: The Story of Integration since the Supreme Court's 1954 Decision* (New York: Viking Press, 1964). James Wilfrid Vander Zanden, in "The Southern White Resistance Movement in Integration" (Ph.D. diss., University of North Carolina at Chapel Hill, 1957), characterizes North Carolina's position as one of delay rather than resistance, "and delay by virtue of inactivity rather than primarily by activity" (p. 187).

for amusement and study by political scientists and laymen. Indeed, in the South, the period from 1945 to the present has been the era of political science.

Remarkably little, however, has been published in book form by writers within the state. Now outdated by the intervening years, Jack D. Fleer's *North Carolina Politics* describes with considerable flair the internecine battles within the Democratic party and the growth of the Republican vote in presidential elections during the period from 1940 to 1966. More recent developments are discussed in a series of uneven essays by nearly a score of writers in *Politics and Policy in North Carolina.* Chapters range from Merle Black's critical analysis of the self-image of North Carolinians to Ferrel Guillory's examination of the anomaly of a governor and lieutenant governor of different parties.[52]

A political campaign of 1964 and another of 1946 are examined closely in a book and an article, respectively. A High Point lawyer and businessman, James R. Spence, wrote *The Making of a Governor: The Moore-Preyer-Lake Primaries of 1964*, an account based heavily on statements of the candidates. This chronological review fails to portray the emotional depths to which the campaign reached on the precinct level; still, it is the best analysis of a postwar political campaign in North Carolina. In an article on the Folger-Chatham congressional primary of 1946, Ralph J. Christian is less successful in reconstructing the story of the liberal-conservative battle in North Carolina's Fifth Congressional District. Although Chatham subsequently became one of the more moderate southern members of

52. Jack D. Fleer, *North Carolina Politics: An Introduction* (Chapel Hill: University of North Carolina Press, 1968); Thad Beyle and Merle Black, eds., *Politics and Policy in North Carolina* (New York: MSS Information Corporation, 1975). Donald R. Matthews and his colleagues at the University of North Carolina at Chapel Hill issued a convenient compilation of election returns in *North Carolina Votes* (Chapel Hill: University of North Carolina Press, 1962), but Christopher Crittenden, in a review, noted that the book reprinted erroneous figures for some of the earlier elections (*NCHR* 40 [April 1963]: 247–48).

Congress, in 1946 he campaigned on the slogan "more business in government and less government in business."[53]

Since 1949 North Carolina has been a controversial subject of inquiry by many political observers of the South. For this attention the state is partially indebted to this statement: "The prevailing mood in North Carolina is not hard to sense: it is energetic and ambitious. The citizens are determined and confident; they are on the move. The mood is at odds with much of the rest of the South—a tenor of attitude and of action that has set the state apart from its neighbors."[54] Thus did V. O. Key, Jr., in *Southern Politics in State and Nation*, place the stamp of academic respectability upon an image that North Carolinians have worn proudly ever since. Hailed by one reviewer as a "new landmark in political science,"[55] this book has had a more profound influence upon the Tar Heel psyche than any other postwar political analysis. For, while Key's twenty-four-page chapter, titled "North Carolina: Progressive Plutocracy," pertained almost wholly to political progressivism, North Carolinians quickly extended the image to economic and social conditions. Nowhere in history can be found a period during which the people of the state exhibited such a buoyant confidence, and W. Kerr Scott, the most progressive governor in memory, exemplified the times by championing huge expenditures for schools, roads, and other services and by prodding

53. James R. Spence, *The Making of a Governor: The Moore-Preyer-Lake Primaries of 1964* (Winston-Salem: John F. Blair, 1968); Ralph J. Christian, "The Folger-Chatham Congressional Primary of 1946," *NCHR* 53 (Winter 1976): 25–53. Folger defeated Chatham in a heated second primary in 1946 but stepped aside and was succeeded by Chatham two years later.

54. V. O. Key, Jr., with the assistance of Alexander Heard, *Southern Politics in State and Nation* (New York: Alfred A. Knopf, 1949), p. 205. Gary C. Ness in "The *Southern Politics* Project and the Writing of Recent Southern History," *South Atlantic Quarterly* 76 (Winter 1977): 58–72, traces the project that produced Key's book, and he provides an evaluation of the work.

55. Bascom N. Timmons, "Dixie Politics Theme of Story by V. O. Key," *Nashville Tennessean*, ca. October 1949.

utilities companies to extend power and telephone lines into all areas of the state. His appointment of Frank Graham to the United States Senate seemed a portent of a changing order.

Within a year after the publication of *Southern Politics*, Key's image of North Carolina was badly marred. In a campaign reminiscent of the general election fifty years earlier, Senator Graham was defeated in a runoff primary. Race as a political issue was therefore fresh in the minds of North Carolinians when in 1954 the Supreme Court announced its decision in the case of *Brown* v. *Board of Education of Topeka*. The race issue was used effectively against Scott in his primary campaign for the United States Senate that year, and had it not been for his popularity among farmers, the former governor might have lost.

Already in the 1950s resident observers began to question the validity of North Carolina's progressive image. These doubts, however, were virtually forgotten after Terry Sanford survived the 1960 gubernatorial campaign in which the race issue was used against him. Sanford's administration effectively exploited the news media in publicizing social and economic progress, and North Carolina again received favorable national attention.[56] Though Sanford's accomplishments were not as progressive (nor those of his successors as nonprogressive) as the news media portrayed them, North Carolinians clung to the adjective bestowed upon them by Key and other observers.

A new generation of political scientists has recently begun to publish reevaluations of the North Carolina image. In an article titled "North Carolina, Bipartisan Paradox," Preston W. Edsall and J. Oliver Williams, both North Carolinians, admit that the state has not lived up to its reputation in the postwar period. They point out, however, that in 1949 Key could not have foreseen the radical changes that would be mandated by a

56. The positive image projected by Sanford brought the state unprecedented publicity. See, for instance, Malcolm Ross, "North Carolina, Dixie Dynamo," *National Geographic* 121 (January 1962): 144–83.

militant minority, a responsive Congress, and an activist court.[57] Between the administrations of Kerr Scott and his son, Robert, North Carolina underwent changes that even Frank Graham could not have anticipated in 1950.

A journalist, Neil R. Peirce, in his recent book on the southern border states, concludes that the word "progressive" gives North Carolina too much credit. His superficial chapter on North Carolina is titled "Progressive Paradox," and in it he states, "This is a state of paradoxes: behind every fact which can be cited as proof of its progressiveness lurks another which suggests just the opposite."[58] Jack Bass and Walter DeVries, in *The Transformation of Southern Politics*, are even less generous in analyzing North Carolina's claim to progressivism.[59] For Key's chapter title of "Progressive Plutocracy," Bass and DeVries substitute "Progressive Myth," concluding that the "energetic and ambitious" mood observed by Key has given way to complacency. They write, "The progressive image the state projected in the late 1940s has evolved into a progressive myth that remains accepted as fact by much of the state's native leadership, despite ample evidence to the contrary. Although North Carolina has changed with the times, it is perhaps the least changed of the old Confederate states. Because of its moderation, it yielded more easily to the forces of change, but it missed the dynamic reaction to resistance that so swiftly

57. Preston W. Edsall and J. Oliver Williams, "North Carolina, Bipartisan Paradox," in William C. Havard, ed., *The Changing Politics of the South* (Baton Rouge: Louisiana State University Press, 1972).

58. Neil R. Peirce, *The Border South States: People, Politics, and Power in the Five Border South States* (New York: W. W. Norton, 1975), p. 113.

59. Bass and DeVries, *The Transformation of Southern Politics: Social Change and Political Consequence since 1945* (New York: Basic Books, 1976). Numan V. Bartley and Hugh D. Graham, in *Southern Politics in the Second Reconstruction* (Baltimore: Johns Hopkins University Press, 1975), while giving little attention to North Carolina, suggest that the liberalization expected to be derived from industrialization and urbanization was stunted by the racial division aggravated by the court rulings and federal action. The authors find more continuity than change in the politics of the South.

transformed political and social development elsewhere in the South. Nor has it experienced the impact of urbanization as much as most other border South states have."[60]

The point that these revisionists make—that North Carolina has not exercised an aggressive leadership for southern change—is entirely defensible, and their writings will undoubtedly influence the self-image of Tar Heels. None of the political scientists, however, adequately recognizes the differences between the *level* and the *rate* of progress. The statistics of economic growth—or of political participation or school desegregation—are more geometrically impressive when compared with a lower base. The generally accepted premise that North Carolina in the late 1940s led the South in certain desirable characteristics is sufficient to explain, in specified instances, why the rates of advancement may have been surpassed by states starting from a less favorable position. Furthermore, political scientists tend to assume that the definition of progress is agreed upon and that change is synonymous with progress. Many North Carolinians, including some historians, do not accept such an equation. Urbanization, for instance, instead of being an index to progress, may in the long run be viewed as retrogression; an increase in employment in a particular industry, instead of reflecting a healthy economy, may indicate rising inflation and a decrease in individual productivity; expanding college enrollments, instead of producing a more highly trained citizenry, may be evidence of deterioration in the quality of education. In short, the historian may have good reason to accept only with caution the measurements of progress used by social scientists. Still, without the works of social scientists, only a few of which have been mentioned in this paper, the era since World War II would be essentially a wasteland of scholarly activity.

The poverty of historical works for the period is evident

60. Bass and DeVries, *Transformation of Southern Politics*, p. 219.

also in the work of graduate students in history. Apparently not a single doctoral dissertation has been written on a broad North Carolina topic of the period. One, William T. Moye, "Charlotte-Mecklenburg Consolidation: Metrolina in Motion," deals with the failure of a county-city merger referendum; and several others overlap the postwar period in chronology. Of the latter, three have considerable pertinence: Robert Cannon, "The Organization and Growth of Black Political Participation in Durham, North Carolina, 1933–1958"; Augustus Merrimon Burns III, "North Carolina and the Negro Dilemma, 1930–1950"; and Clark Cahow, "The History of the North Carolina Mental Hospitals, 1848–1960." At least two masters' theses in history are worthy of mention: John William Coon, "Kerr Scott, the 'Go Forward' Governor: His Origins, His Program, and the North Carolina General Assembly"; and Arthur M. Miller, "Desegregation and Negro Leadership in Durham, North Carolina, 1954–1963."[61]

The inescapable conclusion that historians have virtually ignored recent decades as a subject of research and writing

61. William T. Moye, "Charlotte-Mecklenburg Consolidation: Metrolina in Motion," Ph.D. diss., University of North Carolina at Chapel Hill, 1975; Robert Cannon, "The Organization and Growth of Black Political Participation in Durham, North Carolina, 1933–1958," Ph.D. diss., University of North Carolina at Chapel Hill, 1975; Augustus Merrimon Burns III, "North Carolina and the Negro Dilemma, 1930–1950," Ph.D. diss., University of North Carolina at Chapel Hill, 1969; Clark Cahow, "The History of the North Carolina Mental Hospitals, 1848–1960," Ph.D. diss., Duke University, 1967; John William Coon, "Kerr Scott, the 'Go Forward' Governor: His Origins, His Program and the North Carolina General Assembly," M.A. thesis, University of North Carolina at Chapel Hill, 1968; Arthur M. Miller, "Desegregation and Negro Leadership in Durham, North Carolina, 1954–1963," M.A. thesis, University of North Carolina at Chapel Hill, 1976.

Graduate students in political science, like their professors, have been somewhat more active in writing on recent issues and events. Not unexpectedly, racial subjects are most numerous. Among the dissertations of this type are Bradbury Seasholes, "Negro Political Participation in Two North Carolina Cities," Ph.D. diss., University of North Carolina at Chapel Hill, 1962; A. B. Cochran III, "School Desegregation in North Carolina: Dimensions of a Public Policy," Ph.D.

leaves a nagging question: At what point in time is the historian willing to become involved in a study of the past? Or, put another way, When does the past become sufficiently "past" to attract the historian's probing attention?

Unburdened by the historian's methodology, political scientists, sociologists, economists, and members of related disciplines have been at work, and their writings, supplemented by those of journalists, propagandists, and even laymen, provide nearly all of the reading material available on North Carolina in the past three decades. The public perception of the recent past, to the extent that it is influenced by the written word, is thus based upon these materials.

Furthermore, the public school curriculum dictates less and less attention to the distant past and, correspondingly, more and more to the recent past and present. History is on the verge of becoming a stranger to the classroom, for the schools no longer teach extensively the courses for which historians

---

diss., University of North Carolina at Chapel Hill, 1972; William Henry Coogan III, "School Board Decisions on Desegregation in North Carolina," Ph.D. diss., University of North Carolina at Chapel Hill, 1971; and Steven Francis Redburn, "Protest and Policy in Durham, North Carolina," Ph.D. diss., University of North Carolina at Chapel Hill, 1970. Three deal with the General Assembly: Donald P. Sprengel, "Legislative Perceptions of Gubernatorial Power in North Carolina," Ph.D. diss., University of North Carolina at Chapel Hill, 1966; Thomas Floyd Eamon, "Factors Influencing Social Conservatism among American Elites: A Study of the North Carolina House of Representatives," Ph.D. diss., University of North Carolina at Chapel Hill, 1975; and Debra W. Stewart, "Policy and Decision Processes: The Impact of Women's Policy Issues on Decision Making in the North Carolina Legislature," Ph.D. diss., University of North Carolina at Chapel Hill, 1975. Another, by Douglas Gatlin, deals with the challenging subject, "Socio-Economic Bases for Party Competition: A Case Study of North Carolina," Ph.D. diss., University of North Carolina at Chapel Hill, 1963.

Kenyon B. Segner's "Forces and Individuals Behind the Community College Movement in North Carolina," Ph.D. diss., University of North Carolina at Chapel Hill, 1966, was written in a School of Education, but it might well have passed muster in a department of history. It traces the phenomenon of community educational centers jointly financed by the state and local governments.

Other social sciences, such as geography, sociology, and economics, have contributed graduate studies, mostly masters' theses, but almost without exception they have treated narrow subjects, often statistically.

write, and historians do not often write for the courses that stress
current events and presentism. With the removal from the
classroom of the moderating influence of historians and the
substitution of the works of more activist disciplines, social
studies education is in danger of becoming indoctrination in
political, social, and economic views that remain untested by
the experience of history.

Whether this danger is sufficient to cause historians to
embrace the recent past as a proper subject of study and writing
is a question that individual members of the profession must
answer. If the answer is uniformly negative, then historians
must be willing to admit partial responsibility for the lessening
of their influence upon contemporary Americans.

Perhaps there is a message for historians, too, in Gavin
Stevens's observation, "The past is never dead. It's not even
past."[62]

62. William Faulkner, *Intruder in the Dust*, quoted in C. Vann Woodward,
The Burden of Southern History (Baton Rouge: Louisiana State University Press,
1960), p. 36.

Contributors

ROBERT M. CALHOON is professor of history at The University of North Carolina at Greensboro. He is the author of *The Loyalists in Revolutionary America, 1760–1781* (New York, 1973). His textbook, *Revolutionary America: An Interpretive Overview* (New York, 1976), received the William R. Davie Award from the North Carolina Society, Sons of the American Revolution. In conjunction with his current research on religion in the postrevolutionary South, he edited *Religion and the American Revolution in North Carolina*, published in 1976 by the North Carolina Department of Cultural Resources.

ROBERT F. DURDEN is chairman of the department of history at Duke University where he has taught since completing graduate work at Princeton in 1952. His research has centered on late nineteenth-century United States and especially southern history. His most recent books are *The Gray and the Black: The Confederate Debate on Emancipation* (Baton Rouge, 1972); *The Dukes of Durham, 1865–1929* (Durham, 1975); and with Jeffrey J. Crow, *Maverick Republican in the Old North State: A Political Biography of Daniel L. Russell* (Baton Rouge, 1977).

H. G. JONES, curator of the North Carolina Collection, holds a Ph.D. degree from Duke University and is the author of *For History's Sake* (Chapel Hill, 1966) and *The Records of a Nation* (New York, 1969). He has taught history in colleges in North Carolina and Georgia and has served as director of the North Carolina Department of Archives and History and president of the Society of American Archivists. A member of the North Carolina Historical Commission and chairman of America's Four Hundredth Anniversary Committee, he is currently working on a pictorial history of North Carolina.

SARAH McCULLOH LEMMON, professor of history and dean of continuing education and special programs at Meredith College, received her education at James Madison University (B.S.), Columbia University (M.A.), and The University of North Carolina at Chapel Hill (Ph.D.). She has published *Parson Pettigrew of the "Old Church"* (Chapel Hill, 1971) and *Frustrated Patriots: North Carolina and the War of 1812* (Chapel Hill, 1973) as well as pamphlets and documentaries for the North Carolina Division of Archives and History. Currently she is chairman of the North Carolina Historical Commission.

WILLIAM S. POWELL, professor of history at The University of North Carolina at Chapel Hill, was formerly curator of the North Carolina Collection there. He is the author, editor, or compiler of numerous books, pamphlets, and articles dealing with North Carolina and with England. He is currently editor of the multi-volume *Dictionary of North Carolina Biography* being published by The University of North Carolina Press.

ALLEN W. TRELEASE has been professor of history at The University of North Carolina at Greensboro since 1967. Starting as a colonialist emphasizing Indian affairs, he published *Indian Relations in Colonial New York: The Seventeenth Century*, based on his Harvard dissertation, in 1960. Subsequently he has turned to the Reconstruction period, his most important publications being *White Terror: The Ku Klux Klan Conspiracy and Southern Reconstruction* (1971) and two articles in the *Journal of Southern History*: "Who Were the Scalawags?" (1963) and "Republican Reconstruction in North Carolina: A Roll-Call Analysis of the State House of Representatives, 1868–1870" (1976).

ALAN D. WATSON, professor of history at The University of
North Carolina at Wilmington, is the author of *Society in
Colonial North Carolina* (Raleigh, 1975) and numerous articles
that have appeared in the *South Atlantic Quarterly, William
and Mary Quarterly, North Carolina Historical Review,* and *South
Carolina Historical Magazine.* Currently he is preparing a study
of the colonial quitrent system in the southern royal colonies of
Virginia, North Carolina, and South Carolina.

HARRY L. WATSON, assistant professor of history at The
University of North Carolina at Chapel Hill, received his Ph.D.
degree from Northwestern University in 1976. He is the author of
"Squire Oldway and His Friends: Opposition to Internal
Improvements in Antebellum North Carolina," which appeared
in the *North Carolina Historical Review* (1977). His forthcoming
book, *"Bitter Combinations of the Neighbourhood": Parties and
Politics in an Old South County, 1824–1840,* will be published by
Louisiana State University Press.

Index

The Editors

Jeffrey J. Crow is head of the General Publications Branch, Historical Publications Section, North Carolina Division of Archives and History. He is the editor of the North Carolina Bicentennial Pamphlet Series, the author of *The Black Experience in Revolutionary North Carolina* (1977), and coauthor with Robert F. Durden of *Maverick Republican in the Old North State: A Political Biography of Daniel L. Russell* (1977).

Larry E. Tise is the director of the North Carolina Division of Archives and History. He is the author of *The Yadkin Melting Pot: Methodism and the Moravians in the Yadkin Valley, 1750–1850* (1968) and the general editor for and author of four volumes in the Winston-Salem in History Series.

Jeffrey J. Crow and Larry E. Tise are coeditors of *The Southern Experience in the American Revolution*, published by The University of North Carolina Press in 1978.

Writing North Carolina History is the
first book to assess fully the historical
literature of North Carolina. It combines
the talents and insights of eight noted
scholars of state and southern history:
William S. Powell, Alan D. Watson,
Robert M. Calhoon, Harry L. Watson,
Allen W. Trelease, Robert F. Durden,
Sarah M. Lemmon, and H. G. Jones.
Their essays are arranged in chronological order from the founding of the
first English colony in North America in
1585 to the present.

Traditionally North Carolina has not received the same scholarly attention as
Virginia and South Carolina, despite the
excellent resources available on Tar Heel
history. This study, derived from a symposium sponsored by the North Carolina
Division of Archives and History in 1977,
asks new questions and describes new
methodologies needed to redress past
neglect. Besides providing a comprehensive evaluation of what has been written
about North Carolina, the essayists offer
fresh perspectives on how historians
have interpreted the state's history and
what directions future historians need
to take. Particularly important, the book
provides a current bibliography and suggests opportunities for future historical
investigation by discussing topics,
themes, and source materials that remain
untapped or underused.